D0170534

A
Performer
Prepares

A GUIDE TO SONG
PREPARATION FOR ACTORS,
SINGERS AND DANCERS

Other Titles from The Applause Acting Series:

ON SINGING ONSTAGE
David Craig

THE END OF ACTING:
A RADICAL VIEW
Richard Hornby

ACTING IN FILM
(book & videocassette)
Michael Caine

DIRECTING THE ACTION
Charles Marowitz

MICHAEL CHEKHOV:
ON THEATRE AND THE ART OF ACTING
(audiotapes)

THE MONOLOGUE WORKSHOP
Jack Poggi

RECYCLING SHAKESPEARE
Charles Marowitz

SHAKESCENES: SHAKESPEARE FOR TWO
John Russell Brown

SPEAK WITH DISTINCTION
Edith Skinner

STANISLAVSKI REVEALED
Sonia Moore

STANISLAVSKI TECHNIQUE: RUSSIA
Mel Gordon

THE CRAFTSMEN OF DIONYSUS
Jerome Rockwood

THE ACTOR AND THE TEXT
Cicely Berry

ONE ON ONE:
THE BEST MONOLOGUES FOR THE NINETIES
Jack Temchin (ed.)

SHAKESPEARE'S PLAYS IN PERFORMANCE
John Russell Brown

A
Performer
Prepares

A GUIDE TO SONG PREPARATION FOR ACTORS, SINGERS AND DANCERS

DAVID CRAIG

An Applause Original
A PERFORMER PREPARES: A Guide to Song Preparation for Actors, Singers and Dancers
Copyright © 1993 by David Craig

All rights reserved.
No part of this publication may be reproduced or transmitted in any form or by any means, electronic or mechanical, including photocopy, recording, or any information storage or retrieval system now known or to be invented, without permission in writing from the publishers, except by a reviewer who wishes to quote brief passages in connection with a review written for inclusion in a magazine, newspaper or broadcast.

Library of Congress Cataloging-in-Publication Data

Craig, David.
    A performer prepares : a guide to song preparation for actors, singer, dancers / David Craig.
        p.   cm.   — (The Applause acting series)
    "An Applause Original" — T.p. verso.
    Includes bibliographical references.
    ISBN 1-55783-133-5 (cl) : $21.95
    1. Singing —Interpretation (Phrasing, dynamics, etc.) 2. Singing–Psychological aspects.
3. Popular Music— Interpretation (Phrasing, dynamics, etc.) I. Title. II. Series.
MT892.C73   1993
783'.043—dc20   92-38275
                                                                                      CIP
                                                                                      MN

British Library Cataloging-in-Publication Data

    A catalogue record of this book is available from the British Library

First Applause Printing 1993

Applause Theatre & Cinema Books
19 West 21st Street, Suite 201
New York, NY 10010
Phone: (212) 575-9265
Fax: (212) 575-9270
Email: info@applausepub.com
Internet: www.applausepub.com

Applause books are available through your local bookstore, or you may order at
www.applausepub.com or call Music Dispatch at 800-637-2852

Sales & Distribution:

North America:
    Hal Leonard Corp.
    7777 West Bluemound Road
    P.O. Box 13819
    Milwaukee, WI 53213
    Phone: (414) 774-3630
    Fax: (414) 774-3259
    Email: halinfo@halleonard.com
    Internet: www.halleonard.com

Europe:
Roundhouse Publishing Ltd.
Millstone, Limers Lane
Northam, North Devon
EX 39 2RG
Phone: 01237-474474
Fax: 01237-474774
Email: roundhouse.group@ukgateway.net

For my Parents
who missed the show

and

For my sister
who had to leave at Intermission

and

For my beloved wife
who, from the start, urged me to get it all down

ACKNOWLEDGMENTS

and gratitude are due Gary Carver: friend, pianist and right hand; Kate Billings, loyal amanuensis; Earl Holliman for permission to use his work; Kip Niven for permission to quote him; Joel Craig: house music copyist; Joe Mays and Michael Harrington, guides into the world of rock and roll.

Special salutations to the composers and lyricists who allowed their work to appear in this book, and to Ted Chapin, Mark Trent Goldberg, and Artie Valando who made effortless the clearance of those words and music.

And to Flora Roberts, life friend.

CONTENTS

Preface

The choice of the title *A Performer Prepares*, a shamefaced appropriation of Constantin Stanislavski's *An Actor Prepares*, is calculated to invoke in the reader a specific response, namely, that the craft of performing songs shares a common, albeit parallel, ground with the craft of acting as it has been defined by that eminent Russian. This common ground is given added credence when one recalls that Stanislavski's final years were devoted to the lyric theater. As a young man he was trained as a singer by the great Fyodor Kommisarjevsky and, as reported by Elizabeth Reynolds Hapgood (Stanislavski's translator), he " . . . always felt instinctively that music could greatly enhance the effectiveness of an actor." Further, I have turned to *Stanislavski on Opera* by him and Pavel Rumyantsev (again, edited and translated by Miss Hapgood) when his remarkable vision gives weight and corroboration to personally held opinions.

A Performer Prepares completes a trilogy whose aim is to define a pedagogy that will support the uninitiated and/or the uninformed actor, singer, and dancer who is asked to stand alone on a stage (or in a room) and sing what he has to say.* Book One: *On Singing Onstage* defines the techniques I teach. Book Two: *On Performing* has the sole purpose of placing that act within the context of show business as it relates to the musical theater. It ranges through all the relevant subject matter the late twentieth-century performer needs to target his expertise toward achieving employment in that marketplace. Book Three, this final volume, attempts to clarify the vast library of theater songs available to the beginner by choosing a "performer's dozen"—thirteen songs placed in categories with

a) a defining essay of each classification;
b) a song assignment that exemplifies the category (with one exception: True Blues);
c) a valid phrasing of the song;

---

* The use of *he* throughout this book is intended only as a substitute for the awkward *he* and/or *she*. No sociopolitical statement is implied.

d) a dialogue between me (DC) and a fictional performer, beginning with the music reading and ending with a professional performance of the song. Expatiations accompany these dialogues when what has been said leaves something to be said.*

In the main, the sung material is taken from the literature of the musical theater. Scenes are omitted on the surmise that the reader is interested not in "how to" act but in "how to" act songs. The technical facts in the exchanges are heard in my studio, but the dialogues have been edited to erase the identification of the performers and to eliminate talk that is discursive and small. They lie in between what was seen and what was heard in the sense that they exist in a dimension in which they can only be read. As a chronicle of events not witnessed by the reader they are, perhaps, less than the truth in that they attempt to report rather than to record what took place. In this regard I think they enjoy an advantage: The reader can bring a personal knowledge of his problems with a specific kind of song and find resolutions in the dialogues that particularize those problems.

As the title indicates, another group has been added to the collective *actor-singer-dancer*—the *performer*. Although this word was in use much farther back in time, it is only in the recent years that I have come to realize that the former defines a homogenized artist who can be expected to excel in one or two interpretive skills but whose ability in the third (more often than not as a dancer or a singer) is no more than passing fair. The performer may be—but need not be—expert in any of the three categories but, more important, he possesses a quite inexplicable quality that, on a stage, enthralls an audience. These artists appeared in what has come to be known as "vehicle" shows, and it was in this genre that audiences once attended Fred Astaire, Bert Lahr, Bea Lillie, and Ethel Merman (among others), just as in a later generation, Sid Caesar, Nancy Walker, Zero Mostel, and Lena Horne (among others), and latterly, Barbra Streisand in *Funny Girl*, Robert Lindsay in *Me and*

* The dialogues are evenly divided between the sexes. Although the techniques I teach are neuter, by virtue of their subject matter the performances of songs often have a distinct sexual orientation. This is not always due to a fixed element in the lyric. Times change not only the tastes of the public but, for the performer, alter the allowability factor. Songs denied women in the past may be acceptable today and in some cases add deeper truths to the statement of the lyric. See *On Singing Onstage*, pages 55-62 and 82-88.

My Girl, and Tommy Tune in *My One and Only* are applauded.

Surely *My Fair Lady* and *The Music Man* would not have triumphed had not *actors* and *singers* of the calibre of Rex Harrison and Robert Preston and Barbara Cook first given them vocal life. (Excluding Miss Cook, their performances have been preserved in the film versions of these musicals.) The successful *Sweeney Todd*, *Les Miserables* and *The Phantom of the Opera* were interpreted exclusively by singing casts and in particular by *singers* as gifted as George Hearn, Colm Wilkinson and Michael Crawford. The watershed *West Side Story* and *A Chorus Line* have forever dispelled the notion that *dancers* are mute for reasons other than the silent nature of their art. And just as surely, no amount of performing expertise will preempt a singer from claiming Freddy Eynsford-Hill, the Phantom and/or Georges Seurat in *Sunday in the Park* as his own; an actress will always be cast to play Professor Higgins's mother and Laurey's Aunt Eller; and the dancer holds a rightful claim on the ingenue in *Finian's Rainbow*, Tulsa in *Gypsy*, and the cats in *Cats*.

The category "performer," as differentiated from "actor-singer-dancer," is not easily defined because there are those who seem at home in either grouping and others who are sui generis. However, for me, one factor distinguishes all great performers: Because they are uniquely themselves they are always more interesting than anything they sing, dance, or act—no matter how well they do one, two, or all three. It is their very singularity that shapes the productions in which they appear, and without them, revivals of those musicals (or plays) are destined to suffer the weight of comparison, namely, Merman in *Gypsy*, Walker in *On the Town*, Harrison in *My Fair Lady* and Mostel in *Fiddler on the Roof*. This does not imply that comparison reveals the second-rate, only that productions invite nostalgic recollection. Critics may claim reportorial impartiality, but in our times any woman who plays Gypsy's mother invokes, in her personal notices, the name of Ethel Merman. In the future she will probably be lumbered with a reference to Tyne Daly and her dynastic successors.

The metamorphosis of the actor, singer, dancer into the hyphenate actor-singer-dancer began when musical comedy evolved into musical theater. It is not untenable to suggest that as early as 1927 Oscar Hammerstein's *Showboat* and later, in 1943, his *Carmen Jones* and *Oklahoma!* broadened the range of subject matter available to librettists. As enhanced plots and richer characterizations slowly and inexorably replaced the inane librettos whose sole purpose, until then, was to support glittering songs performed by star performers, "vehicle" musicals began their slide into history.

The "concept musical" is not a manifestation of a new musical theater, but it does pass as a new wrinkle whose definition remains fuzzy. Originally a symbol of auteurism, it now appears to suffer from a severe case of gigantism that inflates production costs and, in turn, the price of a ticket. Taking its cue from the old (for example, Rodgers and Hart's *Jumbo*) and the new (film and MTV), it offers the public visually stunning musicals whose simplism is sheathed in sumptuous splendor. This very splendor is its raison d'être, a contradiction of the older formula—the performer(s) whose presence, requiring a musical, justified its production. Extravaganzas are nothing new. They have been with us as far back as Mr. Ziegfeld. Viewed as magnificences, his Follies editions and the likes of *Cats*, *Starlight Express*, *Les Miserables* and *Phantom of the Opera* have much in common. But where gorgeousness once was employed as a setting in which to present the finest performing talents of the time, today's audiences are seemingly indifferent to who does what on the stage. A similar manifestation of this phase may even be found in opera houses. Donal Henahan, ex-music critic of *The New York Times*, has written, "In the absence of enough important singers [and conductors] to fill out a thirty-week season, the Metropolitan is training audiences to find alternative thrills in [the] sumptuous stage designs . . . and elaborate direction." Although major roles boast one, two, and even three understudies, the paying customers, once all too eager to ask for their money back if the star of a piece was "indisposed," is either unconcerned or unaware that B is standing in for A or that C is standing by to cover both of them. When I see one of these behemoths, I cannot refrain from wondering how a Merman, a Lahr, or a Lillie would have tolerated them. One can almost hear them as they call to the director sitting out front in the darkened theater, "Is all that going to go on while I'm working?" An ironic afterthought: Despite its passage into theater history, the era of musical comedy survives in the hearts, minds, and ears of the world because its scores are played and sung in endless recapitulation. The Gershwins, Jerome Kern, Irving Berlin, Rodgers and Hart and Hammerstein, Cole Porter, and Harold Arlen, among others, may not be alive (except in revivals) but their work is, and it is doing very well indeed. Alas, those performers who danced, clowned, and sang their songs have long since become victims of their ephemerality. Many of them are with us on recordings but these are less-than-prime testimonials. Unless they appeared on the screen and on cassette, the great singing, dancing, and/or comic artists are treasured memories only for the audiences who saw their work. They share this fate with the renowned actors of the eighteenth, nineteenth, and early twentieth centuries, all of whom had the bad luck to carve out their niches on the stage at a time in history when the stage was all there was on which to carve it.

It is this disappearance of the performer that concerns me. As a teacher I am only too aware that most of my students who are hell-bent to enter the musical theater have never seen the kind of performer who, transcending all else that is visible, fills the stage with his uniqueness. In recent years I find I am more and more impelled to cultivate in the young artist the courage to affirm a sense of his own essence (the primary building block of the performer as I have defined him) before moving on to the subject of the interpretation of sung text. The latter, essential to all acting studies, is one I have come to consider of secondary importance. It is true that all text has a subtext beneath it. It is equally true that for me neither the text nor its subtext has real *musical* theatrical significance until the "I" who sings it is unequivocally affirmed.

Plays and musicals take place on stages. Beyond that shared venue they have little in common. When placed beside the complicated structure of a musical, a play can seem simplistic. Even in their rehearsal periods, from first reading to opening night out of or in town, the stately pace of the creative development of a play makes a musical seem a bedlam in its preparatory phase. The mini-armies of creative people who labor to make a musical "work" illustrate this disparity. There is music to be taught to and learned by casts and choruses who will be singing its solos, duets, trios, quartets, and choral arrangements; orchestrations to be created, scored, copied, and rehearsed; staging and choreography to be devised, taught and rehearsed; hundreds of costumes to be designed and fitted—all of these elements (and many more) create a state of logistical complexity that can be daunting to an actor more accustomed to the slow pace of a play's rehearsal period in which he and the director, the captain of rehearsals, create a climate in which the actor is free to explore, investigate, personal-ize, and interact. But it is a given that it is the actor alone, in rehearsal, who will be expected to take responsibility for breathing life into his role and, in ensemble, into the life of the play. A play, then, may be said to mature through elastic channels that may not be calculated or guessed at before the process begins.

In contrast, musicals develop along more predetermined routes. The director's concept of the piece has already been "put into the works" in scenery-building shops, and the composer, the lyricist, and the librettist have, from the beginning, been partners in the enterprise. By the time the cast comes into the picture the musical has already begun the journey toward its final destination. It is not my intention to downplay the contribution of the cast—depending upon the particular artist(s) in a major role(s), this can be enormous—but to point out that no matter the importance, it must not—in fact, cannot—disturb the original intentions of the creative staff.

Today, the creation of a musical is a prime example of content decreeing form put to the service of concept. While there are exceptions to this, they are exceptions. For the actor, the awful truth is that musicals are staged. Very little time is allowed or even available for slow inward-to-outward growth. Improvisational work in the early days of rehearsals, as in the case of *Les Miserables*, may be allowed but time is money and the calendar remains unyielding. Nor is there much freedom in the land of musical theater. Just as one is enslaved by music and its shackling of melody, rhythm, key, and time signatures, the same can be said for the performer's placement within the context of the setting for the scene. And within that imprisonment, like boxes within boxes, there are strictures that determine the shape of things: the need for brevity (overtime can be costly) that justifies painful surgeries that cut not only lines but entire roles from the piece; and, above all, the driving energy—the pacing—that propels a musical and can work havoc with an actor's "moments."

The singing performer who reads this volume with no ambition or desire to work in the musical theater may find some of the subject matter confining. It is agreed that the demands of concert and stadium stages that present the work of "pop" performers and groups, and the nightclubs, cocktail lounges and small boîtes that employ chanteurs and -teuses are far removed from the criteria applied to the musical theater. However, it is this writer's opinion that show business refracts, separates, comes together, duplicates, and splits again with dramatic changes in styles that, in the beginning, seem immiscible but, in time, become congeries of the whole enchilada.

Introduction

BY WAY OF EXPLANATION

Songs can be sung with lungs, throat, and mouth regardless of an absence of mind. To perform a song sanely is an act exclusive of its vocalization. Three elements of the performer's art reveal sanity or in–:

FOCUS: The *to whom* am I singing?

PHRASING: The clarity of thought and the sensitivity to language that shapes what is being sung.

BODY LANGUAGE: The physical appearance of the performance that is the performer's personal signature.

I have written at length on these three subjects in *On Singing Onstage*, and they will be discussed again within the pages of this volume. Simply restated:

FOCUS

Unifocus songs are songs sung to one "spot" because the lyric speaks (sings) to an explicit "you."* The exception: when the explicit "you" implies "you-all," as in:

"Forget all your troubles and just get happy
<u>You</u> better chase all your cares away."**

House numbers are songs in which the lyric speaks (sings) to everyone present.

Internalized focus songs are those in which the singer of the song is also its receiver.

Unifocus

Unifocus songs are embraced by the actor (as distinguished from the singer) with evident relief since they most resemble the actor's own turf: working *to* another person. Of course, in singing, the

---

*See *On Singing Onstage*, Focus, pages 197-199
**"Get Happy" by Harold Arlen and Ted Koehler, from *9:15 Revue*.

"other person" must be created out of the fabric of the actor's imagination and placed through and beyond the fourth wall. Before the concept of unifocus is presented to the beginner, what had seemed an unfamiliar generality now enjoys a familiar specificity. "To whom am I singing?" is no longer a flabby concept defined as "everybody" or "anybody" but a personalized centered focus that is the receiving end of the song. The actor (and I now include the singer and the dancer) is so seduced by this coziness that often what is not a unifocus lyric is forced to become one. A song that concerns the theater-at-large is then crushed into a narrow field of reference. Does the neophyte performer realize this? Not until he is so informed. Singers are less guilty because for them singing is, in the beginning, an acoustical/musical experience that has nothing to do with an organic, dramatically motivated performance of the song. A song intended for everyone or anyone is not so much alien to their studies as it is irrelevant; they will sing what is printed on a page of music even if their choices of focus are confusing to the listener. The discovery of sane focus has an immediate effect on their work: a seeming well-spring that gives artistic truth to the sight and sound of the vocalized music.

House Numbers

House Numbers present no discomfort to the innate performer, whether he is a singer or a dancer. Unencumbered by the baggage of acting techniques (as taught by acting teachers who are ignorant of the rules of the game of singing as set apart from acting), they revel in being the one who diverts the many. These performers are often described as "entertainers". (When confronted with a unifocus song, they have only to learn what actors, by the definition of their craft, already know. One need only bring to their attention an understanding of "to whom am I singing?").

Internalized Focus

This focus choice defines a song that is a soliloquy in the strict Elizabethan meaning of the word. Although all songs can be said to be soliloquies (one person is singing, alone, on the stage), some songs can be said to be *more* soliloquized than others.* The sung lyric seeks to work out the performer's problem, as in:

*I am speaking here only of solo performances. Duets, trios, quartets, and choral arrangements are not within the context of this book.

> "Why was I born? Why an
> What do I get? What am I

or:

> "Steady, steady
> Am I ready?
> Really ready
> This could be my once in a lifetime."**

The singer is addressing the lyric to himself, singing out a problem that does not require an audience to attend it. But the performer must be made aware that an audience *is* present and it is imperative that he hold its attention. A performance that disregards this truth need not bother to be sung in public. The problem can just as readily be worked out (sung) in the privacy of the singer's home. When privacy goes public it is imperative that the audience (no matter how small) be acknowledged. Remember: Songs are always sung in the present, at the time and in the place in which they are sung. When auditors are present, the performance must bear witness to that fact.

Phrasing

Bad (or no) phrasing is an indication that the performer has not made a memorized lyric his own or, worse, ignored the subject entirely. But audiences tend to hear what they hear. When a song moves through the fourth wall in a garbled fashion, the listener cannot be expected to rescramble nonsense into sense. Good phrasing makes effortless a comprehension of what is being sung. The attention of the audience lies somewhere within the margins of that comprehension, and it is sustained by the continual flow of current generated not only by what is seen but, just as important, by what is heard. Just as Focus manifests a sane presentation of the performer, good phrasing of words and music offers a sane presentation of the song.†

---

*"Why Was I Born?" by Jerome Kern and Oscar Hammerstein II, from *Sweet Adeline*.
**"Steady Steady" by Milton Shafer and Ronnie Graham, from *Bravo Giovanni*.
†See *On Singing Onstage*, pages 33-45.

By Way of Reference

forty-odd years I have been teaching, a glossary of terms own out of the need for a language the student and DC could for instant comprehension of the criteria upon which criticism was based. Below is a short lexicon to help the reader understand this intramural idiom when it appears in the dialogues that follow. Neologisms were invented only when preexisting musical and/or acting terms were not there to borrow.

"*Air*." All music printed in the score that has no sung text printed beneath the melodic line. With this as its distinguishing factor, "Air"—no matter the length of its metrical footage—

    a) always appears at the top of the song, preceding the vocal. In the trade it is called the Vamp or the Intro. (see below);

    b) always appears at the end of the Verse as it moves into the Chorus (see below);

    c) always appears between "8s";

    d) precedes the Release, or Bridge, if there is one (see below); and

    e) describes the music that accompanies the last held note at the end of the song (the Rideout—see below).

"*Air*" *will always be found in these five placements* and may be present more often within the body of the song.

Base. Sung material at any audition for a musical should be performed standing up. Sitting down on a stool or a chair is not recommended as a professional presentation of your work.* A standard Base—position of the feet—should be approximately twelve to fifteen inches apart. At that spacing the Base is neither too narrow nor too wide and allows for further widening when the melody rises and more "grounding" is required for the support of the vocal line. Weight should be firmly planted on both feet. When weight is transferred to one side of the body, the Base is described as "sitting". This position of the Base more aptly suits an easy, conversational lyric. What is essential to remember is that feet, as well as hands, betray a thoughtless mind.**

*See Category 13, Contemporary, pages 296-297. Performances in musicals, concerts or nightclub acts are staged and sitting while singing may be an element of the staging process.
**See *On Performing*, Question 9, pages 75-77, and many of the dialogues in this volume.

Come and ***Go Home***. All performances should take place in the optimal geography, neither too close nor too far from those who are auditioning you. Most often, on a stage, this is the desirable Center (C) and down "in one" where everyone, given a choice of location, dreams to stand. Movement away from Center within the performance of the song must be either to the Left or Right (L or R) since "in one" is as far down as one may go and moving upstage, farther away from the auditioner is, in the main, unwise. When the singer moves to the Left or Right an aesthetic shape to the appearance of the performance is achieved by remembering to Come or Go Home (return to C) in time for the finish of the song (Rideout).

Down and ***Up***. When the performer moves closer to the audience he is moving Down—as he retreats, the move is described as moving Up. (This is not to be confused with "going up," a reference to forgetting lines or lyrics. Sometimes this is also described as "drying up" or "going dry.") Just as Center is the ideal, Down is better than Up.

Diphthong. Two vowel sounds within a syllable that are glidingly pronounced and, for the neophyte singer, a bane. For example, in Cole Porter's "Night And Day," the title contains a diphthong in each key word. When the words are spoken they are not abusive to the ear; when sung, they close the throat and raise the lower jaw and wreak considerable damage on the singer. The rule: Sing the first vowel and at the last possible moment close into the second element of the Diphthong as in NAH . . . EET and DEH . . . EE.

Elision. The graceful vocalization of the lyric line, moving on one column of breath from the ending of a word into the beginning of the next word. For example:
"MAH . . . EEKUH . . . NTREE . . . TIH . . . ZUH . . . VTHEE . . . "
Music is sung on vowels, not consonants. (*l*'s, *m*'s and *n*'s, can be pitched but the consensus of opinion does not commend the practice except in vocal exercises.) There are times when the

explosion of a consonant has dramatic value and, indeed, it is good to remember that vowels become words when and if consonants surround them. When fear or sloppy vocal production impels the singer to close into the consonant too soon, the practice of Elision prevents that closing by eliding the consonant to the beginning of the word that follows it. In this manner, the throat is kept open and the legato line of the musical phrase is maintained. This *bel canto* style of singing is still the recognized mark of a knowledgeable singer.

Finger Tape. For learning purposes, a recording of only the melodic line of the song set apart from its accompaniment. When a performer has no one to teach him the song, a Finger Tape is of great value in pinning down and freezing the exact notes as scored by the composer.

Focus or **Spot**. As previously explained, the "to whom" the song is being sung.

Frame. I use this word to describe a specific physical action that *immediately precedes the vocal line*. As a general rule, it sets up the first hearing of the song's title, "frames" a joke about to be told, and, of course, indicates (in the nonactor's use of the term) valuable subtextual thinking.*

Glottal or **Glottal Stop**. The interruption of a column of breath to achieve a comma in the vocal line. It is not to be confused with a breath.

Music Reading. A "reading" of the song onstage in order to allow the performer to concentrate on notes, rhythm, choice of key, and phrasing. No performance, not even the hint of one, is permitted. The objectivity required of a Music Reading is easier to write about than to maintain. The seduction of making music emotionalizes and thereby destroys the purpose of the Music Reading. The performer must learn to keep up his guard.

Nod. The indication to the accompanist that the performer is

---

*See *On Singing Onstage*, the "Three," pages 159-163.

ready to start. The Nod is used only for auditions. During the performance of a musical it is the task of the conductor to bring the orchestra in; at an audition, with only a pianist as his accompanist, the performer must be the decision-maker. When an accompanist does not receive a Nod, he rightly assumes that the performer is waiting for him to begin. This sets into motion the absurdist condition wherein the performer accompanies the accompanist. It further establishes a primacy the pianist neither desires nor merits.* An afterthought: A Nod should not be so subtle that the accompanist fails to see it. There is nothing more pitiable than two Nods.

Promenade. The Come and Go Home, referred to above, is executed by performing a Promenade. One may think of it as a walk to the Left or Right, but there is so great a "fix" on the walk in order to give it its style that everyone agreed to add a special word to identify it.

Rideout (as referred to above in "Air"). Just as all songs have Vamps (see below), all songs have Rideouts. And just as Vamps may be as short as one note and as long as the composer or the arranger chooses to make them, so, too, do Rideouts come in all sizes. They may be no more than a mere chord or Sting (again, see below) or extend all the way to what has been called a Roxy Rideout.** A Rideout begins on the downbeat of the last-sung word and the song is considered to be finished only when the Rideout has played itself out—no matter its length. The performer plays through it with decreasing intensity so that when the Rideout has ended he is visibly free of the song. Of course, in a performance before a paying audience, this is no longer true since the purpose of the entire enterprise is to elicit a positive response—applause. At an audition, no matter how affectionate the response, there is only silence. It is important to remember that an audition is not, in the strict sense, a performance of the song. It is a demonstration of the performer's work. A good audition is never greeted with a hand; it sets into motion decision-making conferences that may include the scheduling of callbacks or, better still, the offer of a job. I have always found it wise to learn how to rid yourself of a song already

*See *On Singing Onstage*, Don'ts and Do's, pages 73-75.
**See *On Singing Onstage*, The Rideout, pages 26-27.

sung and to step back into the reality life that was "on hold" from the moment you nodded to your accompanist. Going for a hand you will never get leaves you alone in an intolerable silence.

Vamp (as referred to above in "Air"). All songs have, as introduction, music that sets

a) the key of the song;

b) the tempo in which it will be played and sung; and

c) (if deemed necessary) music that will set the ambience of the song by painting the Vamp with specific tonal colors.

The first (a) is of prime importance given the number of possible keys a song can be played in; (b) is less urgent but it does inform the singer how fast *fast* will be or how slow *slow* will be. The audience is unconcerned with (a)—in what key a song is sung is of significance only to the performer. They may, in the case of (b), enjoy the foreknowledge that it is a ballad or an uptempo song they will be hearing, but for the performer it establishes an affective imprint on his thinking.* In the case of (c), choice is given to the performer. There are many songs that benefit from a kind of musical scenery, preset into the Vamp. Both the performer and the audience share in the Vamp's ability to create a mood. One can live without (c), struggle along without (b), but (a) will always be required unless, of course, the performer possesses perfect pitch. It would, even then, not be recommended. A song that begins with no instrumental announcement seems to me unnecessary self-advertising. Vamps, like Rideouts, come in all sizes. They can be as simplistic as:

a) a *Bell Tone* (one note—the starting note);

b) a *Sting* (a Bell Tone harmonized with the starting note accented at the top of the chord); or

c) one, two, three, four, five, six, eight bars—or for that matter, as much music as the composer or the arranger deems necessary (always keeping in mind that too long is provocative and long, longer, and longest are the simple, comparative and superlative equivalents of tedium); or

d) a *Vamp 'Til Ready*—an open-end Vamp that comes to its

---

*From *Stanislavski on Opera*: " . . . How lucky you singers are. The composer provides you with [one of] the most important element[s]—the rhythm of your inner emotions. That is what we actors have to create for ourselves out of a vacuum. All you have to do is listen to the music and make it your own."

finish at the moment the performer begins to sing.

Verse. That section of the song that precedes the Chorus. Do all songs have Verses? No. When they do, should they be sung? That depends. A Verse exists to reveal expository information (just as a play has, at its top, the exposition that gives pertinence to the subsequent action of the piece). Without a Verse, the Chorus lacks a coherent specificity. But Verses do add to the length of time allowed a performer at an audition. They can be an irritation to the auditioner(s) when schedules are tight. Discretion is recommended. In a general performance, the choice belongs to the performer.

When a Class begins, the performer is assigned his material but there is always confusion about what is expected of him. DC explains the rules of the game:

1. *Have* two *copies of each song: one copy* for the accompanist who will mark on it all pertinent musical information—the key the song will be sung in*; new Vamps and Rideouts pasted over the altered parts; the Verse's excision if it is not to be sung; new or added lyrics legibly inserted; cut or extended "Air" "fills" noted; repeats and/or skips notated; and a *second copy* of the song for the exclusive use of the performer, to treat in the same way an actor marks his script (the phrasing "plot," subtext information, altered lyrics, focus choices, implicit cues, physical "business"). All this information should be marked so that the performer can pick up the song at any time in the future and rest easy in the knowledge that he can reprise his performance without resorting to impaired memory.

2. *Learn the music of the song with particular attention to detail.* Too often, the performer begins to sing a song before he knows exactly what the composer has written. Wrong notes, then, must be blasted out of his internal ear. When he is sure of himself and the song, he will take a Music Reading (see above).

3. In *On Singing Onstage* I have described five technical exercises the performer works on a song.** Simply stating the complicated:

   a) *"One."* What does the song *say?* In his own words, and

---

*Opera scores and lieder are printed in keys that should not to be tampered with, but it must be apparent, even to the beginner, that the published key of a "pop" or theater song is not intended as the performer's private arrangement.

**See *On Singing Onstage*, pages 117-168.

beginning with "This is a story about a man, a woman, a boy, or a girl," the performer renders an objective monologue in which the tale of the song is told. Further information is added: the sex of the singer of the song (male, female, or possibly either); his age (maximal, minimal, optimal); education (un-, minimal, high school, well-schooled); economic status (lower lower class up to and inclusive of upper upper class); his geographic classification (urban, suburban, rural)—all this rendered as *objectively* as possible. Since none of the above is explicit in the lyric, the performer must attempt to stay within the bounds of the intention of the "One" and conjecture must be rooted in *objective* inference drawn from stated facts in the lyric. Does the performer "do" a "One" in the *performance* of a song? Yes. But it is not discussed in Class. DC assumes the performer's understanding of what a lyric means is drawn from a cognizance of what it says.

b) *"Two."* What does the song *mean?* In his own words and, this time, beginning with "This is a story about me . . . ", the performer constructs a dialogue between himself and a vis-à-vis. The latter is, of course, imagined and therefore the "dialogue" is a monologue constructed with one major intention: *to impel the performer to move.* If the "Two" can be delivered without a continuous physical life, it is rejected.

DC suggests that the choice of vis-à-vis be *conflictive with the performer.* Just as all drama can be said to draw its life from the acknowledgment of "A wanting something B won't let him have," so the performance of a song gains and holds the attention of the audience when it is not presumed to be interesting merely because it is being sung. It is conflict that builds tension and it is tension that sustains the connection between the performer and his audience. Furthermore, the "Two" creates the energy (heat) that produces a *personal, physical life,* the primary goal of the "Two". It is this continual flow of body language that is the hallmark of a *workable* "Two". In the performance of a song, does the performer first "do" a "Two"? *No.* A "Two" is a *technical exercise* placed on a song—an invented monologue the telling of which keeps him in a constant state of movement. In the *performance* of a song, this goal is not only not sensible but, were it employed, would result in a performance so physicalized that it would appear bizarre. However, the performer has learned that no text (lyric) exists without the ever-present ballast of subtext. He will always *sing* the written song but he will *play*, to a specific focus, what the song means (to him). His physical language, when called for, will be the outward manifestation of thoughts that create movement and that are significant to the text. This "personal" body language precludes the limited stock gestures beloved by singers of all kinds of music that are passed from performer to performer and, in some cases, taught by teachers who themselves are innocent of alternative solutions to the problem.*

c) *"Three."* The physical appearance of the "Two" is now placed over the spoken lyric. This element of the five exercises is difficult to perform. The silent "Two" must be played with almost total commitment (since the heard lyric is whispered) while the physical "frames" *precede* the lyric they relate to in a seamless flow that, in the beginning, may strike the performer as something akin to rubbing his stomach while, at the same time, patting his head.** In the performance of a song, does the performer "do" a "Three"? Yes, in the sense that, *when and if body language is employed*, it will precede the words it births.

d) *"Four."* The same exercise as the "Three," but the lyric is whispered on the note pitches the composer has assigned to them. The "Two" remains the dominant element. What was spoken in the "Three" is now sung. As in the "Three," DC recommends a whispered rendering of the melody since concentration on the "Two" is menaced by unrestrained vocalization.

e) *"Five."* Again, the "Two" is played full-out but the performer sings the song as written: melody and rhythm are given their due as the "Two" conforms to the demands of the printed song rather than to its own truths.†

Does the performer do a "Five" in a performance of a song? No. He

---

*Again, from *Stanislavski on Opera*: "Singers usually imitate the mannerisms of [great] performers and for that all they need is to have a good aural (sic) memory."

**The words "almost total" appear to cancel out the strict meaning of "commitment." Only those who have successfully worked a "Three" would agree with this fractional reference to a word that is either total or not committed at all.

†The descriptions of the "Two," the "Three," and the "Five" are simplistic. For a detailed elaboration, see *On Singing Onstage*.

has (correctly) not done a "Two."

The confusion experienced by the performer when he first begins performing asssigned material is understandable. Overstuffed with technical information, paralysis takes over. When singing a song was once nothing more than singing the song, innocence spared him any discomfort. Now, do's and don'ts constrict and, worse, rob him of the enjoyment of simply singing out. But all technique exists, finally, to support and to liberate. When it is new and in need of constant attendance to its rules, some degree of self-consciousness is to be expected but the inevitable moment arrives when the performer flies free of it. It is then that technique has learned its place and disappears into that part of the right brain where it waits to function in its own arcane fashion. *

DIALOGUES

The dialogues that follow attempt to dramatize twelve of the thirteen categories by dispensing with numbing pedagogic prose. The characters depicted and their professional standing are an out-and-out fiction. The performing information they contain is fact. It is hoped that within them the reader will find answers to hitherto unanswered questions. Omitted is DC's habit of throwing cues to the performer as he sings. These proddings may be no more than a "Why?", "You're kidding!", "What did you think about that?", "What happened next?", and other equally simplistic verbal pokings. Delivered by DC at a specific moment (before the new line has arrived), their purpose is to keep the performer alert to what is *going* to be said and to prove, in their fashion, that any cue correctly timed is better than none. It would be impossible to imitate this on paper because their effect depends on the spontaneity of the cue and would read meaninglessly. For those readers

---

*In his book *Opera—Dead or Alive*, subtitled *Production, Performance and Enjoyment of Musical Theater*, Ronald E. Mitchell writes: "Intelligent actors cannot leave everything to nature. Most of them are obliged to go through a learning and improvement stage during which they lose some naturalness as they increase their physical flexibility. . . . [One] must take the risk of remaining in this apprenticeship forever. If one remains in it, the training was a total waste of time. The successful artist is the one who, having learned his craft, recaptures the spontaneity of movement and the genuine quality of speech and song. One's mature acting must have nothing of the classroom in it. . . . "

whom I have taught, it will be further corroboration of the fictional nature of the dialogues.

It must be emphasized that the dialogues are best understood if the reader comprehends the disparate goals of the actor as opposed to those of the performer. At first the actor may resist DC's insistence that what the song *looks like* must be considered as significant to its successful rendition as the *internal truth* of its life: The *who is singing* shares equal importance with the *why* and the *to whom* the song is being sung. For actors assured of a hiding place behind the characters they play, this can be a difficult adjustment to make, but make it they must, for *they are the songs they sing*. The natural performer unconsciously celebrates that *he is the song*. *Who is singing* is the mark of his calling, his inclination. However, in its extreme manifestation, it can become a solipsistic approach to the work that ignores the two other elements integral to great performing. My personal conviction holds that it is not a satisfying work-method in any arena of show business since it fails to recognize both the presence of the audience and the impulse that creates the need to sing. It is this reality that informs the content of *A Performer Prepares*.

A PERFORMER'S DOZEN

Stephen Holden, in *The New York Times*, has described the music written for the theater as " . . . a literature that begins to look like a peculiarly American form of classical music. Refined in its craft yet remarkably adaptable in performance, it occupies a special historic place. Conforming neither to the European classical tradition of written music intended for strict interpretation nor to the oral tradition of American jazz and rock, it stands as a bridge between opposite musical worlds. Like any other music, this literature can continue to live only through performance."

It is this literature I have attempted to categorize. With only two exceptions, its provenance is the vast available library of theater and/or screen musical. The categories will make it easier to choose what to sing for general or audition performances.* Like all subjective categorizing, the divisions are arguable and fuzzy at the

*For further information concerning the subject of choice of song and "what to sing?", see *On Singing Onstage*, pages 182-183.

outer margins of each group. The classifications are given some degree of validity because they have been around a long time and, although compositional styles change, they remain precedented and timeless. As for the selection of songs, it is only my intention to offer illustration by way of example. As a result of the confining nature of any listing, there is some musical material left without a home, thus the need for a catchall: the twelfth group. Each category will be

> a) described in its particular section;
> b) followed by an assigned song;
> c) followed by a fictional dialogue between the performer and DC that creates and builds to the final performance of the song.

The categories are

> **1**. Show Ballad
> **2**. Narrative Show Ballad
> **3**. Dramatic Show Ballad
> **4**. True Blues
> **5**. Pop Blues
> **6**. Theater Blues
> **7**. Swinging Ballad
> **8**. Up-Tempo
> **9**. Waltz
> **10**. Patter Song
> **11**. Showstopper
> **12**. Catchall
> **13**. Contemporary*

The sample song from each category includes its printed lyric and the lead sheet of its melodic line with basic harmonic information and a suggested plotting for a reasonable phrasing of the song.** The lead sheet is *not an exact copy of the published sheet music.* Changes in the arrangements, made during the course of the dialogues, are added. They are not to be thought of as holy writ. I recommend the singer purchase the published sheet music if he plans to perform it.† It is then suggested he begin to use his imagination to discover his own personal choices. For the reader,

---

*The Contemporary category refers to those songs that are identified with the world of "pop" music as distinct from theater music.
**For detailed information on the "how-to's" of phrasing from both lyric and/or music, see *On Singing Onstage*, pages 33-46.
†For a more detailed discussion of sheet music, see *On Singing Onstage*, pages 3-17 and 19-31.

however, the lead sheet should be kept close at hand in order to follow and to understand the exchanges between the performer and DC in the body of the dialogues. Each dialogue is in two sections. The first is a music reading that shapes the *vocalization* of the song. The second is the arrival at a *performance* of the song.

For the actor, preparation is an integral element of his art. In a play it is the why and the how of his entrances onto the stage and it is the play from which the actor extracts the "facts" of his character that will become the taproot of his performance. But just as surely as the *play's* the thing for the actor, the reverse is true for the performer: the *singer* is the song. The performer is quite literally the instrument of the song's birth and, by virtue of this parentage, the material will be stamped with his singularity. Sanford Meisner, the preeminent acting teacher, has written that acting is " . . . a scary paradoxical business. One of its central paradoxes is that in order to succeed as an actor you have to lose consciousness of your own self in order to transform yourself into the character of the play. It's not easy but it can be done."* *A Performer Prepares* presents the counter-argument: *Singing is a scary business but it is never paradoxical. In order to succeed as a performer you have to surrender to the total exposure of self; to reject characterization and evasion of who you truly are. It is not easy but it must be done.* The most often heard exchange in my classes after a first-rate performance of a song:

DC

That was splendid! How did you feel?

STUDENT

It was so easy. I felt as though I didn't *do* anything.

The student speaks what appears to be the simple truth, but as Oscar Wilde remarked: "The truth is never simple." It takes a great deal of "letting go" before it becomes easy. The dialogues that

*From *Sanford Meisner on Acting* by Sanford Meisner and Dennis Longwell. Copyright © 1987 by Sanford Meisner and Dennis Longwell. Published by Vintage Books, NY.

make up the body of this volume involve DC and students who will be moving through a painful process, learning to make it easy or, still more difficult, learning to make it *look* easy.

"An American In Paris"

Love Is Here To Stay

Words by Ira Gershwin

Music by George Gershwin

26

"Love Is Here to Stay"

VERSE:
The more I read the papers
The less I comprehend
The world (✓) and all its capers (,)
And how it all will end (✓)
Nothing seems to be lasting
But that isn't our affair (✓)
We've got something permanent (✓)
I mean (,) in the way we care (✓)

CHORUS:
It's very clear our love is here to stay (✓)
Not for a year but ever and a day (✓)
The radio and the telephone (✓)
And the movies that we know
May just be passing fancies (✓)
And in time may go (✓)
But (,) oh my dear
Our love is here to stay (✓)
Together we're going a long long way (✓)
In time the Rockies may crumble (,)
Gibraltar may tumble (✓)
They're only made of clay
But (✓) our love is here to stay (✓)

"Love Is Here to Stay" from *The Goldwyn Follies*, lyrics by Ira Gershwin, music by George Gershwin. Copyright © 1938 Chappell & Co. Copyright renewed. International Copyright Secured. All Rights Reserved. Chappell & Co., Inc. sole selling agent. Used by permission.

1

Show Ballad

The Show Ballad is a basic building block in the construction of a musical and, as such, it can be found in every musical theater piece. Composers and lyricists may somewhere, someday, try to get away with writing a score without one, but the attempt will be futile. There may be scores whose ballads are craftily camouflaged (the following two ballad categories are where they can be found), but just as in the opera house, the genders are hell-bent to stand side by side and sing of their mutual affection (in Act One), to stand apart in disaffection (as Act One ends) and, at Finale time, to reunite and reprise. Like ballads of all kinds, the Show Ballad is melodic and slow, but this first ballad group can be identified by its easy, unpushed rhythmic beat and three features common to the genre:

a) Because its lyric statement is more or less general it can be lifted out of the score of the musical to which it belongs and sung, out of context, with no loss of its essential meaning.

b) Of the three ballad groups, they are generally the easiest to vocalize. They have to be. They were and are written for the world to hum and sing.

c) Most often they are unifocus songs that A sings to B (boy to girl or the reverse).

It is virtually impossible to list the composers of Show Ballads in the musical theater and the songs for which they are most known without risking unpardonable omissions, but the following standard songs will perhaps suggest recognizable features that are characteristic of the category:

- Rodgers and Hart: "Where or When," "I Could Write a Book," "I Didn't Know What Time It Was," "I Married an Angel," "Have You Met Miss Jones?" "My Heart Stood Still," "Dancing on the Ceiling," "I'll Tell the Man in the Street," and "You Are Too Beautiful."
- Rodgers and Hammerstein: "People Will Say We're in Love," "A Fellow Needs a Girl," "If I Loved You," and "You Are Beautiful."
- George and Ira Gershwin: "Embraceable You," "He Loves and She Loves," "Mine," "They Can't Take That Away From Me," "Love Is Here to Stay," "Who Cares?" and "Of Thee I Sing."
- Irving Berlin: "Always," "I Got Lost in His Arms," "I Used to Be Color Blind," "How Deep Is the Ocean?" "Let's Face the Music and Dance," "They Say It's Wonderful," and "Be Careful, It's My Heart."
- Cole Porter: "I Concentrate on You," "I Love You," "In the Still of the Night," "I've Got You Under My Skin," "Mind If I Make Love to You," and "What Is This Thing Called Love?"
- Frank Loesser: "I've Never Been in Love Before," "My Heart Is So Full of You," "Somebody Somewhere," "I'll Know," and "My Darling, My Darling."
- Jerome Kern: "The Way You Look Tonight," "Make Believe," "Why Do I Love You?" "The Song Is You," "I'm Old-Fashioned," "All the Things You Are," and "They Didn't Believe Me."
- Jule Styne: "Time After Time," "You'll Never Get Away From Me," "How Do You Speak to an Angel?" "Who Are You Now?" and "Small World."
- Kander and Ebb: "A Quiet Thing" and "We Can Make It."
- Lerner and Loewe: "On the Street Where You Live," "Another Autumn," "Here I'll Stay," "The Heather on the Hill," and "Almost Like Being in Love."

The above list ignores Harold Arlen, Arthur Schwartz, Burt Bacharach, Shire and Maltby, Stephen Sondheim, Strouse and Adams, Jerry Herman, Bock and Harnick, Leonard Bernstein,

Andrew Lloyd Webber, Cy Coleman, Noel Coward, and . . . and . . . but they, along with other composers and lyricists, will appear in later categories.* The Show Ballad, whatever its permutations, is and will always be the sine qua non of a musical theater score, and no performer's repertoire may be considered complete without one or more of them close at hand.

THE SONG

The Show Ballad I have chosen, "Love Is Here to Stay," is by George and Ira Gershwin, written at the peak of their talents. The song carries a tragic weight—it is the last song George Gershwin wrote before he died on July 11, 1937, at the age of thirty-eight. Written for the score to the film *The Goldwyn Follies* and sung by Kenny Baker, it was later reprised by Gene Kelly in the Academy Award-winning musical *An American in Paris*. For me, it is quintessential Gershwin. The Verse is both simple and complicated. The lyric matches the grace of the music as it swoops, turns, and finally settles into descending scales and a final short variation of the first theme. The rubato upbeat " . . . It's very . . . " keeps the Chorus at bay, which is all to the good since, as soon as the downbeat arrives on the word " . . . clear," the recognition factor that accompanies it is irresistible.

The form is ABAC and the second "8" (the B theme) is unique in that, ideally phrased, it should be sung in one breath. It rarely, if ever, is. The last "8" (C) is a variation on the B theme with a surprising quarter-note rest before " . . . our love is here to stay" that kicks the song out of the sentimental and somehow makes the title doubly affirmative.**

The dialogue that follows singles out the Ingenue, but the song may be sung by a Juvenile, a Leading Man or a Leading Lady. There is no preferred gender, nor does color of skin, hair, or eyes delimit who may or may not sing it. The Character Man and Character Woman are barred only if their chronological age

---

* For the reader with no knowledge of the above-listed songs, I recommend the recordings of Ella Fitzgerald, Frank Sinatra, Mel Tormé, Tony Bennett, Mabel Mercer, Sarah Vaughan, Bobby Short, Carmen McRae, early Streisand albums, Michael Feinstein, Steve Ross, and others. They have all recorded albums exclusively devoted to musical theater "standards."

** See *On Singing Onstage*, pages 25–26 for an explanation of "8s"and song forms.

mitigates against the vow that love is here to stay. For senior performers, choose a song that celebrates the fact that it stayed.

THE DIALOGUE

EM enters. She is a young lady cursed and blessed with the classic "look" of the Ingenue, a presence in musical theater (along with the Juvenile) as elemental as Harlequin and Columbine are to Italian commedia dell'arte. The blessing? Easy typecasting. The curse? Too easy typecasting. This is a bind not uncommon to all show business arenas. Young persons eager to seek a professional life in the theater (as well as in film and television) commit the understandable and pardonable sin of finding corroboration for that career choice in the attractive vision looking back at them from their morning mirror. In one sense this is justified; the world celebrates beauty and happily pays to view it. But there is an ambivalence in the celebration. Women and men who come packaged with too many of nature's blessings are not taken as seriously as those who, by virtue of their less alluring appearance, are judged to be more real and thus more consequential artists. An added burden: It is assumed that beauty cannot play any wider of the mark than what the eye sees. Were EM a skillful soprano her professional life in the musical theater would be abundant. Unfortunately, the outward aspect and the vocal sound are not well matched. Nevertheless, DC is aware of the young lady's acting skills and her earnest desire to improve her singing. Her natural voice is more than pleasant; she is musical and she likes to sing (an asset in a Gershwin song). Her ongoing study work with a singing teacher may very well redeem what the thrifty gods have withheld. The assignment of "Love Is Here to Stay" allows her to sing a Show Ballad that does not—in fact, must not—be soprano'd into its grave.

EM sings through her first music reading. The song has been keyed down to C Major from the key in the published copy (F Major) to service EM's chest voice. When she is finished, and before DC can comment, she begs for a lower key.

DC

I don't think you can risk going any lower. The melody lies low in the voice, and if we cheat it lower for you it'll sound like an open admission that you can't sing the B naturals* on " . . . The radio" in the eighth bar and " . . . In time . . . " at the top of the twenty-fourth bar.**

EM

Well, I can't.

DC

You can't if you've already made up your mind. A B natural is not out of the question for you even now. You have to remember to take a good low breath, get some support under it, and indulge in some positive thinking.
> (EM *tries again. It is better but the B naturals still loom like*
> *approaching mountain peaks.*)

That's better. Much better. The problem, I think, is that you're shortchanging yourself when you sit on the notes right before those trouble spots. It doesn't leave you time to get in enough air. There's no money to be made holding on to that last word " . . . day" in the line " . . . but ever and a day." And the same goes for " . . . way" in " . . . going a long, long way." Get off them after you've held them for three beats. No longer. Then you'll have enough time to breathe and to deal with the high B's that follow. Even more important, you'll get rid of what you just finished saying and you'll be able to get on with what you're going to say. Let's just try the first one. Come to it from the top of the Chorus. It'll be easier that way.
> (EM *does so, remembers to get off the word " . . . day,"*
> *allowing herself sufficient time to take a valuable "swimmer's"*
> *breath. The B natural on " . . . radio" comes singing out.*)

How did that feel? It sounded fine.

---

* In the sheet music it is scored as an E natural. EM's key would place it on a B natural.
** From here on the reader should keep the lead and lyric sheet near in order to follow and understand the dialogues.

EM

I couldn't believe it was me!

DC

Good. Let's go on, then. I'm in the Verse now. About your ad-lib reading. You're singing the lines like a nursery rhyme.
"Mary had a little lamb (*Stop*)
Its fleece was white as snow (*Stop*)
And everywhere that Mary went (*Stop*)
The lamb was sure to go."
What I hear is
"The more I read the papers (*Stop*)
The less I comprehend (*Stop*)
The world and all its capers (*Stop*)
And how it all will end."
You're pressing on those external rhymes. Rhymes rhyme. They don't rhyme more or better by vocal indication. Furthermore, try to think of the full length of the line—its subject and predicate—and not as one note attached to another. In that sense, ad-lib singing is very much like speaking. Tell me the words as you hear them and this time in American English.

EM
(*Speaking*)

"The more I read the papers the less I comprehend the world (*She stops here for a "comma."*) and all its capers (*Stop*) and how it all will end."

DC

That's better. Let's do it again and this time, slow it down a little. It's a shade fast. Don't forget, lyrics are not small talk but light verse so, although the *reading* of the line obeys the rhythms of speech, the *singing* of the ad-lib should not be so . . . well, flip. This time sing it.
(EM *sings the eight bars in imitation of her spoken reading and the pianist follows with no trouble.*)

Perfect. And the pianist had no problem staying with you this time because he speaks English, too. What you were doing before was almost an "in tempo" reading of the Verse when you had asked for an ad-lib accompaniment. What happened then was hard for him to follow. He didn't know when you were going to say each word and, I would put it to you, neither did you. Try the next eight bars of the Verse.

EM
(*She sings it conversationally.*)

You know, that's the first time I understood ad-lib. I mean, I understood it in my head before, but I never got it into my mouth.

DC

Good. Just a couple of suggestions. I don't think you need a four-bar Vamp at the top. Two bars and a Sting* should be enough. What you're saying at the very top is not that high off the floor.** And don't forget: To avoid a knee-jerk reaction to the sting, count two slow beats before you begin to sing.

EM

Didn't I do that? I could've sworn I waited.

DC

I'll pass on that. Oh, yes, there are some possible glottal stops† that'll help you to slow up that ad-lib reading when you perform the song. One after " . . . the world and all its capers" so you can spike " . . . and how it all will end," which, after all, is the payoff line that underlines your concern for the future. You could have said: "The more I read the papers the less I comprehend the world and all its capers. Don't you agree, my friend?" " . . . And how it all will end" is a commentative line, a real zinger.

* See Introduction, page 16.
** See *On Singing Onstage*, the Vamp, pages 23–24.
† See Introduction, page 14.

EM

Got it. You said there was a possible other glottal. I don't see where.

DC

You rightly chose a breath before " . . . I mean in the way we care." But how do you feel about a glottal stop after " . . . I mean?"

EM

I don't see what you're driving at.

DC

Well, the lady is on the verge of saying something intimate that perhaps she hasn't said, or even thought of saying, before. Also, " . . . I mean" is like a stutter, a stop while the person speaking may be having second thoughts about saying what's on her mind. Or it may be nothing more important than searching for just the right words. A moment ago, you said—and I quote—"You know, that's the first time I understood ad-lib. I mean . . . " and then you halted, at a loss for words to explain what you meant and how to put it, before you went on with " . . . I understood it in my head before, but I never got it into my mouth." Do you remember?

EM

I see what you mean. (*She speaks.*) " . . . We've got something permanent. (*She stops, then goes on.*) . . . I mean (*She stops again and there is a noticeable change of gear.*) . . . in the way we care."

DC

Great! Also . . . (DC *turns to take in the class.*) when you're in ad-lib it is a good idea to break up the *last* line of the ad-lib before the tempo arrives on the *next* line.* In this case . . . (*Back to* EM) it not

* See *On Singing Onstage*, paragraphs 1 through 5, pages 16–17.

only puts on the brakes before sliding into the Chorus but, remember, this is a Gershwin standard that is particularly endearing. As soon as you sing " . . . It's very clear our love is here to stay . . . ", everyone will react the way they would if they'd spotted a kitten or a puppy in a pet shop window. The song has that same kind of immediate emotional appeal. Cheating its arrival can only work in your favor. I wouldn't want to rush " . . . It's very"—the upbeat into the Chorus—because as soon as you say " . . . clear" the accompaniment will come in, in tempo, like a feather bed mattress under you. Try it from " . . . Nothing seems to be lasting."

> (EM *sings the last eight bars of the Verse, with the breaths and glottals as marked, and* DC *allows her to sing through to the end of the Chorus.* DC *and the Class are with her all the way.)*

A beautiful tune! Of course, you'll work on those B naturals now that you know how to go about it.

EM

Right. I think I got off on singing and, pun intended, forgot to get off the note before each of them and, then . . . well, there they were, but I wasn't.

DC

I'm not worried about it. You can work on that at home on your own time. However, good as it was, there are refinements we can add. Let's talk about that second "8," beginning " . . . The radio and the telephone and the movies that we know," etc. (*To the Class*) The story goes that Oscar Levant* remarked, after Gershwin played the newly composed song for him, that he thought it would never achieve popularity because the second "8" didn't allow for a breath anywhere. Even worse, the final note jumped up a fifth just when the singer had pooped out. Levant was clearly a better composer than a clairvoyant. The song has never fazed singers.

---

* A close friend of the Gershwins' and, in his own right, an eminent pianist, performer/personality on radio, one-time actor in films, professional wit, composer of a piano concerto, a nocturne for orchestra, and a string quartet but remembered mostly for his great standard "Blame It on My Youth" and the less than great "Lady, Play Your Mandolin."

They ignore the long line, breathe after " . . . telephone" and after
" . . . fancies" and go on with their lives—just as EM has done. (*To*
EM) Ideally, if you could get all the way to " . . . fancies" on one
breath it would be, at least, a nod to Levant's and Gershwin's shade,
but if not, I wouldn't risk life and limb to prove you could do it
while the rest of us watched your eyes pop and your complexion
turn scarlet. What is important is that you may not grab a breath
after " . . . the movies that we know." So, do as you did—breathe
after " . . . telephone" and " . . . fancies" and settle for the best of all
possible worlds and continuing good health.

EM

Yes. If it's a question of giving him what *he* wants and what *I* can
do, I'll stick with the second choice. Any suggestions for the rest of
the Chorus, leaving out that damn B natural on " . . . In time . . . "
before the crumbling Rockies?

DC

A few. I like a glottal stop before the " . . . oh" in the line " . . . But,
oh my dear. . . ." Ira Gershwin puts a comma after " . . . But" and a
glottal stop is just that—a "comma" that intrudes on the column of
air you just inspired. It gives the word " . . . oh" the significance the
word deserves. Also, you weren't guilty of it, but just in case it
didn't happen on purpose, there is no breath ever after " . . .
Together we're." The rhyme will take care of itself. It's one
sentence sung on one column of air: " . . . Together we're going a
long, long way." Oh, and by the way, you can spread on those
"long, long's" and come in late on " . . . way." All you have to
remember, of course, is that you have to get off " . . . way" to get
enough breath for that B natural coming up. But we've spoken
about that before. You won't have as much time as you may think
you have. Incidentally, that first B natural* on " . . . In" is not
important. You could even think of it as a sixteenth note on the *low*
B natural—a throwaway—and jump the octave on to the open "ah"
you'll be singing on the word "time." The jump is easy and the
"ah" will stop you from closing into that damn diphthong. Just put

* In the sheet music it is scored as an E natural. EM's key would place it on a B natural.

an "ee" preceding the word " . . . the." (DC *sings in the key of the printed copy.*)

in Tah - eemthe

(EM *tries it in her key and experiences no problem with the B natural.*)

Very good. Just one last suggestion. Can you handle any more?

EM

I'm running down.

DC

I'll make it short. Whether you breathe or put a glottal stop *after* " . . . tumble" depends on whether you plan to breathe *before* " . . . But our love is here to stay." If you breathe there, a glottal stop will get you through " . . . they're only made of clay." But if you want to take that quarter note rest *after* " . . . But"—as it's scored—you'll need a breath *after* " . . . tumble" to get you through that jump up to D natural on the word " . . . But." (DC *sings both phrasing choices.*)

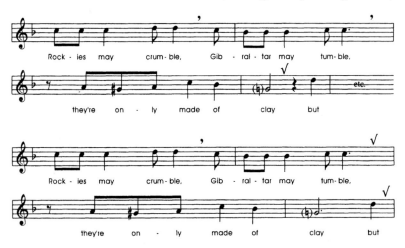

EM

I like the second one. And looking at the music, it seems to be what Gershwin had in mind.

DC

Fine. But it's important to choose one or the other and stick to it so that your accompanist knows he has to fill the "Air" after " . . . But." And—on my honor, this is my last word—sit on the word " . . . here" in the last title for a bar and a half—six counts. (*He sings.*)* As for going down, as written, on " . . . to stay" or staying on the fifth—or even daring to go up to the C. . . .

EM

Forget it.

(The Class laughs.)

DC

I knew you'd reject that. Well, why don't we wait until your performance gets to the Rideout before we make any decision? You've done very well. I don't think a "hand" would be out of place here. (*The Class willingly responds.*) The next time you're up we'll see how you see the song and, of course, how much of what we've covered today you can manage to remember when your concentration is on performing it.

EM

One final question. This is a unifocus song,** isn't it?

DC

Are you serious? Is "My Country 'Tis of Thee" a house number? (DC *changes the subject and speaks to the Class, the accompanist and* EM.) "Love Is Here to Stay" is not only an archetypal Show Ballad but,

---

* This suggestion is scored into the lead sheet.
** See Introduction, pages 9-10.

more to the point, it's an archetypal Gershwin tune. The classic standard "How About You?", composed by Burton Lane to Ralph Freed's words, begins with Mr. Lane's single contribution to the song's lyric—its opening line: " . . . I like a Gershwin tune—How About You?". It is purported to be contributed by Mr. Lane in gratitude for Mr. Gershwin's mentorship when the young composer was still in his teens. Exactly what is a Gershwin tune? For this writer it is music and words of unfailing optimism and good humor. So strong is this hallmark of the brothers Gershwin that no singer of their songs can be comfortable in a "blue light" or find a scintilla of solace in self-pity. Even the "bluest" of Gershwin's blues are saved from bathos by a joke: "But Not for Me" is all about loneliness, but in its Verse the singer writes letters to the current Miss Lonelyhearts and signs off one of them with a rejection of all those " . . . [Pollyannas] . . . who tell you fate supplies a mate. It's all bananas." The second Chorus lyric ends with one of Ira Gershwin's best puns: " . . . When ev'ry marriage plot ends with a marriage knot, And there's no knot for me." The gist of all this is that sloppy, sentimental readings of a Gershwin song disserve the authors' intentions. Even the accompaniment should be light and swinging and with no pedal-smeared harmonies. When you allow the signature of a composer to point the way, it will lead you, if not to a "right" performance, away from a "wrong" one.* (*To the accompanist in rapid delivery.*) Remember to re-edit the printed Vamp from four down to two bars and mark it at the top "ad-lib." The Verse stays as printed, but in the last line after " . . . permanent" we could have a soft sting to fill the "Air" when she stops for the breath. I think, too, another sting like that after " . . . I mean," for the same reason. On the last word " . . . care," pedal that G ninth and let her have " . . . It's very" on her own. As soon as she hits the downbeat on " . . . clear," mark the copy "in tempo." The Chorus accompaniment should have a nice, easy swing. The last four bars are all that have to be fixed. Fall out on a sustained down-beat on that diminished C chord and let her have " . . . Our love is . . . " for herself. You can come back in, in tempo, on " . . . here to stay." And, oh, yes, mark " . . . here" as a whole note tied over the bar to a half note. Don't worry about the word " . . . to"—just get set to ride her out on " . . . stay."

---

* See *On Singing Onstage*, pages 19–31.

EM

Will I ever be able to talk to a pianist like that?

DC

It's like anything. Knowing what you want and the lingo to say it. It's worth pointing out that, like most penultimate words before a Rideout begins, the *to* of an infinitive—in this case " . . . to stay"— is not a power word. Holding on to it is plain bad musical taste. There is no value in singing

" . . . Our love is heeeeeere tooooooo stay"

and it makes it next to impossible to conduct, since the hold on " . . . to . . . " is pure whim. Neither the performer nor the accompanist (conductor) has any idea when he will get off it and sing the last word. To make everyone happy, those final bars should be sung:

" . . . Our love is heeeeeere . . . "

(six beats, a breath on the seventh beat if needed) and, on the last quarter note, a throwaway on " . . . to" and into the Rideout—" . . . stay"—in tempo as rehearsed.

A week has gone by. EM is once again on stage. She asks for a warm-up music reading. DC thinks the idea is not only a good one but in her case (EM is new at the game) probably a wise one. EM does herself proud. The points covered in the music reading—the easy delivery of the ad-lib Verse, the slowing up of the upbeat into the Chorus and the suggestions for breath marks and glottal stops—are all remembered. The infamous B naturals are well intentioned—still a little shaky, but DC knows this is due more to self-consciousness than a failure to remember how to go about it —and well on their way. He suggests EM go to Center stage for her first performance of "Love Is Here to Stay."

(EM *moves to Center stage and, after a moment of playing generally into the theater, nods to the pianist. As she comes Center,* DC *stops her.*)

DC

If you remember, we cut two bars out of the original four-bar

Vamp you were used to. Now it's only two bars long—or should I say short?—they and a sting are all the time you have to come front, establish a committed Center focus, and give it its life. After all, it *is* the one specific man who receives the song, and he may not want to hear it, or maybe he feels the times don't warrant a commitment of any kind, especially to you. And all this before you sing "The more I read the papers," etc. You don't have any time to linger. I'd get over to Center easily, but without any feeling of rush, a moment after you've nodded to the pianist to begin. Let's try the Vamp again.

(EM *tries for a cleaner, less jerky arrival at Center in the Vamp. The work is better.*)

You're getting it. Just a couple of suggestions. After you leave the pianist after the nod and come front, don't jerk your head to Center. Remember, *he's not there until you put him there*. First deal with singularizing a Center focus. Then make the adjustment by recognizing a specific man in a specific place (in which you, too, stand).* It may be a short Vamp but you still have those two beats after the sting. You don't have to feel rushed. Deal with each element of each moment that gives life to the Vamp. Practice this at home as slowly as you need to and then, when you've got the component parts down pat, pick up the tempo of your thinking until it matches the amount of time the Vamp and the sting allow you. Try it now, without the accompanist.

(EM *works at staying* generally *focused into the theater and then puts her eyes Center [the* specific *focus] and slowly follows through with her head. After two or three tries it is perfect.* DC *asks the pianist to bring in the music to the Vamp and, again, in two or three tries, she has it down pat.*)

EM

Why do I always make what's so easy so damned hard?

---

* DC suggests, for all performances of Vamps:
   1. In the beats before coming Center, stay to the Left or Right of a Center spot in order to allow yourself the trip to go there when the time and the timing is right;
   2. Then, instead of moving eyes and head to the Center spot at the same time like a military maneuver, eyes must move *first* to the Center focus and then the head follows. In other words, *recognize* the presence of Center before you *relate* to it. Once these two actions are performed mechanically, it will occur to you that it is what you do in life.

DC

There's nothing wrong in working on the mechanics of something. In fact, I think it's probably a good thing to know that when you do something on a stage that works, you know how you did it. Now you can repeat this anytime you care to and those out front will have no idea that it was once born of a technique that, after all, is nobody else's business but yours and mine. And, of course, the Class's.

EM

You said before that you had two suggestions? I think I can handle another one.

DC

Okay. After you come to that Center focus and give it its life, *he* is now there. He has a life. What is he doing? More important, what is he saying? I like to think a song doesn't begin from a dead stop with the first line printed on the music copy. Give the man something to do or say—an *implicit* cue you can react to—so that the line " . . . The more I read the papers," etc. has its justification.

EM

Can you give me an example?

DC

Yes. It doesn't have to be a literary masterpiece. Actually, I try to keep it as much in the vernacular as I can and, as I've said before, in some kind of conflict with me. How about . . . HE: You look funny. Don't tell me your mother's coming into town again! SHE: No, it's just that (singing) "the more I read the papers the less I comprehend the world and all its capers" (and worse, still) "and how it all will end."

EM

So what you mean is that the first line is actually the second line only the audience doesn't hear the first one.

DC

Exactly. By the way, this *implicit cue* you write for yourself need not come from him (the audience). You can make up a line for yourself that will trigger the first line of the song.

EM

What would that look like?

DC

Well, here's one. After coming Center and creating the man, you shake your head, sigh, and say, silently, to him, "God! Did you see the MacNeill-Lehrer show last night?" and then, in mock despair, you segue into the top of the Verse. Now, I don't want you to think that this is my best effort. They're just off-the-top-of-the-head examples to demonstrate that *a song should be moving before it sings*. Actually, I don't like to show how or what I do. The thing is to do it your way, not to imitate mine. Georgia O'Keefe, the late, great American artist, once said that she had never been able to find a teacher to help her with her landscape painting because " . . . they always wanted to teach me how *they* painted *their* landscapes, not how to paint *mine*." And now, I think we can quit for the day. Your third and last time up should see the beginnings of a performance. By the way, about your complaint that there's a lot to cram into those two bars of Vamp and sting at the top of the song. I just remembered another quote, this one from the late Orson Welles: "The enemy of art is the absence of limitations." There is no question that in the beginning all technique is going to be constrictive. But with practice it somehow gets programmed into our thinking, disappears into the network of that thinking, and—to end the Class with a third and final quote, this one by Katherine Anne Porter—becomes " . . . a complication of simplicities."

EM's final time up on stage has come around. There is an air of expectancy one always senses as the Class warms to the prospect of a performance. It is a kind of silent "rooting" born of an understanding of what the performer is going through as he goes for it. EM nods to the pianist, times and plays the Vamp well, and sings the ad-lib Verse as rehearsed. As the first "8" of the Chorus comes to an end, DC reluctantly stops her.

DC

The phrasing and the singing of the song are coming along very nicely. But I don't have an inkling of what's on your mind.

EM

I'm thinking how much I love him and how I always will.

DC

But you're *saying* that. You're in mono with this script. We need some stereo.

EM

I don't think there's much subtext here. She's just saying what she's thinking.

DC

No one ever says what he's thinking. The song—all songs—are benign weapons that challenge the other person's (in this case the man's) script, since I assume he isn't a donkey pasted on the opposite wall waiting to have a tail pinned on to him. I don't mean to lay too heavy a hand on this particular tune, but it requires a little more than a pretty, smiling face and a little too much laying on of the charm.

EM

I can't help being pretty and charming, now, can I?

DC

You're joking, I know. But the last thing you have to worry about is the way you look. Or your charm. Anyway, charm is something I tend not to trust. By the way, someone once said it's what the violet has and the camellia has not. It's a quality one doesn't "play"—it *is*. It doesn't *get done*. But I've just changed my mind: The first thing you have to worry about *is* the way you look. What you should have on your mind the moment you enter is, "Okay, cool it! I know what you're thinking, but there's a helluva lot more to me than what you're looking at." Anyway, what you're registering is redundant. The song *is* charming. What you need is a reason to sing this violet of a song. And that reason is most probably born of the relationship between you and the man. I'm not suggesting a conflict as heavy as, let's say, "you care for him and he doesn't give a damn about you." The song wouldn't sustain it. But how about: You know he cares for you, but he isn't sure or able to make a permanent commitment? Perhaps he's made that mistake before you met him and was badly burned—and you know that's the way he feels. The song, then, is a weapon you use to fight his indecision. What's at stake is nothing less than your future happiness in an unstable world. And while you're busy working through your "script" you will, incidentally, be singing a charming song.

EM
(*She has listened to* DC's *criticism with growing interest.*)

I like everything you're saying, but is there never a time a singer sings a song because "why not?" or because, well, because it's a good song?

DC

Yes, often. When the entertainer's persona or extraordinary voice is what sells the tickets.

EM

Like Ella Fitzgerald?

DC

Exactly. But Ella Fitzgerald is one of the great vocal stylists of our time. Are you? We are working on the *art* of singing. Stanislavski has written that " . . . on a stage we must have life but not only that, it must be the life of your imagination which you make real for us." You must see the difference?

EM
(She has been silent, then speaks.)

I see. *(Pause)* May I have another try? Oh, and by the way, you aren't interested in hearing what I'm thinking?

DC

Absolutely not. That's your business.

EM leaves the stage and returns a few minutes later. Even her nod to the pianist is more energized and, upon coming Center, she invests the focus with a bittersweet recognition of her partner. The song is personal and wholly effective. DC and the Class are held by the warmth of revealed, unrestrained love. And because the song is what it is—a Gershwin song—any young man would be powerless to resist her (if indeed she was working to a young man). There is no need to say anything more. The response of the Class speaks for itself. EM is a little shaken but obviously touched in a new way by having sensed the power of singing out of a personal need.

DC

How do you feel?

EM

You know, this is the first time I felt the difference between singing at someone and singing to someone. The first way is, well, you sing the song. But this time I sang it because . . . because there was . . . intention, a purpose. The purpose was always on my mind and the song, well, it somehow got sung.

DC

Of course, songs don't somehow get sung. There's a good deal of subtext, if you will, that concerns breathing, phrasing and the demands of the vocalization of a line. You can never surrender entirely to the dramatic impulse that drives the song, not if it lures you out of control of the mechanical elements that support the act of "singing." But I think what you just experienced has introduced you not only to the special demands of singing that the actor must learn to juggle but also to the idea that what you know you know, as an actor, need not be discarded when you sing what you want to say.

EM

That's what I meant. This time I didn't feel like a total alien. But what I also felt was that the song began to work for *me*. Up till now, I always felt the song made me its victim. Now all I have to do is get it all together. Right?

DC

Right. Let's just say that today begins the journey. The trick will be not to slip back to the old habits but to work on making it always fresh and new while, at the same time, you work more and more on the "sound" of your singing without forfeiting what you learned today. It begins . . .

"Gypsy"

Small World

Words by Stephen Sondheim

Music by Jule Styne

Moderato

Fun - ny,_____ you're a stran - ger who's come here, come from an - oth - er town. Fun - ny,_____ I'm a stran - ger my - self here. Small world, is - n't it? Fun - ny,_____ I'm a man who goes trav' - ling, rath - er than set - tling down. Fun - ny,_____ 'cause you love to go trav' - ling. Small world, is - n't it? We have so much in com - mon

50

"Small World"

CHORUS:
Funny (,) you're a stranger who's come here
Come from another town (✓)
Funny (,) I'm a stranger myself here
Small world (,) isn't it (✓)
Funny (,) I'm a man who goes trav'ling
Rather than settling down (✓)
Funny 'cause you love to go trav'ling ⌣
⌣ Small world (✓) isn't it ⌣
⌣ We have so much in common (✓)
It's a phenomenon (✓)
We could pool our resources
By joining forces from now on (✓)
Lucky I'm a man who likes children (,)
That's an important sign ⌣
⌣ Lucky (✓) you're a woman with children
Small world isn't it (✓)
Funny isn't it ⌣
⌣ Small (✓)
And funny (✓)
And fine (✓)

"Small World" from *Gypsy*, lyrics by Stephen Sondheim, music by Jule Styne. Copyright © 1959 by Norbeth Productions, Inc. and Stephen Sondheim. Copyright renewed. International Copyright Secured. All Rights Reserved. All rights administered by Cappell & Co. Used by permission.

2

Narrative Show Ballad

To place all ballads under one rubric would make one "slow song" indistinguishable from another when there are distinct and definable characteristics to justify three divisions. The Show Ballad, as described in the previous chapter, betrays its label in the im- or explicit "I love you" of the lyric. This second category, the Narrative Show Ballad, still maintains the slow tempo and the primacy of melody, but its lyric statement is broader. It may help to move a plot line forward and/or to furnish character information, but like its sibling, it too can be excerpted from its home score and remain comprehensible. Unlike the Show Ballad that more commonly finds A singing to B, the Narrative Show Ballad may be a "house number" (A no longer needs B to hear it) or a soliloquy whose delivery is best served by an internalized focus.* A personally held opinion: Whereas the Show Ballad seems to resist a departure away from an easy but nevertheless insistent 4/4 time signature, the Narrative Show Ballad lends itself to a wide variety of vocal and orchestral interpretations. These arrangements may have little to do with the original printed notation of the song. On the contrary, a distinctive treatment can give the work a new and richer meaning. Other less apparent characteristics that set the two groups apart: In place of "I love you" we may now hear of self-revelation, the lack or loss of a loved one, or a script born of a

* See Introduction, pages 9-11.

prevailing plaintiveness.

When librettos graduated out of the state of inanity in which they once dwelled, their corresponding scores moved with them. As song forms became more complicated, sung words became more revealing. The Narrative Show Ballad has arguably done away with the simpler Show Ballad, but every so often the latter reappears—Rodgers and Hammerstein's "Some Enchanted Evening," "If I Loved You," "I Have Dreamed" and "Younger Than Springtime," Frank Loesser's "I've Never Been in Love Before"—and it can be heard as late as 1989-90 in Cy Coleman's score for *City of Angels* ("With Every Breath I Take"). Because the public continues literally to venerate them, Ballads, in all their guises, are heard in and out of the theater, here, there, and everywhere.

A partial list of keepers of the flame who perform in person and/or have recorded theater music would include: Bobby Short, Steve Ross, Michael Feinstein, Mel Tormé, Frank Sinatra, Tony Bennett, Ella Fitzgerald, Barbra Streisand, Sarah Vaughan, Lena Horne, Carmen McRae, Julie Wilson, Maureen McGovern, Rosemary Clooney; and the great jazz instrumentalists of the past and present: Art Tatum, Oscar Peterson, Bill Evans, Marian MacPartland, Stephane Grappelli, Barry Tuckwell, and countless others. One may turn to opera heavyweights who have recorded theater music, beginning with Eileen Farrell and on to Kiri Te Kanawa, Teresa Stratas, Joan Sutherland, José Carreras, and Thomas Hampson. This admittedly abridged listing of recording artists affirms that ballads may be interpreted in a variety of arrangements without detracting from the essential quality of the material.

The following examples identify the Narrative Show Ballad category:

• Rodgers and Hart or Hammerstein: "He Was Too Good to Me," "It Never Entered My Mind," "Blue Moon," "Little Girl Blue," "My Funny Valentine," "Spring Is Here," "You'll Never Walk Alone," and "My Lord and Master."

• George and Ira Gershwin: "The Man I Love," "Someone to Watch Over Me," "But Not for Me," "Looking for a Boy," "Somehow It Seldom Comes True," and "A Foggy Day."

• Irving Berlin: "Better Luck Next Time," "Fools Fall in

Love," "Get Thee Behind Me, Satan," "How About Me?" "Say
It With Music," "White Christmas," "You're Laughing at Me,'
"All Alone," "What'll I Do?" and "Remember."

• Cole Porter: "Make It Another Old-Fashioned, Please,'
"Get Out of Town," "Were Thine That Special Face," "Why
Can't You Behave?" "Pipe Dreaming," "Every Time We Say
Goodbye," "So Near and Yet So Far," and "It Must Be Fun to
Be You."

• Jerome Kern: "In the Heart of the Dark," "Lonely Feet,"
"Yesterdays," "Smoke Gets in Your Eyes," "The Last Time I
Saw Paris," "Why Was I Born?" "Try to Forget," "Don't Ever
Leave Me," "Here Am I," and "Long Ago and Far Away."

• Kander and Ebb: "Isn't This Better?" "I Don't Remember
You," and "It Couldn't Please Me More."

• Harold Arlen: "Any Place I Hang My Hat Is Home,"
"Cocoanut Sweet," "Happiness Is a Thing Called Joe," "I Never
Has Seen Snow," "I've Got the World on a String," and "One
for My Baby."

• Stephen Sondheim: "Love, I Hear," "Sorry-Grateful,"
"Anyone Can Whistle," "Green Finch and Linnet Bird," "Not
While I'm Around," "Pretty Lady," and "Good Thing Going."

• Noel Coward: "If Love Were All," "Mad About the Boy,"
"World Weary," "London Pride," and "The Party's Over Now."

• Burton Lane: "How Are Things in Glocca Morra?" "Hurry!
It's Lovely Up Here," "On a Clear Day You Can See Forever,"
"There's a Great Day Coming Mañana," and "Something Sort
of Grandish."

• Lerner and Loewe: "Another Autumn," "I Loved You Once
in Silence," "If Ever I Would Leave You," "Gigi,"* and "How to
Handle a Woman."

• Cy Coleman: "I Walk a Little Faster" and "It Amazes Me."

Again, the omissions are glaring. My purpose is only to help the
reader, familiar with even a limited number of the above titles, to
discern the textural differences between the Show Ballad and the
Narrative Show Ballad.

---

* "Gigi" may also be described as an eleven o'clock number (see page 73), but that
classification would be misleading. The song is originally from a film.

THE SONG

I have assigned Jule Styne and Stephen Sondheim's "Small World" from *Gypsy* to a Character Man. In the context of the musical as performed today, it is sung by the Leading Lady. However, the original intention was to create a duet for her and her leading man to be sung at their first meeting. Unhappily, it was felt by the authors that Jack Klugman, although an actor of infinite skill whose contribution to the musical was immeasurable, was not able to sustain the duet. By default, it became yet another solo for the star who was already carrying a heavy load of six songs, including the triumphant "Rose's Turn." Out of context, it becomes a song that either sex (ideally tilting toward the "character" category) may sing regardless of race or color of skin. All that is required is a simple readjustment of pronouns. Like the preceding Gershwin song, "Small World" is justifiably described as a "signature song"—pure Styne.

The author holds the opinion that only Jule Styne approaches Irving Berlin's unique creative gift for composing simple songs that, on second and third hearings (or better yet, upon singing them), betray their far-from-simple textures. "Asking for You," "I'm Just Taking My Time," "Just in Time," "Make Someone Happy," "People," "The Music That Makes Me Dance," "The Party's Over," "Who Are You Now?" "Can't You Just See Yourself?" "I Still Get Jealous," "Time After Time," "What Makes the Sunset?"—these standards bear the mark of his genius for crafting straight-to-the-ear and -heart melodies. He has worked with Bob Merrill, Sammy Cahn, Comden and Green, Bob Hilliard, and E. Y. ("Yip") Harburg, but his masterpiece *Gypsy* was written with Stephen Sondheim and is regarded as one of the enduring musical scores of the twentieth century. Originally played by the memorable Ethel Merman (it was the last role written for her), stock productions reprise it with anyone who dares to grapple with the relentless score, and by Angela Lansbury, Tyne Daly and Linda Lavin in major revivals. Each consecutive production reclaims the enduring quality of the piece. In the long arc of the history of musical theater, *Gypsy* may be one of the last successful *musical comedies*, paced to move at full throttle with only the necessary pauses taken to sing a score that never stops the action but always can be relied on to stop the show. I do not mean to settle second-class citizenship onto the term musical comedy. Indeed, *City of Angels* may be so described. Musical comedy was the preferred title given all musicals before the more inclusive "musical theater" replaced it.

The words and music of "Small World" have a lovely synchronism. The A theme (the song is AABA) is simplicity itself, but as the B theme of the Bridge begins to undulate, Sondheim introduces a more sinewy lyric while at the same time staying within the bounds of the vernacular, for example, " . . . common" paired with " . . . phenomenon," " . . . resources by joining forces from now on." As remarked above, in the following dialogue the song is sung by a man to a woman.

THE DIALOGUE

LK enters. He is a recognized man. Behind him are stage, film, and television credits, and one may assume that there are more ahead—but he would trade them all to sing. And he can. His problem is that he cannot make the sound he would sell his kingdom to produce, the sound that marks the singer—at least in the way the world defines the word. It has taken a while, but he has begun to accept the fact that his assets are not diminished by this reality and may very well be increased; his voice "looks" like him—a vocal fingerprint. He studies singing without a shred of a sense of humor, and as he pins down the techniques of proper vocal production his voice is becoming, if not a silk purse, a good deal more than a sow's ear. "Small World" has a double edge: It is a song a singer may sing, but it is no less served by the actor-singer when the right Character Man or Woman performs it.*

DC

Have you had any trouble learning this?

---

* There are many songs of which this may be said. "September Song" by Kurt Weill and Maxwell Anderson from their *Knickerbocker Holiday* comes to mind. It has been, is, and will be sung by performers as long as good songs endure, but no one ever spoke-sang it quite the way Walter Huston did in the original production. And, of course, there is the example of the late Rex Harrison's performance of "I've Grown Accustomed to Her Face" from Lerner and Lowe's *My Fair Lady*. Both Huston and Harrisons's versions are available on recordings.

LK

Well, I knew it. It's a helluva song, but sometimes that can be a problem. What I mean is, you really only know the vicinity of it. There were some wrong notes I had to unlearn, but I think I'm on top of it now.

DC

Good. Let's try it, then. (DC *interrupts* LK *after four bars.*) Who taught this to you? I'll lay odds it was your singing teacher. Here we are trying to get you and a song on the stage in one piece and what do we get? A stand-in singing a song from the score of a Berlitz textbook.

LK

And I thought I had every note right on the nose.

DC

That's the problem. You do. Even the first word " . . . Funny" you sing, well . . . funny. You sing, "Funneeeeee," but the word is an interjection like "Hey," "Good grief," "Indeed," "Damn." Let it go. Think of what you're saying.

LK

It's the damned singing. I want to sound like a bird, not a frog.

DC

You sound like what you're meant to sound like: a bird. A frog-like bird but nevertheless, a bird. And this is just the song he'd be singing. Anyway, there are wonderful musical phrases up ahead where you can preen your canary feathers.

LK

But the music is written with the first word held.

DC

A copyist's conceit. He doesn't have to sing it. All the " . . . isn't it's" in the sheet music are written with the same hold. You aren't planning to ask " . . . Isn't iiiiiiiiit?" each time you get to them? Or are you?

LK

I get your point. Well, here we go again. (*He sings the first "8."*)

DC
(*Interrupting*)

That's better. Much better. (*To the Class*) Will someone assure him that we liked that? Liked it a lot?

CLASS
(*To LK*)

I not only liked it, I understood it.

DC

There you are. And I didn't give her a penny to say that. Now, let's clean up the phrasing. To begin with, let's put in a glottal after " . . . Funny" to help you remember to get off it. No need to breathe after that. You just took a breath. That should get you through the end of " . . . another town."

LK

Right. Hey, wait a minute. I forgot to turn on my tape machine. (*He does so.* DC *repeats the suggestion.*)

DC

Then I'd get in a good low breath at that point and sing out real pretty on " . . . Funny, I'm a stranger myself here, Small world, isn't it?" Just remember, another glottal after " . . . Funny" and one before " . . . isn't it?" and don't hold on to " . . . it." Oh, yes, something we ought to mention here. All those "isn't it's," when the two words aren't separated by just a hint of a glottal, sound like a word you wouldn't be using in a conversation with a lady you were trying to join forces with.* Are you with me?

LK

You weren't that subtle. I'm with you.

DC

Well then, moving on. Remember, don't hold on to the "it." Get off and get yourself a well-needed breath for the start of the second "8." (LK *sings the first and second "8," softly separates "isn't" from "it," but gets into a bit of trouble on the higher " . . . isn't it?" that ends the second "8.")* Very good work. How did it feel?

LK

That last " . . . isn't it?" sounded like someone had me by the throat.

DC

Not that bad. You were concentrating on the " . . . isn't it?" and forgot to breathe. Let's see where you can grab a breath . . . (*He scans the music.*) Well, I'll tell you something. Despite the fact that I suggested you get off *all* the " . . . isn't it's," here's one I think might be worth holding since you'll be sliding up to " . . . We have so much in common" right after it. When you're at the top of your range it's wise to stay there and phrase from the demands of the music rather than the words.** Remember, however, not to close into the "t." Stay on the vowel and put the "t" on the next word: " . . . We." (DC *sings.*) " . . . isn't *ih . . . tweee* ha . . . vsoh much . . . " I've always hated that damn "ih" vowel. Of them all, it's the hardest

---

* There are other combinations of words that, unless they are taken up tenderly, add an unintended scatological tone to a lyric. See *On Singing Onstage*, Bad English—Good Lyrics, pages 203-204.
** See *On Singing Onstage*, pages 33-45.

to keep open. A good idea is to check your lower jaw to see to it that it doesn't freeze. In fact, when you practice this at home, sing the "ih" vowel and while you're holding it move your jaw back and forth to make certain it isn't locking on you.

LK

I think I know what you mean. I'll work on it. Oh, yes, I'd like to breathe after " . . . so much in common." I need a beat there before I hit her with " . . . It's a phenomenon."

DC

Very good. We're back to phrasing from lyric. I like that. Can you do the next four bars from " . . . We could pool . . . ." through " . . . from now on" in one breath?

LK

I think so. Is there a safety alternative?

DC

Yes. First be sure, of course, that you get enough breath for the line. If you feel yourself weakening a little as you near the end, grab a glottal before " . . . from now on." You'll find it relaxes you. They're only three syllables and you'll be breathing before " . . . Lucky" at the top of the last "8."

LK

Yep. I didn't think " . . . Funny" and " . . . Lucky" are the same.

DC

No. " . . . Lucky," as it's used here, is the first word of the sentence. I'd put a glottal before " . . . That's an important sign." It'll spotlight the fact that it *is* an important sign. But I'd do the opposite, I think, and not breathe after " . . . sign." Elide it to the next " . . . lucky" and then breathe.

LK

That's nice. This time " . . . lucky" means "You better believe it."

DC

You've got it. From here on in, let's go for some offbeat phrasing. Try and follow this.* A breath after the first " . . . isn't it"—and make sure you get a good one. Then, on one column of air: " . . . Funny, isn't it small"—then a breath before " . . . And funny" and, of course, a breath for the Rideout on " . . . fine."

LK

I like that. Instead of " . . . Funny, isn't it?", you come out with " . . . Funny, isn't it small!" which means, "Damn it! How great that we got to meet!" Then " . . . and Funny," which means "Ironic? Isn't it?" and finally: " . . . Fine" . . . "by me."

DC

That's about it. Why don't we quit for today? You can work on this on your own. The only way you can lay this proposition before her is to nail all the vocal, rhythmic, and phrasing choices we've been talking about. Then you'll be free to do what I know you can do with a piece of material like this.

It is a week later. LK is on stage. His music reading is meticulously rehearsed—a thorough professional.

DC

That's extraordinary! Not one point forgotten. I'm proud of you.

LK

Music readings are easy for me. What I've learned is to record what you say in Class and not argue. I wait until I get home and

---

* The reader can follow the marked lead sheet.

I've cooled off, and then I can hear it without any ego getting in the way. Does that make any sense?

DC

If your music reading is an example of the system, it makes sense. And now—for the performance.

> (LK *moves to Center stage. Once there, he is a man at home. His years on the stage corroborate his residency. To stand without any self-consciousness and work generally through the fourth wall into the theater is no strain for him. A few moments later, he nods in the accompanist and, arriving at the Center spot with a sure sense of timing, he begins to sing.* DC *allows him the first two "8s." As he segues into the Bridge . . .)*

Let's stop here. Unlike the Gershwin song "Love Is Here to Stay," "Small World" has no Verse. It simply begins. And not only that, it begins at the very beginning. The audience has to board an already moving train. To keep the metaphor going, you have to be *on* that train before they board. Not only on it, but be the conductor and the engineer as well.

LK

I know what the problem is. When I'm acting I know what I have to do. And it's so much easier because I know *with whom* I have to do it. In this case, she'd be standing right here. (*He turns sideways and indicates a spot to the Left of him.*) As soon as I have to create her *there* (*Pointing out front*) she . . . well, she fades out.

DC

It's just *because she is not standing beside you* that your imagination must be heightened and made unequivocally specific. Because, you see, she *is* out front. Singing is a lonely life on stage if she isn't there. As an old wag once remarked, "You can be arrested for talking to yourself." And always she's there to the degree that we, the audience, can see her effect on you. This journey the actor must make to that "solo" state which *is* singing—as separate from acting—strips you—the actor—of your methods.

LK

And the new methods?

DC

All of them have to do with the power of your imagination. Think about this. As you just said, she isn't there. But, then again, that leaves you free to create the *she* you need. *Who* is she? *Why* are you singing to her? *What* do you want from her? We know the *when*. It's *now*. Not a moment ago when the song may not have been on your mind. Not a moment from now because we cannot know the future. But now. This instant. What is at stake if she said, "No"? If she said, "Yes"?

LK

The interesting thing about all this is that the difference between singing and acting is that there is no difference.

DC

There are many differences and we can speak of them at another time. But in this instance you're right. There are none. But to get back. You are thin on "situation" and so the first "8" has very little impact other than our pleasure in hearing a song we all like. But that isn't good enough. We want to know who you are. We want to be moved, to see what lies behind the words and the music. Just as *you* must know the language behind the words you sing, *we* want to receive the words we hear and to understand them—perhaps in a new way. Two unattached drifters—he without ties, she with a family. If we forget *Gypsy*, it could be a business proposition he's suggesting in the Bridge. He could be a con man with a shady scheme he's pushing. He could be, on the bottom line, a man in love for the first time in his life. *Who* is he? He is *you*. Who are *you*? We haven't seen him yet.

LK

Whew! I'll listen to that when I'm home. Can we get on to another problem? I'm having a helluva time coming up with a physical life. I feel like a block of concrete up here. That's never happened to me before—at least, not when I'm acting. I never think about my hands or my feet or any part of me, for that matter.

DC

It's all part of the same problem I'm talking about. When your thinking is general, you can bet your behavior will be. Once you have the man in your sights, the problem will disappear. Body language can never be consistently true when the imagination and the mind are not supplying a steady stream of specific information. Stanislavski has said, " . . . Thoughts are embodied in acts and a man's actions in turn affect his mind. His mind affects his body and again his body, or its condition, has its reflex action on his mind and produces this or that condition. You must learn how . . . to free your muscles and, at the same time, your psyche." Important, too: remember, the song escalates; it doesn't merely flow along like a river. It's born of a purposeful mind, a mind that's consistently crafty, desirous, hungry, sexual, determined, childish, frightened, eager—and it doesn't spend itself until the last moments of the Rideout of the song. Let's talk further about this because . . . (*To the Class*) it's a problem so many of you are working to solve. In our reality lives, language may be passive or it may be active. Conversation needn't have anything at stake. In the theater, it must not only be active, but the threat of a care-less audience compels us to keep it so. Jean Cocteau wrote that " . . . active speech is the secret of theater. Otherwise everything stagnates and the audience stops listening—waiting for something to happen and then tired of waiting for something to happen." (*To* LK) In your case, when the lyric merely delivers itself, your hands and feet have nowhere to go. When the words are made active and given purpose, you'll be as free in your singing as you are when you act because you'll be a whole man and not a disembodied voice. In this sense, yes, both interpretive arts share a common characteristic.

LK

You know, when I hear you speak, it all becomes so clear to me. Ideas come crowding in and I feel like I could fly with it right now.

DC

That's because you're playing off the energy I'm feeding out to you. You need to plug into your own power source. Try to heed your advice about listening to these tapes when you're back at home. How did you describe it? That's the time when you're cool, objective and able not only to listen but to hear it as well. (LK *exits. To the Class*) What have we learned here? To quote Stanislavski again: "Words are not an end in themselves." Most of you work hard to memorize the words and the music, to learn the phrasing that gives them their meaning, and to make sensible focus choices: the "to whom" you're singing. With all that behind you, you forget that that's only the beginning, only the matrix, so to speak, upon which you will build your performances. The audience has no knowledge of all the work that went before, nor should they be expected to know or to care. They're there for you to elicit specific reactions—reactions you control by virtue of your art. To forget that goal is to eliminate the essence of what great performing is about.

It is days later. LK is back on stage. The Vamp is not yet over when DC stops him.

DC

Your focus level when you come Center is too high. It looks like you're singing to a Watusi.

LK

That's the first time that's happened.

DC

We know that a Center focus tends to rise and lateral "spots" to widen. What you have to keep in mind is that you are on a stage singing into a theater below you. Furthermore, you are standing on that floor while the audience is sitting on the one below. You want to sing eye-to-eye to the lady. That's too high from our POV out front. You have to lower that Center spot.

LK
(*He does so.*)

Now I feel like I'm working to a pygmy.

DC

How you feel isn't significant. It's we who should be important to you. How we feel. And we thought you were working to God before. Believe me, you look just fine. Now you look like you're singing to and for us. By the way, you'll get used to this level and the pygmy will go.
(LK *makes the change and sings through the song.*)
I don't want to talk about your performance. It's enough to say that it's affecting. But your physical life still has me a little worried.

LK

Worried? Why?

DC

Hands and feet never lie. When your thinking produces awkward, false body language that draws attention to itself, something is wrong. Not so much with your choices but with the richness of its steady flow. In your case, I imagine it's the latter. You're not all there. How did Cole Porter put it: " . . . the eyes, the arms, the mouth of you. The east, west, north and the south of you."

LK

I don't think he meant that in this context. But never mind—what about the overall guy?

DC

I like him. One thing worth mentioning here is that if your feet never move you look like you're nailed to the floor. A good idea is to allot a fraction of your thinking to them. When he's easy, he should be sitting. When things get hot, feet tend to move into a supportive stance. Between "8s," especially. Think of those "Air" pockets as scene changes. Each "8" is there to push the song up—what I mean when I ask each of you to escalate the song. They're the building blocks that keep the song erect—vertical. The "Air" between them, then, is like that old vaudeville phrase " . . . and then I wrote . . . " or "Don't go! I haven't finished what I was saying."

LK

Yes. I need argument from her at those points in order for me to go on.

DC

Well put. One more suggestion. You're coming off too needy in the Bridge. What you're proposing looks like a life-saving plan for survival. "We could pool our resources . . . " isn't a question of covering a bad check. A better approach is to think of it as an imminent family in the making: you, her, and the children. You don't need a heavy reason to sing this song. It *looks* like you. It *is* you. Don't invent another man to sing it for you.

LK

I think that's due to nerves. I don't mean what I'm playing is necessarily good or bad, only that I may be pressing.

DC

Well, as we've said many times before, it's no business of mine or the audience's, for that matter, to know what you're thinking. We only know what we see. But it does seem fruitless to assign a song to a good actor who only has to stand there and sing it, and then find out that he went out and found someone else to sing it for him.

LK

I understand. I'll work on the Bridge. How was the last "8"?

DC

Good. A little obvious on those last three adjectives. You indicated with your hands a *small* world, then played an *amusing* world and a *wonderful* world. Why not try reversing the body language. Open your base slowly and open your arms wide as you start to sing " . . . Funny, isn't it small?" Since that last word is on a high note it could profit from better grounding—all of this to "frame" "small." What you're thinking is: "This is important to me. I'm putting all of my life on the line on this proposal." Don't think you're talking about the size of the world. Then slowly start to close your base—bring your hands together, wipe the smile off your face, and get set for " . . . funny," a word that's pure irony—now it means " . . . strange." Then start the "beats" of your Rideout with a cooler reading of the last word: " . . . fine." You said last week you'd think of it as " . . . fine by me."

LK

That's nice. Oppositional body language to the lyric. I like that. (*He nods to the pianist and sings the last "8." The Class reacts noisily.*) That felt great.

DC

It looked it. I think we'll be able to wrap this up with one more session. You're well on the way to singing a ballad. Something you said you'd never be able to do. And it'll be better and better and you'll sing it better and better, I promise you.

LK
(*Exiting*)

What a high! I tell you, singing is a real high! One chorus of a song has as much punch as playing the scene would've had.

DC

I remember an interview with Peter O'Toole in *Time* magazine. The interviewer asked him if he regretted anything. He said "No," but after what the interviewer described as a "delicious pause," O'Toole said, "Well, sure. I'm not a [French] singer."

Send In The Clowns

"A Little Night Music"

Music and Lyrics by Stephen Sondheim

Lento

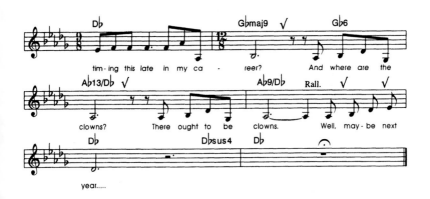

tim-ing this late in my ca - reer? And where are the

clowns? There ought to be clowns. Well, may-be next

year.....

"Send in the Clowns"

Isn't it rich (✓) Are we a pair (✓)
Me here at last on the ground (,) you in mid-air (✓)
Send in the clowns (✓)
Isn't it bliss (✓) Don't you approve (✓)
One who keeps tearing around (,) one who can't move (✓)
Where are the clowns (,)
Send in the clowns (✓)
Just when I'd stopped opening doors (✓)
Finally knowing the one that I wanted was yours (✓)
Making my entrance again with my usual flair (✓)
Sure of my lines (✓)
No one is there (✓)
Don't you love farce (✓) my fault (,) I fear (✓)
I thought that you'd want what I want (✓)
Sorry (,) my dear (✓)
But where are the clowns ⌣
⌣ Quick send in the clowns (✓)
Don't bother (✓) they're here (✓)
Isn't it rich (✓) Isn't it queer (✓)
Losing my timing this late in my career (✓)
And where are the clowns (✓)
There ought to be clowns ⌣
⌣ Well (✓) maybe (✓) next year (✓)

"Send in the Clowns" from *A Little Night Music*, music and lyrics by Stephen Sondheim. Copyright © 1973, 1985 Revelation Music Publishing Corp. & Rilting Music, Inc. International Copyright Secured. All Rights Reserved. A Tommy Volando Publication. Used by Permission.

3

Dramatic Show Ballad

The Dramatic Show Ballad maintains its melodic primacy, but it is an increase in the density and consequent importance of the lyric that justifies this third category. Found, most often, at the finish line of a musical, it bears the special designation "eleven o'clock number," a song that resolves the first plot line by assigning that task to a song rather than to the "book." Its placement and importance to the script can be relied upon to give the star of the musical a dramatic and often powerful "curtain." The classic example is Jule Styne and Stephen Sondheim's "Rose's Turn" from *Gypsy*. This category may include songs that are not found at finale time, but they, as well as the eleven o'clock Dramatic Show Ballad, are affirmative, resigned, contemplative, or combinations of descriptive adjectives, but in all cases it is a safe bet that they are self-revelatory.

• Jule Styne: "The Music That Makes Me Dance" from *Funny Girl*.
• Lerner and Loewe: "I've Grown Accustomed to Her Face" from *My Fair Lady*.
• Cy Coleman: "I'm Way Ahead" from *Seesaw*.
• Burton Lane: "What Did I Have That I Don't Have?" from *On a Clear Day You Can See Forever*.
• Jerry Herman: "If He Walked Into My Life" from *Mame*.
• Stephen Sondheim: "With So Little to Be Sure Of" from

Anyone Can Whistle and "Being Alive" from *Company*.
  • Richard Rodgers: "Thank You So Much" from *Do I Hear a Waltz?* and "This Nearly Was Mine" from *South Pacific*.
  • Leonard Bernstein: "Make Our Garden Grow" from *Candide*.
  •Andrew Lloyd Webber: "All I Ask of You" from *Phantom of the Opera*.

Dramatic Show Ballads that are not found at the finish line but carry the same dramatic weight and timbre as the eleven o'clock number:

  • Harold Arlen: "The Man That Got Away" from the film *A Star Is Born*, "I Had Myself a True Love" and "I Wonder What Became of Me" from *St. Louis Woman*.
  • Leonard Bernstein: "Something's Coming" and "Tonight" from *West Side Story* and "Glitter and Be Gay" from *Candide*.
  • Stephen Sondheim: "My Friends" from *Sweeney Todd* and "Could I Leave You?"* from *Follies*.
  • Kurt Weill: "September Song" from *Knickerbocker Holiday* and "Lonely House" from *Street Scene*.
  • Galt MacDermott: "Aquarius" from *Hair*.
  • Jerry Bock: "Vanilla Ice Cream" from *She Loves Me*.
  • Charles Strouse: "One Hallowe'en" and "Welcome to the Theater" from *Applause*.

Like the Show Stopper (Category 11), the Dramatic Show Ballad should be taken up tenderly when the performer is facing the choice of "what to sing." As audition material, these songs (and others like them) require juggling two consequential elements: demanding musical/vocal lines while, at the same time, sustaining the elevated flow of creative energy dictated by their scripts. Away from auditions, the songs can make an "act" top-heavy but, *and this "but" should be stressed*, when the time, the place, and the performer's expertise corroborate the choice, Dramatic Show Ballads reliably induce a heightened audience response.
  To summarize: The three ballad categories (Show, Narrative,

---

* "Could I Leave You," a waltz, masquerades as an eleven o'clock number not so much because it resolves the character's plotline (which it does not do) but because of its stunning, vituperative statement and its placement in the Second Act.

and Dramatic) are not bound by rigid margins. There are ballads, even in the above listings, that may lie within two groups because their lyrics or their placement in their original home scores allows the overlap. (See footnote concerning *Gigi*, page 54.) My intention to categorize theater music is not so much to force a constrictive format onto the mass of available material as to make it less formidable to the reader who confronts the musical theater's rich catalog for the first time. Under the circumstances of an audition, the choice of "what to sing" is often aided by suggestions from the auditioner for a ballad or an Up-Tempo song. These labels, so general that only their rhythms define them, may now be seen to be less so. Away from the requirements of an audition, as in the case of the formatting of an "act," or a one-man show, or in any show business arena where the performer elects what to sing and where to place those choices in order to gain the strongest "build," these categories may help to define the professional performer's already acquired knowledge of the repertoire.

It is important to remember that in general the ballad's slow tempo betrays the performer's ability to sing it. Vocal imperfections are more readily discernible.* Of course, there is the other side of this generalization: A good voice needs a ballad to advertise itself.

THE SONG

"Send in the Clowns," Stephen Sondheim's classic eleven o'clock number (more aptly, ten-thirty number) from *A Little Night Music* is arguably the most important theater song written in our time. Its manifest elegance has in no way hindered the across-the-board popularity it enjoys. If anything, the song suffers from a case of overexposure. Anyone and everyone has sung and recorded it in solo and in groups from symphony orchestras to a single instrumentalist on the jew's harp—and if the latter is not so, wait. The theory that it is wise to stay away from songs that have become overworn by being oversung still obtains.**

What is remarkable about the song beyond the perfection of its poetry and the immediate appeal of the melodic line? To begin

---

* See *On Performing*, Questions 6 & 8, pages 65–72.
** See *On Singing Onstage*, Eight Don'ts to Remember, pages 51–52.

with (from Craig Zadan's *Sondheim & Co.*), " . . . Sondheim began composing his score in the style of Ravel, Rachmaninoff, and Brahms, constructing fughettas, canons, contrapuntal duets, trios, a quintet, a quartet, and a double quartet, all composed in three-quarter time and multiples thereof." The stunning variety, despite this fanciful decision to restrict the rhythms within which each song was to find its life, is indeed a feat. (The time signature of "Clowns" shuttles between 12/8 and 9/8—extended divisions of 3/4 time.) Further, Sondheim wrote the entire song in one night after seeing the scene played by Glynis Johns and Len Cariou in rehearsal.*

Further still, although the short phrases (" . . . Isn't it rich?" " . . . Are we a pair?" " . . . Send in the clowns," " . . . Isn't it bliss?" " . . . Don't you approve?") catered to Miss Johns's limited vocal resources, the song's perfection remains dominant whether it is crudely or lavishly sung.**

Still further, the song's placement in the musical is clearly related to the Desirée character and her plot requirements, yet what it says by and for her it says for all of us. I cannot recall another song that speaks so eloquently of the pain inflicted on a lover cursed with bad timing early or " . . . late" in his " . . . career." The show business references in the lyric—the preceding line, " . . . making my entrance," " . . . sure of my lines," " . . . don't you love farce?" " . . . losing my timing," and, of course, the reference to " . . . the clowns" and " . . . send[ing] them in"—are, oddly, not alien to the general vocabulary we all use.

A final word: The song may be sung by a man or a woman. Nothing in the lyric prohibits this, and in a strange way the script gains another dimension when it is a man who sings it. Within the body of the show, the allusion to the lady's profession (actress) gives substance and corroboration to the show business idiom in the Bridge and last "8." When the singer is male, the same words become the language of an aging, and slipping, Don Juan. However, its assignment here to a woman is not sexist but pragmatic: The lady was asked to play the role of Desirée.

---

* Mr. Sondheim is a notoriously slow writer. In his own words, "I'm very neurotic and very slow, as well as being hypercritical of my own work." In the case of *A Little Night Music*, two songs were cut in the first days of rehearsal and, according to Hal Prince, they were short six songs when rehearsals began.

** For confirmation of "crudely sung" there is the show album. At the other extreme and on record: Cleo Laine's superb version. I speak only of the vocal performance of both ladies.

"Send in the Clowns" has no Verse and the song form is AABA. The first two "8s," as is not uncommon, are six bars in length, the Bridge is nine bars long, and the last "8," aptly named: eight bars. The last "8" is reprised with a new lyric and the ironic " . . . Don't bother, they're here" is replaced with the rueful but optimistic " . . . Well, maybe next year."

THE DIALOGUE

Like LK in the preceding dialogue, TB's recognition factor is high. She has appeared in films, on television, and, to a far lesser extent, on the stage. Due to professional schedules and not to a lack of desire, her stage appearances have been only forays and flirtations. More to the point, she has never worked on stage in a musical. Her interest in doing so has been kept clandestine while she studies voice and other ancillary performing crafts. Only the announcement of a projected production of *A Little Night Music* has impelled her to leave the comfort of the closet to audition for the leading lady role of Desirée and, subsequently, to get it. The original composition was tailored to the talented Glynis Johns, whose contribution to the play as well as to the song was vast in every way but vocal. In consequence, the part has always attracted beautiful, witty women who sing no better than they need to. The score asks little of her: one group number—"The Glamorous Life" sung by Desirée, her daughter, her mother and Liebeslieder Quintet; one duet—"You Must Meet My Wife," more aptly described as a solo sung by her leading man (a singer) but in which she is asked to fill in some of the "Air" in the second Chorus with jokes better delivered in *Sprechgesang**; and, of course, the lovely "Send in the Clowns." Although the first two songs do not demand glorious singing, " . . . Clowns" does gain from a sophisticated vocalization.

TB

I'm intimidated by this song.

---

* From *The Concise Oxford Dictionary of Music*: "Sprechgesang or Sprechstimme—Spoken song, speech song. Type of vocal performance between speech and song."

DC

Why?

TB

I've been trying to work out the reasons for it. For one thing, it's a classic song everyone knows. And the poor dears have to wait till the end of the show to hear it. And . . . well, I guess I don't want to let them down. And mostly, I don't want to let *it* down.

DC

We can get rid of the first reason. If they're waiting for it they'll be doubly glad to hear it. As for your second point, there are thousands of classic songs. If performers allowed themselves to be struck mute because good and even great songs had previously been sung, no one would ever hear anything but the first performance of them. True, you're not any of the women who've sung this song, in or out of the show, but it's just as true that they're not you. This may be a distinct advantage. As for letting the audience and the song down, the argument isn't worth addressing. Few of the women who've sung it are as beautiful as you and fewer still sang it as well as you will.

TB

That remains to be seen. Meanwhile, I'll settle for the kindness of teachers.

DC

More to the point: The dilemma here is how to work the song in Class. What you'll be asked to do in the production of *Night Music* is in the hands of the director and would be impossible for us to guess at. There are infinite ways to sing a song, and it would be dangerous to outguess what he'll ask of you.

TB

Somehow that doesn't bother me. For one thing, I have my own idea of what the song's about. And it does come late in the show, so the audience doesn't have to be briefed about why she sings it. I'm sure the director and I will be in agreement . . . more or less.

DC

Fine. Let's hear it in a music reading before we concern ourselves with the performance.

(She sings through the song. The phrasing is fairly obvious.)

Good. There's not much you can do in the way of dramatic and extravagant phrasing. The score is marked "lento" and the lines are short, which will make the "Air" between them even longer. Not breathing when the idea might seem valid becomes a worthless conceit. But there are a couple of places where a glottal stop would work to your advantage and even an "over-the-bar" placement you can work in just before the last line.*

TB

You mean putting glottal stops after phrases like " . . . I thought that you'd want what I want," after " . . . sorry . . . " and before " . . . my dear"? And between " . . . Don't bother" and " . . . they're here"? And after the " . . . well" in the last line before " . . . maybe next year"?

DC

Yes. Don't forget, you'll be breathing more often than you'll need to because the song is so slow. But when a word or a phrase can be spiked to make your thinking clearer, a glottal stop will be a relief. I'll leave that up to you. It's only important for you to remember that, because you won't be holding onto the last word of those short phrases that begin each "8," there'll always be those long "Air" pockets you'll have to deal with.

TB

I think I understand. Oh, yes—I thought I might try going for

---

* The reader is referred to the phrased copy of the lyric on page 72.

over-the-bar phrasing after " . . . But where are the clowns" and breathing after " . . . quick." (*She sings.*)
    " . . . But where are the clowns (⌣) Quick (✓) send in the clowns."

DC

I don't know about that. For one thing, the choice of over-the-bar would be more valuable if you saved it for the next to last line. (DC *sings.*)
    " . . . There ought to be clowns (⌣) Well (✓) maybe (✓) next year."
And by the way, there's a place where a glottal stop after " . . . maybe" is next to impossible because of the slow tempo. You might as well breathe and insure that you have enough breath for the Rideout.

TB

I like that a lot, but why not both places?

DC

For one, this is a "classic" song, and it should be sung pretty much as written. Over-the-bar phrasing should be taken up tenderly. It brings attention to itself. It's a trick, and a trick over-done is better left undone. My vote would go for saving it until the very end. And in the case of a word like " . . . quick," I don't think you'll need the glottal stop. The word is onomatopoeic. The explosive "k" eliminates the need for it. Try it and you'll see.
    (TB *sings the lines:* " . . . But where are the clowns? (⌣)
    Quick (✓) send in the clowns.")
If you really explode that "k" at the end of the word, it says it all. I'd even give up the glottal and take a breath after " . . . don't bother." Remember, you're dealing with that slow tempo. May we hear it?

TB
(She sings.)

    " . . . Quick send in the clowns (✓) Don't bother (✓) They're here." That feels good.

DC

Better yet, it sounds good. Another point of order. The line " . . . Don't you love farce?" Could you relish the "v" of " . . . love" and the "f" of " . . . farce"? You have a tendency to make the "v" do double duty. All I hear is " . . . Don't you luhfarce?"

TB

I was trying to elide the words.

DC

But what about that appreciation of irony you spoke about? Farce is such a rich, double-edged word. You want to put hot light on it. Try it.

TB
(She sings, caressing the "v" of " . . . love" and the "f" of " . . . farce.")

" . . . Don't you love—farce?" Oh! I do see what you mean. *(She makes a note of this on her music copy.)*

DC

Finally, remember the "isn't it's" in "Small World"? Well, here they are again. This time the slow tempo really brings the unintended vulgarism to everyone's attention.

TB

It might add some spice to the performance. *(She sees* DC's *face.)* Only kidding.

DC

All right, then. May I hear the whole song sung with everything we've been talking about added?
(TB sings through the song, observing breaths, glottal stops

and over-the-bar phrasing as suggested.)
That's fine. Even the key is friendly.

TB

Listen. Do I have to sing this so slowly?

DC

I'm afraid so. If you were singing it out of context, anything goes. But in the body of the score, the music is marked "lento." You can't argue with the wishes of the composer. What will be your biggest problem is not so much singing it as working to keep it from sinking. Your mind's going to have to move faster than your mouth. Strange as it may seem, you'll have to tell yourself you're singing a rhythm number to keep from falling asleep up there. And if you don't stay awake, your body language will start moving in slow motion and the performance will look like a silent movie.

TB

How do I deal with that?

DC

Your inner emotional life will have to move like a kaleidoscope.

TB

That's why I asked you if I had to sing it so slowly. I could feel myself nodding off.

DC

I know. This is the most difficult kind of song to keep alive because the speech is so deliberate, it almost ceases to be "speech" as we know it. Try speaking in this tempo and you'll see how bizarre it sounds. (DC *speaks, drawing out each vowel to match the tempo of the song: "Iiiiiihsn't ihhhhhhht riiiiich? Aaaaare weeee a paaaaaair?"*) Not easy to do. The audience, of course, won't find it bizarre. *They* "speak" music. But for *you*, the one who must sing it, it's absolutely imperative that you quicken your thinking in order to keep the song moving in the stately rhythms called for by the composer. Mind you, it's possible. If you can think of this as a plus factor and not something you're lumbered with, you'll see that it allows for all kinds of responses above, below, before, and after the slow unwinding of the lyric. A good idea is to think of the words you sing as the tip of an iceberg. What lies below it is a vaster, denser language.

TB

And the body language?

DC

My guess is that it'll be minimal because the song is contemplative, ruminative. Perhaps we'll find one or two original moves, but for now I wouldn't give it too much of my time.

TB's next appearance on stage begins with a reprise of the music reading.

DC

Very good. Everything's as we planned. Are there any trouble spots for you?

TB

None that I can think of. As I said, there are no problems *singing* it. It's keeping me from falling asleep that I'm having trouble with.

DC

Well, let's start and see what we see.

TB

It's also a question of pushing myself out to center stage.

DC

In Mr. Sondheim's own words, " . . . stop worrying where you're going—move on."
>   (TB *crosses to Center stage, pauses for a moment and then nods to the pianist. The Vamp begins but she stops after the first few bars have been sung*).

TB

It feels dead.

DC

It looks dead. And that's because your relationship to the Center focus is trivialized. " . . . Isn't it rich? Are we a pair?" has no reason to be said. You have to create Desirée's character as well as her problem and it must happen in the Vamp. How do you see her? Not necessarily at this moment, but generally, as she moves through the play?

TB

I see her as a modern-day woman with a sense of drama. After all, she *is* an actress. And if she tends to be a bit theatrical it's probably because she's the star of her life.

DC

That sounds very interesting but I saw none of it. Where is her wit? Her sense of irony? Let's not forget her appreciation of that. And you must run from any hint of self-pity. She doesn't know the meaning of the word. And you must *be* all of this from the very beginning of the Vamp.

TB

I thought we had to wait until we came Center before we begin to play. I couldn't possibly get all that into two bars!

DC

But you should be working this song not out of context, but as you would perform it in the play. Stanislavski has said, "You need great inner technique in order to seize at once the intense inner rhythm of the scene and its focal points . . . [but] you do not get your rhythm *after* the music has begun—there is not time for that. You must set your rhythm ahead, *before the music starts*, as though you were yourself determining it for the accompaniment. Therefore the ballad should already be taking shape in your feelings before the first note is played on the piano." And so . . . What are the scenes focal points? Why is she compelled to sing those opening lines? And are they straight to him?

TB
(She has been listening intently. As she speaks she weighs her words for maximum clarity.)
She's told Fredrik why she's invited him to her home for the weekend. They had made love the first time they re-met and she'd begun to hope that there was the possibility that she could, as she puts it, " . . . find some sort of coherent existence after so many years of muddle." And that maybe he, too, is, as she says, " . . . in need of rescue."

DC

And the possibility . . . ?

TB

It doesn't happen. He rejects her. Very gently but, yes, he rejects her.

DC

So now. We have this modern-day woman, this actress. This witty, proud woman, the star of her life, impelled to hide the pain of rejection . . . .
(DC beckons the pianist to start the Vamp. TB, with no evident sign of shifting gears, begins to sing. There is a wistful, hollow

*smile on her face as she addresses the first two lines of the song
to herself. She risks staying away from playing to Center
[Fredrik] until the split second before " . . . you in mid-air."
The effect is powerful. DC stops her after the first "8" has been
sung. She is obviously moved.)*

Very interesting. I think you should take it home now and build a
performance that isn't off the top of your head. The Class isn't for
rehearsing. No matter how effectively this is evolving, we need to
see prepared work.

TB

I understand. It's been very helpful. Especially your reference to
Stanislavski.

DC

There is something else he said that I'm fond of because it's
apropos here. (DC *turns to take in the Class.*) He said, "In all ballads,
no matter how brief they may be, there is the seed of a larger piece
of work. In each there is a plot, conflict, solution and a through-
line of action and given circumstances all leading to a super-
objective." (*To* TB) You'll find that this is very true of "Clowns."

TB

Do you think that wise man heard the song in the air before
Mr. Sondheim did?

DC

Well, let's just say he heard a good many things before anyone else
did. But getting back to the subject at hand, let's not forget that the
song isn't the end of the musical.

TB

Yes. And she does end it all with " . . . Well, maybe next year."

For TB's last appearance she elects to skip the music reading.

DC allows her the time to sing through the song without interruption. The Class is respectful and silent. TB, after finishing the Rideout, turns to DC.

TB

It's awfully quiet in here.

DC

Oh, I'm sorry. It doesn't mean there was nothing to say, only that I'm trying to get my thoughts in order.

TB

I know I'm still struggling with that damned slow reeling out of the script. It does narcotize, doesn't it?

DC

Yes, we spoke about that. But you must accept two facts. One: It's slow and it'll always be slow and there's nothing you can do about it. As soon as you stop thinking of that as a negative aspect of the song, it'll stop being one.

TB

You said two facts.

DC

The other fact? We've spoken about that, too—many times. The illusion created by a well-performed song is that it is *your song*— just as much yours as the dialogue appears to be. If that is so, then I assume you chose the words, the melody is yours, and the tempo in which you feel the script must be heard is of your choosing. Why, then, has she chosen to deliver this script to sing to him—and to herself, as well—in such a measured tempo? Clearly no rage speeds up the tale. There is no neurotic hysteria born of self-pity that revs her up when she thinks of how their lives first crossed, re-crossed and now are separating again. To think up phrases like: " . . . Me here at last on the ground, you in mid-air," and " . . . One who keeps tearing around, one who can't move." And how about " . . . Don't you love farce?" and, of course, " . . . Losing my timing this late in my career" . . . that's no easy trick to think up language like that off the top of your head. Thought is needed. The humanness of the comedy amuses you . . . bemuses you. I'm saying all this to get you to accept *her rhythms* rather than thinking, God! This is slow! It isn't slow, it's Desirée—it's *her* song. And if you're playing her, then, as I said, it's *your* song.

TB

I think I know what you're trying to do. And I think I even understand it. And I'll work on it. For now, what about focus? Did my choices of when to work to him and when not to make any sense?

DC

Absolutely. I particularly liked looking him straight in the eye for " . . . no one is there" and *not* singing to him on " . . . Don't bother, they're here." The first is an indication of her wit and the second, her sense of irony. But I'd like to review the body language. You're timing what little you do very well indeed. That's probably due to the easy tempo that allows everything to happen in its own time. But I do have a few suggestions. You stayed at complete "zero" for the first "8." I think you can frame the title in the "Air" just before it. After all it *is* the title and not a fill line. It doesn't need an obvious move, but something to spike the interest of my eye. We only hear it once again at the end of the second "8" and then you can move all over the line because there's no need to "frame" it more than once, as you know.

TB

Well, if I bring them out . . .

DC
(*Interrupting*)

Don't concern yourself with what they'll do!

TB

Yes. But then where do I take them as I move into the second "8"?

DC

Bring them together; play with your little finger. I don't care. Just don't let them drop down to zero again. One hand may make a simple indication of who's tearing around and who's paralyzed. But remember, we agreed last week that there's no need to decorate the song with a lot of hand and foot activity. The lyric is interesting enough to keep the audience at attention. I do think that wherever your arms are for the last lines of the song, they should open in the "Air" immediately following " . . . Well" before " . . . maybe," in order to frame " . . . next year." And then you can bring them down, slowly, one at a time, while you play through the Rideout.

TB
(*She has been taking notes of what* DC *has been saying.*)

And the choices? Were they valid?

DC

We began to work the song a few weeks ago with the agreement that your director will have the task of bringing the song into the fabric of the whole piece. For now, I think you've captured a good working substructure you can go with . . . one that isn't so frozen that it would resist change.

TB

One good thing to say about this song: because it's so slow, it's roomy. I've got plenty of time to deal with filling the "Air" before I sing each line—and that's a joy. My problem's always been sluggish thinking, but "Clowns" makes me feel like I'm taking a head trip. I've got enough time left over to send back postcards from the song.

DC

Singing Sondheim means that you will never get it frozen. Every time you sing "Clowns" new revelations will occur to you. It's like peeling a pearl until you get down to the seminal irritant that made you need to create the song in the first place. Then building from that moment on out, each time, is the only way you can beat him at his own game.

TB

I'll be grateful, I suppose, that that's true when I'm doing the bloody show. Until then, it's like holding on to a jellyfish.

DC

You can fight that with what, on the stage, is called "presence." Another way to say that is that you must occupy time as well as space. When you're in front of the camera, all you're asked to occupy is space. The rhythms of a scene are manipulated by the director and the editor. They give the film its tension by mixing and scissoring, cutting, clipping, consolidating, and splicing the performances long after the actors have gone home.

TB

Well, we could argue some of that.

DC

Perhaps. But we can't argue that, on a stage, it's all you and all your doing. What the audience hears may be sifted through sophisticated sound systems, but what it sees, well, that's what I call "presence." Taking stage. Someone once asked me whether it was necessary to know what you want from an audience or do you just want to share the song with them? "To hell with that!" I said. "Their attention! That's what you want! You want their attention!"

4

True Blues

The Blues categories that follow share the rhythms of ballads but little else. They are similarly and undeniably slow. Unlike ballads,* their provenance is not the theater but Tin Pan Alley, and even before that, the unique musical expression of an historic black culture. The arc that began with the spiritual and moved on to W. C. Handy's published "Memphis Blues" in 1912 and from there to Jerome Kern's "Blue Danube Blues," Gershwin's "Rhapsody in Blue" and the second movement of his Concerto in F, Darius Milhaud's "La Création du Monde," on to Samuel Barber's "Excursions" is a long arc indeed. Purists will claim that it first appeared at the turn of the century when black musicians like the above-mentioned W. C. Handy and Big Bill Broonzy wrote and sang their blues. And they are right. But the word "Blues," so loosely applied as a categorical descriptive, has been appropriated by even the unlikely likes of Philip Braham's "Limehouse Blues" and Noel Coward's "Twentieth Century Blues," both songs more than a light year removed from Fats Waller's "Empty Bed Blues" as sung by Bessie Smith.

Its musical form is difficult to place within a specific structure. For the precisionist, it is composed of twelve-bar phrases sprinkled

---

* The word "ballad" as used here refers to ballads from scores for the stage and screen. Category 13, Contemporary, considers the "pop" scene which, of course, includes ballads by the score.

with flatted thirds and sevenths (blue notes) and three lines of lyric filling four lines of music, but the very nature of its improvisational character resists rigid codification. Of one thing you may be sure— they always sing of pain, of tortured and/or unrequited love and, at its most primitive, of raunchy sex. As with ballads, I have placed them in three categories: True Blues, Pop Blues, and Theater Blues.

The original Blues ("Jelly Roll Blues," "St. Louis Blues," "Beale Street Blues," etc.) is so indigenous to the "black sound" that one must pick up this kind of song gingerly no matter the skin color of the performer. The pure rendition of True Blues is available on rare recordings which, once heard, would frighten off even the most intrepid imitator of the real thing. In general, Blues of all kinds are house numbers and most often "blue," but even at their most scatological and, speaking oxymoronically, they may even be funny Blues. An example, Wallace "Pine Top" Johnson's Blues:

"You got bad blood, baby, I believe you needs a shot
You got bad blood, baby, I believe you needs a shot
I said turn around here, baby, let me see what else you got
My needle's in you, baby, and you seem to feel all right
My needle's in you, baby, and you seem to feel all right
When your medicine go to comin' down
I want you to hug me tight.
I'm in your pussy, put your legs upside the wall
My needle's in you, baby, and you seem to feel all right
When your medicine go to comin' down
I want you to hold me tight.
Bad blues!"*

I have never assigned a song from this first category because I have never helped to stage an audition that called for it, and, more to the point, I have never taught anyone who could have naturally performed it. Of course, much ethnic vocal music has been classicized. The spiritual may even be heard in concert halls in solo

---

* The lyric to "Bad Blues" is from *Blues From the Delta* by William Ferris, published by Anchor Press/Doubleday.

recitals where it tends to cluster in a closing group of a program of international art songs. In those instances, the soloist is, de rigueur, black, but just as often, Caucasian choruses sing out "Sometimes I Feel Like a Motherless Child" and "Ezekiel Saw the Wheel" like Protestant hymns, while they and their audiences remain comfortably unaware of the agonies and ecstasies that initiated the words and the music. But, True Blues as a distinct and separate musical statement remains safe in its own special corner, where its soloists are less concerned with interpreting music and text than with stating the facts of their lives. This alone alchemizes song and performance. The one exception that comes to mind is Laurence Olivier's Archie Rice in John Osborne's *The Entertainer* on stage and on film. Beset by money woes, a shattered career, and the sudden death of his son, the drunken Archie Rice during a moment of painful recollection, attempts to imitate a black woman whom he had heard, years before, sing:

"Oh, Lord! I don't care where they burn my body.
Oh, Lord! I don't care where they burn my body.
'Cause my soul's gonna live with God!"

It is a stunning piece of work that achieves its correct "blues" effect without recourse to imitation.

The category True Blues does not have an accompanying dialogue for the reasons stated and a biased "personally held opinion" that like "The Marseillaise," "Hatikvah," and "God Save the Queen," True Blues should be sung by native citizens. Let others sing their own anthems.

"Jump For Joy"

I Got It Bad (And That Ain't Good)

by Duke Ellington and Paul Webster

"I Got It Bad (And That Ain't Good)"

VERSE:
The poets say that all who love are blind
But I'm in love and I know what time it is (✓)
The good book says "Go seek and ye shall find" (✓)
Well I have sought (,)
And my (,) what a climb it is (✓)
My life is just like the weather (,)
It changes with the hours (✓)
When he's near I'm fair and warmer (,)
When he's gone I'm cloudy with showers (✓)
In emotion (,) like the ocean ⌣
⌣ It's either sink (,) or swim (✓)
When a woman loves a man (✓) like I love him (✓)

CHORUS:
Like a lonely weeping willow lost in the wood (✓)
I got it bad and that ain't good (✓)
And the things I tell my pillow no woman should (✓)
I got it bad (,) and that ain't good (✓)
Tho folks with good intentions tell me to save my tears (✓)
I'm glad I'm mad about him (✓)
I can't live without him ⌣
⌣ Lord above me (✓) make him love me the way he should ⌣
⌣ I got it bad (✓) and that ain't good (✓)

"I Got It Bad (And That Ain't Good)" from *Jump for Joy*, lyrics by Paul Webster, music by Duke Ellington. Copyright © 1941, 1986 (copyright renewed 1969) by Robbins Music Corporation. International Copyright Secured. All Rights Reserved. All rights controlled and administered by EMI Robbins Catalog, Inc. Used by permission.

5

Pop Blues

Categories 5 and 6, Pop Blues and Theater Blues, share a common recognition factor: they have little to nothing to do with the "blues" described as True Blues in the previous category. The purity of True Blues is absent and in its place are the popular and the mundane—hallmarks of Pop and Theater Blues. I do not mean to imply that this produces a coarsening effect; what was echt is now ersatz only in the sense that the word "blues," as it is applied to popular song, is an umbrella word that covers songs more blue in tone than blues in form. Most of the songs that find a home in these two groups are an indelible part of the history of American popular music. Unlike True Blues, their natural habitat is the pop world of recordings and CD collections, on sound tracks accompanying films and TV, and performed live in nightclubs throughout the world. Although you may hear on record Ella, Sarah, Billie, Carmen, Lena, Mabel, Whitney, Dionne, Nat, Sammy, Billy and Bobby sing the blues of your choice, the music loses nothing when Frank, Mel, Tony, Hoagy, Libby, Barbra, Peggy, Maureen and Mildred launch into their versions. Although True Blues is more appealing and effective when it is sung by a raw, primitive voice, Pop Blues permits far wider margins of allowable vocal delivery. Eileen Farrell singing "I Gotta Right to Sing the Blues," for example, proves the lady has, indeed, a right to sing them.

The line that separates and distinguishes Pop Blues from

Theater Blues is hazy, but although Pop is rarely Theater, much of Theater Blues may be Pop. More often than not, Pop Blues can trace its origins to arrangers/composers/conductors of historic big bands, to films, and to Tin Pan Alley. They represent a major list of "standards." Theater Blues traces its origins back to scores expressly written for the musical theater. This is, however, an admitted generalization.

Examples:

- Ellington's "Mood Indigo," "Do Nothin' Till You Hear From Me," "Solitude," "Prelude to a Kiss" and "Paris Blues."
- Hoagy Carmichael's "Hong Kong Blues," "Washboard Blues," "Rockin' Chair," and "Georgia on My Mind."
- Harry Akst's "Am I Blue?" and Ray Henderson/Buddy De Sylva/Lew Brown's "Birth of the Blues."
- Alec Wilder's "Rain, Rain (Don't Go 'Way)" and "I Wish I Had the Blues Again"
- Harold Arlen's "Blues in the Night," "Happy With the Blues," and "I Gotta Right to Sing the Blues."*
- Billie Holiday's "God Bless the Child" and "Lady Sings the Blues."

THE SONG

I have chosen Duke Ellington's "I Got It Bad (And That Ain't Good)" not alone for its Pop Blues "sound" but its strength as a theater piece. (The demanding jump of a ninth in the first bar of the Chorus's theme allows for immediate vocal preening.) Furthermore, the published copy has both the familiar bathetic first Chorus lyric as well as a second lyric, less often sung and therefore apt for theater auditioning and a fresher reprise. Finally, Ellington dressed jazz in legitimate designs that, as propounded by Nicolas Slonimsky, "revolutionized the concept of jazz: no longer . . . restricted to small combos of 'unlettered' improvisers, his [Ellington's] scores were to take on the dimensions and scope of classical compositions while retaining an underlying jazz feeling."**

---

* By virtue of the density of their lyrics (Johnny Mercer, Peggy Lee, and Ted Koehler in these cases), Harold Arlen's Pop Blues can easily slide into the Theater Blues category, despite the fact that they are songs written for films.
** From Nicolas Slonimsky's revision of (Theodore) *Baker's Biographical Dictionary of Musicians*, Sixth Edition (New York: Schirmer Books, 1978).

The song form is AABA. The Verse, like many of Ellington's Verses, is shaped in long Brahmsian phrases only a singer dare attempt. The major second interval that appears with insistent frequency in the Chorus (in the first and second bars of the A theme and, with one exception, in every bar of the Bridge—the B theme) is planted in the Verse in the first, fifth, ninth and tenth bars. There is a certain sequential sameness in the melody of the Verse, but this may be due to the rigid rhyme structures that dictate the melody.* As for the lyric, it is archetypal—unrequited love with all the cliché stops out. This can be disheartening for the modern woman, but there is something about an Ellington song that beguiles the ear of the listener. One is powerless to resist those voluptuous melodies or, in this instance, that broad jump of a ninth in the first bar of the Chorus (and repeated in the second and last "8"). The recommended second Chorus lyric, at least in the first two "8s," strikes the writer as somewhat less offensive and even the second Bridge soft-pedals the dependency theme—a hallmark of the Blues.

One final note: As stated above, the notion that only a black vocalist dare sing the Blues is unjustified in the case of Pop and Theater Blues. For this reason, I am strongly opposed to dialect readings of any sort unless they are genuine. The sophistication of the harmonic changes that is the essence of Duke Ellington's inventions is too distant from the primitive language found in the preceding True Blues category to allow for this kind of indelicacy.

The last two decades have seen an increase in the number of Oriental students in the Classes I teach. The black performer's disheartening struggle in the theater community for full-status representation has begun to diminish if not disappear due in large part to the greater exposure of the work of black composers, lyricists, playwrights, actors, dancers, and comedians. Today, the Oriental artist is the slighted minority. Nontraditional casting** is a controversial battleground, but I am convinced that, like the black actors, actresses, and performers whose lot is less oppressive today, the show business community of Oriental and Latino artists whose

---

* In the eternal debate of "Which came first—the words or the music?" one is tempted to guess that the Verse was "first came the word" and the music dictated the Chorus's lyric.
** The term has gained currency in recent years due to the labors of those who feel no role should be denied anyone because of race, creed, or color. It is a slow evolutionary process.

talent, at least in my Classes, cannot be overpraised, is on the brink of a similar assimilation.

THE DIALOGUE

AB enters. She is a third-generation (Sansei) American; a leading lady and a beautiful woman who creates music with that particular flow of sound that marks the trained singer. It is her pleasure and her cross to have played and played again Lady Thiang in *The King and I* and to reprise, yet again, "Something Wonderful"—a fate far from something wonderful. The assignment of material on the basis of color or race is a policy I find both repugnant and irrelevant. An argument might be made that Paul Webster's lyric for the Duke Ellington classic "I Got It Bad" is not that far removed from Lady Thiang's lament.

DC

Any problem with notes? Words? I believe we decided to sing the second printed Chorus because it's less well known?

AB

No. And yes to the second question. The Verse is a little busy. I'd never heard it before, but I like it. And, of course, I know the Chorus. I guess everybody does.

DC

Yes. Ellington's "standards" are part of the national collective unconscious and you're right about the Verse. But it sits easy in the throat and I think singing it helps to balance off the somewhat commonplace Bridge in the Chorus. The song's famous for that jump of a ninth in the first bar of the first, second and last "8s." What's important is that the song works—and you'll be singing the hell out of it.

AB

I hope so. It's, of course, a house number. And the Verse looks like it's meant to be sung in ad-lib.

DC

Yes, and all the way. In fact, right through till its end. The Chorus is in tempo and that first bar is like hearing an old friend. We should choose the best key we can find to advertise your voice without upstaging the dramatic power of the phrase.

AB

Actually, I can sing it in the printed key.

DC

Without slipping into "head" on that E natural?*

AB

Well, yes. I use what they call a "mix." It sounds like chest, but it's really a mix of chest and head. I like to use it. These days they ask for keys that can kill you if you don't know how to get up there without slipping into a bad imitation of Katisha in *The Mikado*. (*She sings.*)
   "Hearts do not break!
   They sting and ache
   For old love's sake,
   But do not die,
   As witnesseth
   The living I!
   Oh, living I!"
      (*The swoop down from head to chest imitates the classic bad
      contralto. The Class responds.*)
See what I mean?

---

* The human voice is divided into two registers: the combined falsetto, or "head voice," and the "chest register." This division is admittedly a facile one. In his admirable *Dictionary of Vocal Terminology* (published by Joseph Patelson Music House, Ltd. 1983), Cornelius L. Reid points out that the "chest register" is a term reserved for the lower mechanism in its isolated form. Singers who employ it exclusively are described, again by the uninitiated, as "belters." Those women who push it "too high into the middle and upper pitch ranges . . . [shut off the head voice] and high notes become difficult or impossible to produce."

DC

Well, I don't presume to tell you how to sing. For now, why don't we all settle back and listen?

> (AB *sings through the song. The mix on the E natural is all she promised. It rings out on "*. . . lonely," "*. . . things," and "*. . . Lord above *me" at the top of the first, the second and the last "8" bars.*)

Lovely. Let's talk about that ad-lib in the Verse. You're sitting on the word ". . . love" in the first bar and again in the third. I'd give the first one up.

AB

For a reason?

DC

Yes. For the sake of variety. You'll be reversing it in the fifth bar and putting a hold on "ye" in ". . . ye shall find" and on "sought" in the following bar: ". . . I have sought and my what a climb it is!" Enough is enough. As for that rhyme—". . . time it is!" and ". . . climb it is!"—just sing what it's about. It'll rhyme. You don't have to point it out. I don't recommend killing rhymes, but as I say over and over again, rhymes rhyme. Concern yourself with what they're saying. If a rhyme is part of the speech, short of murdering it, I wouldn't pay it too much attention. Going on—there's a glottal after ". . . sought" and after ". . . my"; another after ". . . weather" and a slight ritard on ". . . hours." The ritard extends into the next two bars, beginning with ". . . When he's near," etc. and ending with ". . . cloudy with showers." The next two bars should be moved for the sake of contrast—slow followed by fast—and the final two bars are yours to sing as you feel them.* Have you got it?

AB
(*She laughs.*)

On tape. (*She is recording her time on stage.*) We'll see how much I

---

* The reader may follow the lyric and/or lead sheet copy of the music.

remember next time up. One thing I did want to ask. We all know this is Ellington. You can't sing it square-on-the-nose as it's written, but at the same time, how freely may I sing it for a theater audition? I know anything goes in a club where the arrangement of a standard is as important as choosing to sing it in the first place, but don't they get a little uptight when you do that sort of thing for a legit audition?

DC

Yes. But, of course, it would always depend on the nature of the piece for which you're auditioning. If it were for your old friend *The King and I*, this wouldn't be the song you'd choose to sing in any case. On the other hand, for *Sophisticated Ladies*, it'd be ideal in that context—not too square.

AB

I meant particularly on the very last title. I'd like to go for something rangy there. (*She asks the pianist to follow her and sings.*)

Is that too much? (*It is gorgeously sung.*)

DC

Not for me. (*The Class cheers.*) It's unanimous. (*To the pianist*) I think you can give her more complicated harmonies on that rising phrase.

PIANIST

Also, how about if I bow out and let her have the last word in the clear for a heavy count of four? Just silence under that floating sound?

DC

Lovely. Then, when she's off the note, one soft sting to cap it. (*To* AB) I think that's enough for today. When I see you next we'll hear how this all comes together.

The Class applauds. A beautiful voice placed at the service of a beautiful song—the perfect musical partnership.

AB is on stage. The amended, rephrased plotting is laid into her music reading. Minor vocal variations have been added to the melodic line. They are slight and, as previously observed, they prove that, indeed, she has no difficulty "loosening" up a song ill-served by unswerving allegiance to the printed copy of the sheet music.* Again, DC and the Class are enthusiastic.

DC

Well, that's frozen. We all approve. Let's move on to a first performance.
     (AB *moves to Center stage. Before she begins . . .*)
Would you lighten her up a bit? You look like you know what you're going to sing. But how do you know what you're going to sing? How do you even know what you're going to do? Someone may yell "Fire!"—in which case you'll be running out of here along with the rest of us. Remember, it's a kind of madness to be in the country of a song you haven't even thought of, much less begun to sing.** If we can be said to live from moment-to-moment, the moment for "I Got It Bad" is still in the future.

AB

Have I done that again? It must have been left over from the mood of the music reading.

---

* I have not indicated these minor alterations. They are better left to the individual performer who may be relied upon to hear his own "music."
** See *On Singing Onstage*, Don'ts and Do's, pages 73-75.

DC

But you won't be having a music reading at an audition or a performance. Funny, though, that you should bring that up. I know I'm only supposed to be listening to you in a music reading, but often when I look up at you standing there, singing in the wings . . . (DC *turns to the Class.*) . . . and this is true of so many of you . . . (*He turns back to* AB.) . . . I think, Oh! If only she'd settle for this as her performance! Perhaps not a finished one, but the reading is so damned straightforward. It looks like you. It *is* you. Then you cross to Center stage and bring along all the baggage of acting classes, this Class, acquired technical information . . . burdening everything you do with "ideas." In the music reading your mind is only on singing the song—and even enjoying it—and what I see is the lady I know, herself; you're interesting because you're simple. You're aware of the task at hand and you're doing it. But I think you think that isn't enough when you're performing— that you're uninteresting until you *make* it interesting. If only the addition of focus and intention were added to your music reading, how well it would work! I'd see just you—willing to take the rap for yourself.

AB

I know what you mean. In the wings I have nothing to do but start singing when the Vamp's finished. And I love to sing. But when I come out here, I think I've got to do something.

DC

Do nothing.

AB

I know we all say this but doing "nothing" is probably the hardest thing you're ever asked to do in the Class.

DC

I think that's because you think of it as something you have to *do*.

What do you *do* when you wait for a bus? Or do you think of that as nothing? For a green light? For an elevator?

AB

That's easy. I think. Of thousands of dumb things.

DC

Well, why don't you try to think of some of them now?

AB

But of what?

DC

Offhand I can think of, well . . . how about "This is me." "God! I like being here!" "I bet you're thinking what the devil are we going to do with a Japanese?" "Don't worry about it. Wait 'til you hear me sing. You're going to love it!"

AB

That last one may take a bit of doing, but I get your point. Let me walk away and come back on again.
(AB *exits. Some moments later she reenters, crosses to Center stage and begins her performance of . . . herself. Out front, we see a beautiful woman who, because of her appearance, is both intriguing and mysterious.)*

DC
(*Before she can nod to the pianist*)

Perfect. How do you feel?

AB

Not as difficult as I thought it would be. I suppose I thought of nothing as a kind of death. I seem to work harder trying to get rid of myself than I do accepting the fact that it's impossible and not even worth the bother.

DC

Worth the bother? It's yourself you're trying to hang on to! Remember, then . . . (*Taking in the Class*) . . . when you enter and move to that geography you'll be working in, there's no song "on" you and certainly *not the song you plan to sing.* In fact . . . (*Back to* AB) . . . there's no song "on" you when you nod to the pianist. There's no song when you come front, but not yet Center. It's only when you do come Center, in the Vamp, and recognize the presence of the theater, and immediately thereupon endow that "spot" with whatever and whomever you need to furnish *you*—I mean you, yourself—with a specific place, a specific world, and, most important, an implicit cue based on some element of conflict within yourself or between you and that object, that in turn creates the need to invent a song that, *at that instant—and only then*, will emerge from your mouth the first lines of, in this case, "I Got It Bad." Now that was one long sentence! But out of time as we know it—I mean in music time—all this is done so quickly during the life of the Vamp that at the moment of the arrival of the vocal downbeat it'll seem to us that it is not Ellington who wrote this music, not Paul Webster who wrote those words, but . . . you.

AB

I can't tell you how grateful I am that my recorder got that all down. I don't think you've ever described it in such detail.

DC

Oh, I've described it before. You just never heard it. Perhaps you weren't quite ready to hear it.

AB

Why can't we hear it until then?

DC

Because you have other things on your mind. Remember, you're easier today. More comfortable with yourself. The old fear of being up there is leaving. All that noise in your head doing its suicide number—"I'm not good enough," "They won't like me," "I wish I was somewhere else," "Did I turn the oven off?"—all that's quieting down and the woman who lives in the real world is able to hear what's going on. And what's going on, after your nod, is four bars of ad-lib music: the Vamp. As I've said many times, it is the most important "Air" in the song. How you play it sets the song on the right track or derails it before it begins. Something else I've said many times before: A badly performed Vamp cannot birth a good performance. Of that you can be sure. Just as with grammar, bad gets worse. Good gets better. This has taken up more time than usual, but I think it's been worth it.

AB is back for another try. She forgoes a music reading, crosses to Center and begins her performance. Its first phrases are much improved. Good is getting better. It is simpler, less "actor-y," and still beautifully sung. Her focus choices are knowing. The Class, more complaisant than DC, is clearly enraptured.* The rise to the soaring A natural on " . . . and that ain't good" (with the pianist bowing out on the last word) seems to send the note off into space. After a slow count of four, the pianist's "Chinese bells" sting sounds a heartbreaking and inevitable ending to its flight.

DC

Beautiful! Lovely! You're a bloody canary up there. Except for one thing—it won't work. (*The Class is stunned.* AB *waits.*) Hard as it may be to hear, we must talk about the reason you and we . . . (*Taking in the Class*) . . . are here. A classic example of the singer determined to sing the song instead of the problem that compels her to sing it.

---

* Since the assigned songs in classes I teach are chosen from a rich lode of theater music, the power of a well-*sung* song can blind the aggregate critical eye. Not until the work evolves into a well-*performed* song does the Class perceive the progress of good, to better, to best.

AB

I don't understand. I thought I had her just where she wanted to be. And I felt the Class was with me.

DC

They were. They love to hear you sing. I love to hear you sing. And as for having her where she wanted to be—you did. Awash with self-pity. But who gives a damn? People have their own problems. They'll love to listen to you sing, but are they moved? Are they touched? You're stuck in tar. And once you're in it, it's hard as the devil to get out of it. Unless you play her drunk—a possibility, but not valid for an audition or anywhere, for that matter, unless you're doing a comedy routine. (*To* AB *and the Class*) Songs like "I Got It Bad"—and there are thousands of them— invite you to play the "victim"—the "loser." For me, its biggest sin is the sin of mindlessness. It's as if, in the most inhuman way, you cut off the complexity of your thoughts, your questions, your memories—*what* you are singing about and *why*. We hear what's happened because we hear the words; we know the situation. But the uniqueness of the dilemma as it relates to *you*—we don't know it. But, don't you see, that's want we *want* to know.

AB

It sounds like I'm doing what you're always cautioning us not to do. Instead of *doing* the song, I'm letting it do *me*.

DC

As I said, singing the "blues" is a seduction. It's a siren song. You have to strap yourself to the mast in order to deal with the "why" you're singing them. It's just too pleasureful to stand there and whine. Joseph Heller, in an interview, confessed this about his writing: " . . . the [scenes] you want to be touching really require my not having those feelings in the course of [writing] them. The effect I have is different from what I want the effect to be on the [reader]." Let's take this advice and turn this upside down. Is there something worthwhile going for this relationship?. Let me see . . .

(DC *scans a copy of the song.*) Well, we have " . . . When he's near I'm fair and warmer," " . . . When a woman loves a man like I love him," " . . . I'm glad I'm mad about him," and " . . . I can't live without him." Even " . . . Tho folks with good intentions tell me to save my tears" implies how you feel about anyone who doesn't understand.

AB

In MacArthur's classic words from World War Two: I shall return.

DC

I think so. By the way, it was you up there on stage and the trip you took was necessary. You just took the wrong one.

A week has passed. It amuses DC to see that AB has dressed not in black, as before, but in light colors. He chooses to ignore it for now. AB again performs the song. The change in approach is immediately apparent. No longer the victim, there is even an undercurrent of optimism in her performance. " . . . Lord above me, make him love me the way he should," in the final moments of the Chorus, seems to imply that the only reason he doesn't is that he hasn't gotten around to it yet. AB is aware that good went from better to best.

AB

You know, the interesting thing about all this is that I actually enjoyed singing the song. Really! For the first time. Instead of delivering a list of complaints to my shrink, I was busy explaining to myself and to everyone out there why I stick with him.

DC

I could see that. In fact, you were so true to that thinking that when you arrived at the last line, " . . . I've got it bad and that ain't good," you looked, somehow, amused with a weakness you'd long ago forgiven in yourself. In fact, you've so consistently converted subjectivity into objectivity that now there are moments you could leave the audience and go for an internalized focus. A thought that occurs that makes you take your eyes off the theater in order to indulge in a moment of fanciful musing.

AB

Any ideas where?

DC

Well, perhaps right after " . . . The good book says go seek and ye shall find." You could leave us there to remember what " . . . Well, I have sought and, my, what a climb it is!" barely describes. And how about the moment before " . . . and the things I tell my pillow" (implying "you wouldn't believe!") and then a return into the theater for " . . . no woman should"? You may find there's a wry joke there if you go for it. But gently. And certainly a line like " . . . Lord above me make him love me the way he should" can be thrown high up to the gods.

THE CLASS

This has been really interesting. I mean, how effective the first performance seemed to be, but how much more dramatic the second one was. I was perfectly happy watching her eat her heart out, but she really grabbed me by letting me see who she was and how she dealt with her life.

AB

For me what was interesting was that I was thinking—thinking quite apart from the song. The first time around I surrendered to the music and the words without realizing it.

DC

What you must all take away from this is the idea that, in the performance of any song, electing to play a victim or a loser is a no-win choice. What holds and wins the attention of the audience is an *active imagination*. A human life is on the stage and it is dramatic because we are, all of us, human. We want to see how others deal with their problems. To make a passive surrender to the song instead of *working it out* presents an aspect of yourself that asks for understanding and forgiveness in a place—the theater—where you cannot hope to receive them. When you have to sing in the country of the "Blues," you'd be wise to keep your mitts up. I think that wraps it up for today.

(AB *starts to exit.*)

By the way, that dress you chose to wear . . .

AB

I didn't think you noticed.

DC

I noticed. I think it should be given a hand.

(*The Class is confused.*)

AB
(*To the Class*)

What he means is that singing the blues in a flowered print instead of last week's basic black made it a lot easier to perform.

DC

As I always say, "Wear sneakers and you sing sneakers."

(AB *exits to a hand.*)

"Raisin"

A Whole Lotta Sunlight

Lyrics by Robert Brittan

Music by Judd Woldin

116

"A Whole Lotta Sunlight"

CHORUS:
There'll be a whole lotta sunlight (✓)
Nothin' but blue in the skies
Bright (✓) yellow blossoms catching butterflies (✓)
And when the leaves are lullabying in your ear (✓)
Won't need to open up your eyes (✓)
To know the time of year
Time to get out (✓) in the morning
Time to bathe in the glow (✓)
And when that lazy ol' sun sets
Just you let it go (✓)
No need to sit around rememb'ring how it used to be (✓)
There'll be a whole lotta sunlight (✓)
Shining for you (✓) and me (✓)

"A Whole Lotta Sunlight" from *Raisin*, lyrics by Robert Brittan, music by Judd Woldin. Copyright © 1969, 1974 Blackwood Music, Inc. and Raisin Music. International Copyright Secured. All Rights Reserved. All rights controlled and administered by EMI Blackwood Music, Inc. Used by permission.

6

Theater Blues

The Theater Blues category denotes the provenance of this group and, in a sense, it does but the group includes the music of Harold Arlen, the reputed father of Theater Blues, who wrote some of his finest blues for the screen. In the past, adaptations of musical librettos into films tended to enfeeble rather than enhance the source material and, at their worst, work harsh amputations. On the other hand, film scores, as a separate genre, can be notably superior works. The Gershwins, Kern, Rodgers and Hart and Hammerstein, Porter, Berlin, Styne, and Arlen, among others, created music and words for the screen that are the equal of their theater scores. Arlen's "Blues in the Night," "One for My Baby," "The Man That Got Away," and "Last Night When We Were Young" were written for films, and for cabaret, the unforgettable "Stormy Weather" and "Ill Wind" and the unaffiliated "When the Sun Comes Out." Arlen's Theater Blues masterpieces include "I Wonder What Became of Me?" "I Had Myself a True Love" and "Come Rain or Come Shine"—all from *St. Louis Woman*; "Take It Slow, Joe" from *Jamaica*; "I Never Has Seen Snow" and "Don't Like Goodbyes" from *House of Flowers*. In discrete collaboration with lyricists Ted Koehler, Ira Gershwin, E. Y. ("Yip") Harburg, and Johnny Mercer, he created soaring melodies that are the delight of singers.

Unlike most composers, Arlen was a consummate vocalist who

worked at the beginning of his career as a professional singer. I know of no other composer who possesses his understanding of what sings and what requires work to sing. I heard him sing "The Man That Got Away" the week he wrote it, and it has forever colored my ability to make room in the memory of my ear for other interpretations. Along with the songs of Harold Arlen, other examples of Theater Blues:

- Irving Berlin: "Everybody Knew But Me" and "Supper Time."
- Cole Porter: "Down in the Depths" from *Red, Hot and Blue!* and "Love for Sale" from *The New Yorkers.*
- George and Ira Gershwin: "Blue, Blue, Blue" from *Let 'Em Eat Cake* and "The Half of It, Dearie, Blues" from *Lady, Be Good!* And *Porgy and Bess*, with DuBose Heyward: "Summertime," "My Man's Gone Now," "They Pass By Singin'," "Clara, Clara, Don't You Be Downhearted," "What You Want Wid Bess?" and "Oh, Doctor Jesus."
- Jerome Kern: "Can't Help Lovin' Dat Man" from *Showboat*, "Left All Alone Again Blues" from *The Night Boat* and "Blue Danube Blues" from *Good Morning, Dearie.*
- Arthur Schwartz: "Smokin' Reefers" from *Flying Colors* and "Blue Grass" from *Inside USA.*
- Hugh Martin: "That's How I Love the Blues" from *Best Foot Forward.*
- Cy Coleman: "Where Am I Going?" from *Sweet Charity.*
- Harvey Schmidt: "Soon It's Gonna Rain" from *The Fantasticks.*
- Randy Newman: "I Think It's Going to Rain Today,"
- Stephen Sondheim: "The 'God-Why-Don't-You-Love Me' Blues?" from *Follies.*
- Stephen Schwartz: "Turn Back, O Man" from *Godspell.*
- Leonard Bernstein: "Lonely Town" from *On the Town.*
- Kurt Weill: "Lost in the Stars," a title tune.
- Larry Grossman's "All Things to One Man" from *Grind.*

But now we have long since left the blues as a classic song form and moved far into a country where the timbre and the texture of the blues reside, but the blues, as "blues," is a mere whisper or a misuse of the word. The lyrics, too, have a shallower reference to suffering. Ira Gershwin in his *Lyrics on Several Occasions* (New York: Knopf, 1959) has written—"Some sort of grievance is featured in the musical comedy adaptation of The Blues [as evidenced here in "The Half of It, Dearie, Blues" and in Kern's "Left All Alone Again Blues"] but . . . the lyric approach isn't attempting to plumb the melancholy depths of the real Blues." The same may be said for all Theater Blues as a category.

Theater Blues, as set apart from Pop Blues, relies on more complicated melodic and harmonic invention. While Pop Blues can be sung anywhere in the marketplace as long as the performer lives indigenously within its sonic boundaries, Theater Blues packs a more dramatic/musical punch. Propelled by denser scripts that call for heightened interpretive skills along with, but not necessarily, a more voluptuous sound, it is divergent from its blues origins. For this reason, they not only audition well but offer splashy advertisements for the singer. As described in the previous chapter, there is always the risk that a performance drenched in subjective sorrow will not elicit compassion from an audience. Despite the French "*Qui chante son mal enchante*" (He who sings of his woes, enchants), it is best to keep in mind the rejoinder "I've got troubles of my own."* Beyond this cautionary advice, Theater Blues, as a category, provides the performer with some of this country's most beloved songs.

THE SONG

"A Whole Lotta Sunlight" from the musical *Raisin* by Judd Woldin and Robert Brittan is a perfect theater song. As in the case of all blues, the singer's sensitivity to the rubato possibilities that lie within the crannies of the musical phrases adds a voluptuous emotional appeal to this elegant song.

In the unwinding of the Chorus, beginning with the twenty-fourth bar through to the end of the Rideout, the build rises as an element of, rather than a mechanical addition to, the song. Interpretation of the lyric permits wide choices. In the musical, it is sung by the Character Woman to a dying philodendron; I have seen Lena Horne sing it as a call to arms; and in my studio I have assigned it to white and black Character Men as well as Women, and under so wide an umbrella it has emerged as a political rallying

---

* To diminish and even forestall the risk, see *On Singing Onstage*, pages 3-31.

cry (forté), the pep talk of a coach to a football team (mezzo-forté), down to the (piano) hush of a lullaby. Admittedly, there is a "black" sound that pervades the song and gives it a certain piquancy*, but even as I write this, I recall a white Character Man singing it to a drug-besotted son and the emotional impact stays with me still. The bottom line of all great songs is their universality.

THE DIALOGUE

GJ enters. She is a black Character Woman whose credits on film and television are consequential. What she isn't is a singer, but although she would argue the point, DC thinks of her as someone who doesn't sing only because she has never been asked to. True, it is not a trained voice, but despite her reserved attitude toward it, it is a voice that wants to be heard. And should be. It is this unspoken dream—to sing on stage—that brings her to Class.

DC

Did you know this song?

GJ

No. But I know the play. In fact, I've played the part. Not in New York, but I've played it.

DC
(To the Class)

"A Whole Lotta Sunlight" is from the score of the musical adaptation of Lorraine Hansberry's *Raisin in the Sun*, retitled *Raisin* by its authors—Charlotte Zaltzberg and Robert Nemiroff (who was its director, as well) with a score by the lyricist Robert Brittan and the composer Judd Woldin. (*To* GJ) Perhaps you could tell the Class a little about the play to help them understand the symbolism of the song's lyric?

---

* The printed lyric in the sheet music is ambiguous. G's are dropped and added with no discernible consistency. For both the white and black performer I suggest replacing the g in "sitting" (in the Verse) and in "nothing" (in the Chorus). Similarly, in the Chorus, the d should be returned to "ol." However, "lotta," rather than "lot of" in the title, wherever it appears, does not disturb me.

GJ
(*With little warmth*)

Well, everybody knows about the play. The mother, Lena Younger, is hell-bent to get her family out of the Chicago slums to the suburbs, where a new group of tract houses are being built. She has to fight an all-white association who wants to keep her out by returning her down payment on the house she's chosen. Her son, Walter Lee, has his eye on that money to settle some bad debts, but she's determined, and in the end they move in for better or worse. We just don't know. She's a strong lady. A great part. There's a pretty badly off philodendron Lena has kept alive, barely, on her windowsill and for her it's a symbol of the Younger family's resolve to move out into the sun where she knows it, and they, will grow free and healthy. She sings the song to it.

DC
(*To* GJ *and the Class*)

The point to remember is that, removed from the context of the musical, the song may be directed to anything or, for that matter, anyone.

GJ

Yes, that's true. It means cutting the Verse but I don't think that's a big loss.

DC

No argument there. It's a good lead-in for the situation, but given a different slant to the Chorus, it isn't needed. There are Verses that carry weight and make the decision to cut them a hard one. This isn't one of them. Did you have any problem with the music?

GJ

No. It's a little high, I think.

DC

The range is only an octave and a minor third. No strain at all. Especially when you're into playing it. Can you sing it today?

GJ

I can try.
*(She sings through the song, clutching the written lyric like
flotsam to keep from drowning. The key will be all right. The
problem is—will she?)*

DC

That's not bad. Do you know the lyric?

GJ

Not well.

DC

That's all right. Try putting that paper down and sing the song for
me. I'll throw the words at you if you go up.

GJ

I'm really not ready for that just yet.

DC

Try. See if you fail. Maybe with a bit of prompting, you won't.
*(GJ half-heartedly begins, but it is apparent she knows the
words and the crutch of having DC available is resorted to only
once. The song's fervor wipes away her fear of vocal
inadequacy and we can hear, even in this early music reading,
that this will be a valuable song for her. When she finishes, the
Class is quiet. The song has had a prayer-like effect on them.
And on her.)*
Excellent. You have to begin to think of singing as something you
do and not something you dare yourself to do.

GJ

Like I said, I like this song. How freely can I sing it? I hear all
kinds of weird little things as I go along. Hear them in my head.

DC

Well, fairly free, I'd say. Weird? I don't know. The composer has scored the title: " . . . There'll be a whole lotta sunlight" and the following five bars in triplets. Even when the melody's printed more strictly—for example on the upbeat, " . . . And when the" before " . . . leaves are lullabying," etc.—the three quarter notes may also be sung as triplets. Publishers like to keep a song easy for the beginner piano player and guitarist to read. Certainly this song should flow as you hear it, as long as what you hear is not destructive to the composer's intentions. Was there something in particular you wanted to do to the melody?

GJ

Well, yes. In the line " . . . And when that lazy old sun sets just you let it go." I hear another " . . . let it go" like an echo, a repeat. "Let it go" is what the whole thing's about. And it would help to fill that long bar of "Air" after the line.

DC

I see nothing wrong with that. Anything else?

GJ

Let's see. Oh, yes. On " . . . And when that lazy old sun sets just you let it go," I hear: (*She sings.*)

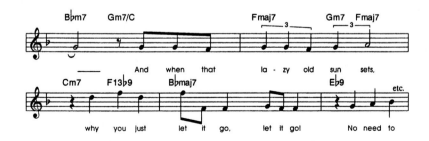

DC

Nothing wrong there, either.*

GJ

I'd like to do something with the Rideout, but I'm not sure what.

DC

The obvious needn't be rejected just because it's obvious. Why don't you jump up to the top on the second syllable of "shining" in the last line," . . . Shining for you and me," and then a neat octave slide down on " . . . for you and me"? That ought to work out quite well. (*He sings.*)

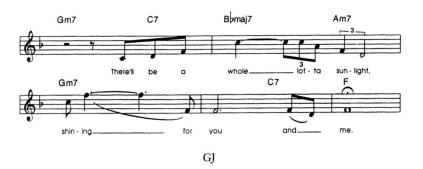

GJ

You think I can do that? You crazy?
DC

Dear lady, why not try it before we find out that we can't? You may be disappointed with how well you do it.
(*She lets that pass and risks it.*)
You'll have to think high on the first syllable of " . . . Shining"—a high, forward "ah" vowel. As high as you possibly can. Then just put the "ih" of the second syllable right in the same place and don't leave it alone. Blow breath right into that placement. It will be an interval of a fourth, but you'll feel as if it's almost the same note.

* The reader may refer to the lead sheet to see this minor variation of the melody away from the printed version.

The slide down the octave on " . . . for you," etc., will be easier, too, if you put the "ng" and the "f" on the low note. (*He demonstrates.*)

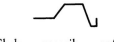

Shah . . . neeeeih . . . ngfaw . . .

And remember, also, the old saw that has a kind of psychological advantage. When you go up, think low, and when you go down, think high. The first half has only to do with an attempt to dispel the fear of singing a high note but the second half—thinking high on a low note—has merit. That octave drop should, in your mind, stay as high as you were on " . . . Shin*ing*."* Try it.

GJ
(*After two attempts*)

I'm beginning to see and hear what you mean. I can feel my jaw going up on the high note and everything dropping when I go down that octave. I suppose the trick is to think of it in the way you said—all one note and only your "ear" changes the pitch.

DC

Simplistic but nevertheless true. It's worth remembering, too, that in your case so much of your singing is born in a climate of negative thinking. You're too smart for your own good. Singing is not an intellectual pursuit. Despite evidence to the contrary, for instance, people still think of tenors—the "highest" of male singers—as mentally deficient. How did the old Italian joke go? "*Stupido, stupidissimo, tenore.*" In your case, you dare yourself to sing and then you put obstacles in your way to make sure you corroborate what you believe to be true—that you can't sing.

---

* For the singer, the concept of "high" and "low" notes is vastly different than it is for an instrumentalist and the nonsinger. The "height" of a pitch is not a question of "high" as we think of it when we see the pianist reach far to the right on the keyboard or, in the opposite direction, to the left for a "low" note. Tone production has its own functional techniques that can be disturbed when the neophyte singer applies misconceptions based on the "imagining" of the piano keyboard rather than having a clear picture of how pitch is produced in the human body.

GJ

I hate to say you're right because then I'll have to sing better. (*She gets a laugh and the charged atmosphere is defused.*) Any ideas for phrasing?

DC

How about a breath after the title, of course, and then phrasing over-the-bar by eliding the word " . . . bright" to the previous phrase—" . . . Nothing but blue in the skies?"* (DC *sings through the song as marked.** GJ takes notes.*)

GJ

Fine. I've got it on my tape. It'll need some practicing.

DC

And don't forget—try to give yourself the benefit of the doubt.

GJ

Like I been saying all along. I like the song.

GJ's next music reading a week later lies somewhere between not bad and almost good. She tries it a second time, sensing that the constraint of a "first reading" had done its accustomed psychological damage—and she is right. The second time around is markedly improved—variations are nailed, the jump up on " . . . Shining" is on its way to a successful rendition, and throughout there is a positive sense that the song lies well within her vocal ability to sing it. DC congratulates her.

DC

Good work. I think we can move ahead now and go for a performance.

---

* See *On Singing Onstage*, Phrasing from Music, pages 40-45.
** To follow this new phrasing, it is recommended the reader follow the lead sheet and the lyric on pages 115-116 and 117.

GJ

What I thought I'd like to do with it is . . .

DC
(*Interrupting*)

Why don't we see it? I have a problem talking about performances before I see them.

GJ

What I wanted to say is that I see this as a house number. To me the "you" in the lyric is really a "you-all."

DC

It works both ways. Playing it to everyone out front objectifies the statement and diverts it away from the more personal. But, as I say, better seen than discussed.
(GJ *crosses to Center, nods in the pianist, but arrives Center too soon. With nothing to play and a long Vamp to play it in, she breaks.*)

GJ

This is one long vamp! What do I need it for?

DC

You may not need it but the composer wants it. And, frankly, I rather like it.

GJ

You don't have to get through it. I do. And what do I *do*?

DC

Don't *do* anything. You're allowed not to do anything. For one thing, you get to Center too soon and the curtain's up. Stay away from Center until you feel the time is ripe.

GJ

But that's what I mean. What do I do?

DC

Do what we're doing. Listen to the music. That's the reality of the world that's going on. Listen to what he's playing. It's lovely music. Enjoy it. But don't "act" listening, just listen.

GJ

When do I come Center?

DC

I don't know. How long do you need to seed a life out of which the first line of the song you're singing can organically grow? Working backwards, subtract that from the end music of the Vamp, and that's when you should be coming front to recognize Center. And, oh, yes, while you're listening, keep your eyes off the floor. It's not a good idea to come up from the floor to Center as if you were ascending through a trap door. Play straight into the theater while you're listening to the music.

GJ

You mean, just stand there . . . listening?

DC

That's what I mean. Just stand there. Don't *do* anything provocative. Just listen. You might find the music has a mood it's setting—one that in its own way is contributing something valuable to the enterprise.

(GJ *takes a moment and nods to the pianist. Her natural sense of what stage demeanor is all about takes over. At a certain*

*moment, somewhere around the end of the third bar of the
Vamp, she comes Center and, at the top of the fifth bar, begins
to sing.* DC *stops her.)*
How did that feel?

GJ

Pretty good. I see now it's a question of changing attitudes. The
first time I felt like I was facing a firing squad and wanted to run
for my life. This time I was just standing there—letting my life
happen.

DC

It looked fine. Now that we've taken care of that, let's try it again,
and this time I promise not to stop you.
(DC *keeps the promise.* GJ *repeats the Vamp with the same
ease, but the performance is the one* DC *feared she would bring
in—a political harangue. When the Rideout ends, the Class is
unmoved but not uninterested. There is palpable tension.)*
Well, now. Where are we?

GJ

In disagreement. God! I hate confrontation.

DC

No more than I, but I don't see why confrontation has anything to
do with this. (*To* GJ *and the Class.*) It's never my intention to reject
the performances you bring into Class. There are innumerable
choices that can make a song "work" and not one of them is the
only way or the right way. How I see a song is no more valid than
how each of you sees it. My job is to make certain that what you
choose to play is expertly executed. But if you hear a "but" lying in
the bushes, you're right. There may not be a correct way or a right
way to sing a song, but there can be no argument that there is a
better way to sing it. (*To* GJ) May I be honest?

GJ

Of course. (*Her jaw has tightened.*)

DC
(*To the Class*)

"Take note, take note, O world! To be direct and honest is not safe."

GJ

You're not talking to a jealous husband here.
> (*The Class relaxes. The tension has broken.* DC *makes a mental note to call upon Shakespeare—the perfect mouthpiece—more often in the future.*)

DC

We've agreed that the song may be done to everyone or to a single focus and that either choice is valid. But I'm not speaking here about what's good for the song. What I am speaking about is what is good for you. You are—(*To the Class*) each of you—the packager of yourself, and you're the merchandise as well. What do you want them to see? Who is the *you* they *should* see? You can manipulate their judgments of you by clever merchandising, but you cannot forbid them from seeing what they see. Auditioners and audiences are, like all of us, imprisoned in their own world of sexuality, tastes, frustrations, likes and dislikes, secret dreams—the whole ball of wax that is the sum of the parts of our social behavior and how we interrelate.

Do you remember when we all first met and you were assigned a "wrong song" to work on—a song that would make more visible what I, and the Class, agreed was recessive about each of you? Well, now you're singing a "right song" based on what is dominant about you. The smart merchandiser seeks a fairer, truer representation of his product—a packaging (acting choices) that retrieves those colors that are on the dark side of the moon and brings them into the light.* Our families, our lovers, and our

* For a detailed description of this section of the critique, see *On Singing Onstage*, pages 55-62.

friends know they are there by virtue of the histories we share. But families, lovers, and friends do not cast musicals or pick up our bar tabs. (*To* GJ) You are a beautiful actress. Making a polemic of this song serves neither the work nor the stage. Were you a manifestly warmer woman . . . (*The silence in the studio reflects the Class's awareness that* DC *is navigating shallow shoals.*) . . . your ideas would work splendidly. But . . .

GJ

No. I've never been what you call "warm." But, go on . . .

DC
(*Treading carefully*)

Why don't you try a different approach? Instead of targeting the song to everyone you think *ought* to hear this script, why not work to someone who *needs* to hear it. I won't suggest anything further. As I have said—and everyone here knows—you are a skillful actress.

GJ
(*She laughs—a "pro"*)

Thought you'd get to me, huh? For a while there you almost did, but then I thought, why not? He could even be wrong and how will I know it if I don't try it his way. I guess this means I'll be bringing it back next week. Like I've been saying all along—it's a good thing I like this song.

It is a few days later. GJ crosses to Center stage with that stride we unconsciously recognize in the veteran actor. Only its reasonable facsimile can be taught. The real thing is the accretion of years of struggle and the hard-won comfort in knowing that it is not the artist but his art that is up at bat. GJ waits a moment, working "front," and then nods to the pianist. There is something regal about her contact with the pianist that on another actor would be unacceptable. She returns to the theater and, in the proper time, adjusts her focus to Center. The Vamp has not only seemed shorter, the sight of her has become more important than our listening to it; in a rapid series of subtle changes, her demeanor alters dramatically. There is love, fear, and a certain timidity coupled with a determination to face the facts—all of this is in the Vamp after coming Center before she begins to sing. The impact of her performance is shattering. So full of its truth is she that when the jump up on the second syllable of " . . . Shining" in the last bars of the Chorus arrives, the open, easy sound quite literally is offered as a gift to whomever she is singing. At the finish, there is justifiable silence. She turns to DC.

DC

We must talk about this. It is so perfectly performed that the Class should know how you went about it.

GJ
(She hesitates for a moment, looks at DC *and turns front.)*

The hardest thing for me to deal with in this Class, other than the singing, is criticism. In a play I'm part of a whole. Other actors are with me. The dialogue and the character I play protect me from myself.* Singing is different. You're alone up here. No matter how you tell yourself a song is a soliloquy—it's still a song. And you're on the stage—hearing yourself, distracted away from what you should be worried about—what we always talk about: Why did I choose to sing what I'm singing? To whom am I singing? And what am I singing about? The funny thing is that when I do all that, I sing better than I ever do when I'm worried about . . . when I'm just plain worried about me singing.

DC

Well said.

GJ

One thing more. I'm learning something else here. When I act, I don't lean too heavily on a director, especially in television. They

* See *On Performing*, Question 2, pages 56-58.

don't exist. I know which buttons I have to press and I press them when I have to. But in singing, somehow . . . (*She chooses her words carefully.*) . . . I need that other "eye" checking me from outside. If it's someone I trust . . . (*She indicates* DC *with a flip of her hand.*) . . . I think of it as another "me" telling me what I'd tell myself if I could split in half and run out front to check whatever it is I'm doing and whether it's working or not.*

DC
(*To* GJ)

I know it's the actor's secret, but I wonder if you could give us an idea of what you're using?

GJ
(*After a moment of indecision*)

I have a nephew. He's a wonderful young man, but his life has been nothing but an obstacle course he runs and loses. Young black men in Chicago live in an awful bind. They can't go forward, left, or right—only backwards. He's a good boy, but all that sunlight I was singing about ain't that easy to come by where he lives. I do everything I can to help him and my sister 'cause I love them, even though I sometimes think it's more than any one person can handle. Least of all me. (*To* DC) When you said, "Bring it into one focus," I thought of him and the rest just . . . fell into place.

DC

I was wondering why you let me get away with rejecting that first performance last week?

GJ

I knew you were right. It was just a matter of putting my brain on hold and working from my heart. I've always known that. It just takes more courage.

---

* See *On Performing*, the Tony Roberts interview, pages 151-152.

DC

Herbert von Karajan once said, "Opera concerns those ecstatic moments when a man or a woman has to use a means of expression other than the spoken word." I feel that way about every kind of singing.

GJ

Well, let's just say that's one thing he said I agree with. Now that I've told you what I was thinking, I want to say that using something or someone you know, someone who's a part of your life, is so much easier than making a song into a case or a speech. (*To* DC) Didn't you once say, if you can't make a song sing, you probably should've said what you were singing about? This time I really felt that. Felt it was more natural singing what I had to say. Did you ever hear this one? Ellen Terry said, "How much easier it is to ask *naturally* for a dirty bonnet to be removed from a chair than to offer *naturally* a kingdom for a horse!"

DC

Even more parochial, Bernard Shaw, her buddy, held to the opinion that if anyone would sing for half an hour each day they'd be in much better health. How do you feel today?

GJ

Not a 4-H winner yet, but getting there. Getting there.

"Baby"

Baby, Baby, Baby

Lyrics by Richard Maltby, Jr.

Music by David Shire

Funky ♩=ca. 104

Ba-by, ba-by, ba-by. Lis-ten to your pa-pa.____ Hey there, pret-ty ba-by, bet-ter hur-ry and get____ here.____ Ba-by, ba-by, ba-by. See your pret-ty ma-ma.____ Don't you know the min-ute that you get your foot set____ here:____ you're gon-na be loved.____ You're gon-na be

138

"Baby, Baby, Baby"

CHORUS:
Baby baby baby (✓)
Listen to your papa (✓)
Hey there pretty baby better hurry and get here (✓)
Baby baby baby (✓)
See your pretty mama (✓)
Don't you know the minute that you get your foot set here ⌣
⌣ You're gonna be loved (✓)
You're gonna be held (ˌ)
You're gonna be kissed (✓)
You're gonna feel warm ⌣
⌣ You're gonna feel fine (✓)
You're gonna get all that I got handy (ˌ)
Silver spoons and candy ⌣
⌣ Baby baby baby (✓)
Lord how you are wanted (✓)
I got all this love dressed up with no place to go
Woh woh woh (✓)
Baby baby baby gonna love you so (✓)
La la la la la la la (repeat three times with a breath between
    each repeat)

"Baby, Baby, Baby" from *Baby*, lyrics by Richard Maltby, Jr., music by David Shire.
Copyright © 1984 by Fiddleback Music Publishing Co., Inc. & Progeny Music &
Revelation Music Publishing Corp. & Long Pond Music. International Copyright Secured.
All Rights Reserved. A Tommy Volando Publication. Used by permission.

7

Swinging Ballad

The Swinging Ballad begins the transition away from the slow to the not too fast. Its rhythm is more assertive; the ballad literally "swings." When the accompaniment goes, so goes the "swing," and often the song is revealed as a ballad rather than an up-tempo song. Charm is its calling card and those who perform it well are charming by fiat of the gods or are made to appear so by the alchemic combination of song and singer. Swinging Ballads can be performed in a limitless variety of presentations (instrumental, sung and/or danced). Their most valuable salesmen were the ineffable Fred Astaire and the still "pop" champion, Frank Sinatra.

Younger performers, children of their times, do not speak the language associated with this category. "The wee small hours of the morning" that Sinatra sang about were set to gentle, swinging balladic tunes. Today's rock and roll and its ancillary descendants are a more fitting accompaniment for those same small hours. This is not to say that Swinging Ballads are no longer written or taken to the public heart. On the contrary, the song I have chosen was written in 1984 and, although the music and the lyric are in a contemporary idiom, the song is very much in the tradition of the genre.

Every theater composer has written songs found in this category, but for reasons one may only guess at, no one writes them better than American composers. To my taste, no American wrote them better than the Gershwin brothers, although I am partial, too, to the Swinging Ballads of Jule Styne and Cy Coleman.

- A most partial list of Gershwin tunes: "Things Are Looking Up," "I Was Doing All Right," "Somebody Loves Me," "Oh, Lady Be Good!" "Sweet and Low-Down," "Funny Face," "S'Wonderful," "My One and Only," "I've Got a Crush on You," "Liza," "Mine," "Let's Call the Whole Thing Off," "I Don't Think I'll Fall in Love Today," "That Certain Feeling," "Do Do Do," "How Long Has This Been Going On?" and "Nice Work If You Can Get It."
- Jerome Kern: "A Fine Romance," "I've Told Ev'ry Little Star," "She Didn't Say 'Yes,'" "I Won't Dance," "You Couldn't Be Cuter," "Pick Yourself Up," "Who?" "Let's Begin," and "Nobody Else But Me" (Kern's last song).
- Cole Porter: "I Get a Kick Out of You," "I've Got My Eyes on You," "You Never Know," "You Do Something to Me," "You've Got That Thing," "All of You," "At Long Last Love," "Do I Love You?" "Friendship," "From This Moment On," "It's All Right With Me," "Just One of Those Things," "You're Sensational," and "You're the Top."
- Irving Berlin: "Isn't This a Lovely Day (To Be Caught in the Rain?")," "Change Partners," "Cheek to Cheek," "Easter Parade," "I Got the Sun in the Morning," "I've Got My Love to Keep Me Warm," "Let's Face the Music and Dance," "This Year's Kisses," and "You're Just in Love."
- Rodgers and Hart: "The Blue Room," "I Wish I Were in Love Again," "Manhattan," "Mountain Greenery," "Sing for Your Supper," "There's a Small Hotel," "You Took Advantage of Me," "Do It the Hard Way," "Ev'ry Sunday Afternoon," "The Heart Is Quicker Than the Eye" and "This Can't Be Love."
- Rodgers and Hammerstein: "Many a New Day," "The Surrey With the Fringe on Top," "June Is Bustin' Out All Over," "A Cockeyed Optimist," "Getting to Know You," "Shall We Dance?" "A Very Special Day," "I Enjoy Being a Girl," and "My Favorite Things."
- Jule Styne: "All I Need Is the Girl," "Comes Once in a Lifetime," "I'm Just Taking My Time," "Just in Time," "Let Me Entertain You," "Some People," "Together Wherever We Go," "You Are Woman, I Am Man," "Can't You Just See Yourself?" "I

Still Get Jealous," "I Want to Be Seen With You Tonight," "My Own Morning," and "Bye Bye Baby."

• Cy Coleman: "Baby Dream Your Dream," "Sweet Charity" ("You Wanna Bet?"), "It's a Nice Face," "You Fascinate Me So," "When in Rome," "Witchcraft," "The Best Is Yet to Come," "I Love My Wife," "Hey, Look Me Over," "We've Got It," "You're a Loveable Lunatic," "Tall Hope," "My Personal Property," and "I've Got Your Number."

• And in cluster: Arthur Schwartz's "By Myself" and "I Guess I'll Have to Change My Plan"; Stephen Sondheim's "Honey," "I Do Like You," "Old Friends," and "Love, I Hear"; Burton Lane's "If This Isn't Love,""Hurry! It's Lovely Up Here," "You're All the World to Me," "The World Is in My Arms," and "Something Sort of Grandish"; Lerner and Loewe's "Almost Like Being in Love" and "Wouldn't It Be Loverly?"; Burt Bacharach's "Alfie," "Close to You," "I'll Never Fall in Love Again," and "This Guy's in Love With You"; David Shire's "Travel," "One Step," and "I Chose Right"; Jerry Bock's "Beautiful, Beautiful World," "Without You I'm Nothing," "Grand Knowing You," and "Ilona"; Charles Strouse's "Put on a Happy Face," "A Lot of Living to Do," "You've Got Possibilities," and "Dance a Little Closer"; Marvin Hamlisch's "One," and . . . .

The above list allows the reader to become familiar with another distinguishing feature of the Swinging Ballad, namely the variety of standard songs that swing from the "almost" ballad to the "very nearly" Up-Tempo (the next category). Too trained a voice may be (but not necessarily) destructive to the song's performance, but an alien ear for—and a discomfort with—jazz can be lethal. Beyond that, they are comparatively easy to sing because . . . they swing.

THE SONG

As the model song for the category I have chosen David Shire and Richard Maltby, Jr.'s "Baby, Baby, Baby," the reiterative title song from their score for *Baby*. The musical enjoyed a moderately successful Broadway run, but its afterlife in the world at large has been rich indeed, exceeding over 250 productions. Shire and Maltby are in the forefront of a new musical theater age. Their voice, literate and free of Sondheimism, is an intaglio, incised with contemporaneity and the personal biographies that feed their words and music. Mr. Shire: "I was riding in a car with Francis Ford Coppola, who happens to like musicals, and I said, 'Richard and I are looking for something to write about that isn't the same old thing.' [Francis] said, 'Why don't you write about something you know? What's the most emotional thing that happened to you in the last five years?' And without thinking I said, 'Being present at the birth of my son.' And that's how *Baby* began. From then on, we started using material that came from our own lives."*

The musical *Baby* examines three couples at a milestone event in their marriages. The first, young and not yet prepared for the surprise fact of their pregnancy, the thirty-something couple who desperately want to but cannot conceive a child, and the over-forty couple with an already grown family, beset by mid-life crisis, who discover a pregnancy they neither want nor can emotionally afford.

The song "Baby, Baby, Baby" is AABA. There is no Verse and the Chorus proceeds in its own infectious swinging fashion with a "doo break" at the finish, this time on "la la la." As is fitting, the music and the words are celebratory. In the musical it is sung by all the concerned characters, but the published sheet music is scored for male solo. However, the song "works" for a Leading Man, young Leading Man, Juvenile, Ingenue, Character Man or a Character Woman, regardless of race or color, as long as the performer is visibly within the fertile years of postpuberty to late middleage.

THE DIALOGUE

DC assigns the song to a Leading Man, a singer who is at home in the classic repertory but whose long-standing affection for the musical theater has brought him to a place where he can study its rules and behavior and, not incidentally, broaden his commercial appeal.

FR is a casting agent's fantasy come alive—the classic *outer* image of the Leading Man polished and cloned to service the musical theater down through the ages, a genetic miracle of design. FR's packaging includes an *inner* asset: He sings. He sings very well

* From an interview with Mssrs. Shire and Maltby in *The New York Times*, November 5, 1989.

indeed. What is wrong with the picture? Nothing. Upon entrance, he is all the director could hope for. What the ear hears when the song is sung will have a similar effect on the composer and the lyricist. The problem is FR: a man imprisoned, hobbled, and hampered by invisible restrictions and constraints. While every man dreams of looking and sounding like him, when he sings he dreams only of the freedom to be the man he truly is, the man behind the clone. In Class, his only mission is to bring together, in one corporeal entity, the man and the singer—to make certain that what the eye sees when he enters onto the stage is not zapped when he sings his songs. For this is the bottom line: Why doesn't the real FR, and not a musclebound stand-in, stand up and be counted at that exact instant when a song begins? Where does the real FR go? And why does he return at the very instant the song ends, once again comfortable in and with himself? DC's assignment of "Baby, Baby, Baby" will be the vehicle that will take him on a journey of self-discovery.

DC

Not a difficult song. Agreed?

FR

No, not at all! But I think I'll need a higher key. G maybe?

DC

Well, we don't want to get it so vocal that it loses that nice, easy, swinging quality I like about it. Why don't we cut it down the middle and settle for F? That'll give you a good, strong note at the end of the second "8" on " . . . .You're gonna be loved."

FR

Okay. I want you to know that this song scares the hell out of me.

DC

Are we talking about the same number?

FR

It's the easy ones that kill me. What, for God's sake, do I do with the "woh, woh, woh's" and the "la, la, la's"?

DC

Let's sing it first. We can talk about the "woh, woh, woh's" and the "la, la, la's" after the Class hears the song.
   (DC *instructs the pianist to raise the printed copy up one key from E flat to F Major. FR sings the song with his customary vocal skill. As always, it becomes a destructive weapon aimed at the song.*)
It sounds like you learned it in Prague.

FR

C'mon. It wasn't that bad, was it?

DC

Not if you plan to sing it to a Czech baby. We've got to take that hanger out of your jacket. None of us can live in this country and remain deaf to the sounds that bombard our ears every day and night of our lives—no matter how far removed we are from its popular culture. Somewhere in your blood is where this song lives, and not even you can turn it all off.

FR

The thing is that I trained to learn how to sing.

DC

Well, you've done it and done it well. Consider it done. You're supposed to enjoy singing when you do it as well as you do. What did you do it for in the first place if not to make music? And why make music if it isn't a joy? Try it again, and this time hang loose. Feel free. God, what I'd give to hear a wrong note come out of that silver throat!

(FR *tries again but doesn't get beyond the first* "*8.*")

FR

You have to remember this is a big departure for me to do a song like this.

DC

I didn't think it was that time. The train never left the station. Damn it, we've got to crack through this iron curtain you sing behind. Do you sing like this at home?

FR
(*Off the hook*)

Oh no! It's a lot easier at home.

DC

Where?

FR

In the bedroom.

DC

Do the Class and I have to make house calls?

FR

It always goes so much better there because I'm not self-conscious at home.

DC

I won't let you off the hook that easily. Instead of treating a song as you would a script, you decide right from the start that it's not as interesting to you as this over-refined compulsion to produce perfect vocal sounds. You're a married man, aren't you? (FR *nods.*) And a father? (*Another nod*) Tell me—tell us—do you remember when you first saw your baby? When you first held him? That first day you and your wife brought him home? Or is it a girl?

FR

My son. (*His voice has altered. A nerve has been touched.*) We have a son.

DC

I'm going to ask you to do something for me, something just a little offbeat. Would you go away from us—far away where we won't see you. Stand behind the portal curtain. Sing the song there, hidden from us—in your bedroom, if you will. Forget we're here. But, standing in that place, sing to your son. Sing to him a few weeks before he was born. Would you try that for me?
　　(*FR looks at DC, decides he is not the butt of a trick or a joke and exits behind the side portal nearest him.*)
No. Go to the other wing, away from the pianist.
　　(*As he does so, DC instructs the pianist to play the Vamp, as the composer has scored it: gently, softly, funky. FR begins to sing from behind the curtain. The voice is warm and intimate. It is a new man we are hearing. The last bars of the second "8" slowly begin their build through the phrase " . . . You're gonna be loved" and continue their passionate outpouring in the Bridge and into the last "8," when there is a softening, an almost heartbreaking reading of "Lord, how you are wanted!" Before FR is aware of it, he has sailed through the "woh, woh, woh's" into " . . . Baby, Baby, Baby, gonna love you so!" It is a promise he is making and it is not a light one. The "la la la's" diminish in sound and texture. There is even a hint of self-amusement as he moves into the third repeat. A heavy silence follows the end of the song.*)

FR

Can I come out now? (*He does, a little sheepishly.*) I've got to tell you . . .

DC

Save it. When you get up the next time I want to hear you sing this song as close to what we just heard as you can, with only one fix. You'll have to come out from behind that curtain. You have to come out from behind all your curtains. Even the ones in your bedroom. You've got business to do. Show business.

Some days have passed. FR is on stage again.

DC

I've been thinking a good deal about that last session. Trying to make sense out of it.

FR

So have I. It seemed to me to be an almost out-of-mind-and-body kind of experience. For the first time in my singing life I forgot to sing—I mean, sing as I've always defined the word.

DC

I believe you. But we have our work cut out for us. To begin with, we have to repeat that music reading—repeat it with a control mechanism that achieves the same effects but does it without resorting to a mystical experience. Even the Dali Lama knows what he's doing.

FR

I understand that. You said, "To begin with . . . ."

DC

Yes. Remember, this was a music reading and nothing more. It's designed to assure both you and me that you know the song, that the key is well chosen, that your phrasing is sensible and musical, and that the pianist knows what you're doing so that he can provide the accompaniment needed to enhance those choices.

FR

What you're getting at is the performance. Right?

DC

I'm afraid so. I said before that I've been thinking about what you did and, mostly, what you fail to do when you slip into the old rut. I came to a conclusion—not momentous, but I think it's important. It's about what lies at the very bottom of your problem. You see, I've been mistaken. All along I've been asking you to sing it a new way—new, in the sense that it's alien to your idea of what constitutes "singing." But now I realize we've been tackling the problem from the outside—in this case, the vocal side. What we're dealing with here, I'm afraid, is a difference of opinion about how the world perceives you, and singers in general, rather than the essential and elemental truths of what makes a great singer.

Now, I grant you that audiences tolerate the quality of a performance in inverse ratio to the quality of its vocal sound: The more the *quality* diminishes, the more the audience unconsciously expects the *performance* to make the song "work." But these two elements of singing that make up the whole—the vocalization *and* the performance—are not exclusive of each other. Norman Treigle and Maria Callas come to mind. When a baritone sang a song by Rimski-Korsakov (to words from a poem by Heine) in Stanislavski's Class, he said in his defense, after a harsh criticism of his work, "I simply recounted the story to you." To which the maestro countered, "In other words, you were not addressing anyone in particular. You did nothing but stir the air and sang to the microbes in it." Am I making any sense? You have, first, to *un*think and then *re*think the very basic precepts of how and why you sing. Not till you do this will I be able to help you shape the man you are into a singing man.

FR

I'm ready to try.
(*He nods to the pianist. No longer protected by the portal curtain, he sings through "Baby, Baby, Baby." It is nowhere*

*near last week's reading of the song, but neither is it the
stilted rendering it once was.)*

DC

What did you think?

FR

It's a beginning.

DC

It was better than that.

FR

May I try it again?

DC

I think we have to move on. Music readings are essential building
blocks toward the performance of a song, but it's the performance
we're concerned with here. And you know the song. I have a
feeling that once you begin to perform it, you'll be singing it as
well as you just did and probably far better.
   *(FR crosses to Center stage. As he stands there, the old habits
   take over.)*
Why do you hold your hands in front of you like that?

FR

I don't know. I had a singing teacher in college who told us to
stand like this.

DC

But why?

FR

She said it was the proper way to stand before you began to sing.

DC

Ridiculous. There's no proper way to stand before you do anything, with the exception, I suppose, of army drills. There's an improper way, I'll grant you, and one of the improper ways that comes to mind is the way you're standing right now. Let your hands go. You look like you're holding on to yourself to keep from drowning.
> (FR *drops his hands to his sides.*)
Does that feel awkward?

FR

Frankly? Yes.

DC

It doesn't look awkward. Where they are now is where they always are—at the ends of your wrists. And from there they can go anywhere. If your nose itches, you can even scratch it. If you'd been holding on to them, you'd have had to undo them first before they could perform a perfectly ordinary task. I want you to stand there. Just stand there. Leave yourself alone. Work into the theater at large. Don't push against yourself.

FR
> (*After a moment of this*)
I feel stupid.

DC

You don't look stupid. In fact, I was just thinking how attractive you look. No, don't look at me. Just listen to me as you busy yourself working front. Try to capture who you are when you're just *you*. What you do when you do nothing.
> (*The Class watches the slow transformation away from a*

"stock" singer to a man—just standing there. * FR *eases into the exercise. At one point he brings his hands together and plays with his ring. It looks natural, but more important, because he isn't doing it as an act to be done, anything he would do would appear so.)*

Don't leave what you're doing. Just hear me. How do you feel now?

FR

It's crazy, but I'm beginning to feel like I could stand here like this forever.

DC

Don't do it right now. Wait a few moments and then, when it isn't going to be performed as something that must be executed rather than another moment among many, nod to the pianist to begin.

*(FR *waits and then turns to the accompanist and nods to him. The "funky" Vamp begins.)*

Stop. You can look at me now.

(He "leaves" the theater and turns to DC.)

Don't play off the music. You went to him in order to nod to him. That's all. The nod affects each of you differently. For the pianist who has been waiting for your signal, it means *play*. And that is *his* life. You can stay with him. I mean, you can relate to him for a moment or two after he begins. But then your life returns to who you were before you left the theater in order to nod him in. As far as you're concerned, the music he's playing, at least for the first two bars of its time on earth, is dead tape. Only when you come Center does *your* life move into a new action; in this case, the baby or its image is born. You have two and a half bars of music remaining that, once he's there for you, will service you with the amount of time you'll need for a reaction to his presence. From that moment on, you're on your own. Your performance will be the result of

---

* The work discussed here is admittedly simplistic and superficial. I am only too aware of the difficulty of "doing nothing" and the all-too-facile direction to just "be," but this book cannot deal in depth with essential acting techniques and tasks. I recommend, among the many excellent publications, the manuals of Sanford Meisner, Stella Adler, Robert Lewis, Uta Hagen, and Gordon Hunt.

whatever you choose to play. In that crucible will be all the elements that make up a partnership with the vocalization of the song—in this case—"Baby, Baby, Baby."

FR

This is a different approach to the Vamp than I remember you gave to TB when she was working on "Send in the Clowns." You even quoted Stanislavski as saying you need to set your rhythms ahead, before the music starts. How does that jibe with the first bars of my Vamp being nothing but dead tape?

DC

TB was singing a song she'll be singing in a production of the musical. She knows the scene that precedes that song. Hell, she knows the whole play that precedes it. The song doesn't begin so much as continue out of dialogue into a musical statement, more heightened and therefore more in need of song.

FR

And "Baby, Baby, Baby"? Doesn't it grow out of my life?

DC

Not at all. It draws on your life, but it can hardly be said to grow out of it—at least, until the curtain goes up. The man who sits in the dugout is a member of the team up at bat, but his life—as it's lived in the game, that is; his baseball life—doesn't begin until he's the next man up. Or better, a moment before that moment. It's the difference between being a spectator and a participant.

FR

I see. So until I come Center and deal with the moments that change that "spot" from nothing into the birth of my son, there's just . . . me?

DC

Exactly. By the way, if TB was going to sing "Clowns" outside the context of the musical, she'd use the same formulas you're using. Out of everywhere and everyone she'd have to come Center, raise the curtain and create a man or, for that matter, anything and anyone who could be the receiving agent of her song. But let's get back to *your* ball diamond.

FR

Before I put down my bat, are there any special phrasing suggestions you could pitch my way?

DC

What's interesting is that you phrased it perfectly when you sang it behind that curtain last week. Just remember not to breathe after " . . . Don't you know the minute that you get your foot set here." It should sing right into " . . . You're gonna be loved." The same goes for " . . . You're gonna feel warm" sliding into " . . . You're gonna feel fine." And, of course, coming out of the Bridge between " . . . Silver spoons and candy" and "Baby, Baby, Baby" at the top of the last "8."*

FR

Thanks. That should do it. Anything else?

DC

I just thought that it's worth adding to that baseball game allusion that what you were doing that first day was playing ball, but it was handball you were playing. The audience isn't a wall you play off. There was no surprise because you were sure that wall would return the ball. But there *is* an audience. And they're not as reliable as a wall. Perhaps they won't return it. What then? Aren't you

---

* The reader may follow this on the lead sheet or the phrased lyric on pages 137–139.

singing *for* them? Doesn't that require their involvement? When there is no involvement isn't that what's meant by "I feel like I'm talking to a wall?" Well, you looked like you were singing to one.

FR

That's really great! (*He laughs and begins to exit.*)

DC

And by the way, remember to try to enjoy it all. Those verbs and adjectives: "better hurry and get here," "see your pretty mama," and in the Bridge, "held," "kissed," "feel warm," "feel fine," "silver spoons"—they're your World Series.

FR's effort to refine his performance took place over a period of weeks. Once the vocal began to match the swinging nature of the song—not an easy achievement for someone devoted to the written score—considerable time was spent on his physical life. The following dialogue focuses on that problem.

DC

There's a major short circuit between what you're thinking and how your body responds to that thinking.

FR

I know. It's my damn arms. I never know what to do with them.

DC

You know only too well what you do with them. That's the problem. You do "things" with them.

FR

I don't understand.

DC

You've purchased a small packet of gestures that you think of as a bank account of coins from which you withdraw one penny here and one penny there when you need them. I wouldn't care half as much if it was generous, lavish paper money you were throwing around but they're thrifty, mean little things of no significant value. Worse, the language they speak is so stock it recalls the singer you once were whose attention to *how* you were singing drowned out whatever inner voices dictated *what* and *why* you were singing it.

FR

That's a helluva diagnosis! What do you suggest, doctor?

DC

Close the bank account. It's nothing but Confederate money. All it's good for is bringing your arms up and then down, one arm up and then down, the other arm up and then down, and for a finale, nothing at all. Gestures. Empty, meaningless gestures. Gestures that add nothing to your performance and only hide who you are behind cliché arm moves that upstage everything you sing.

FR

But what then? I can't just stand there and do nothing. Can I?

DC

You're right, although nothing is a darn sight better than the something you've been doing. (*Taking in the Class*) When your body has no idea what's expected of it, it behaves like a child and does whatever it pleases. The part of your brain that instructs muscles to perform specific body language is out to lunch. Imagination, an insight into the *meaning* of the words you are singing, the *need* to sing them, and a clear understanding of the "action" required at any and every moment—all these are the necessary elements that instruct the body to do its bidding. Then, and only then, will you be free of those "stock" moves that so many of you resort to. Again, quoting Stanislavski: " . . . forget about gestures [when you are practicing]. Action is all that counts, a gesture all by itself is nothing but nonsense." (*To* FR) I don't expect or ask anyone to do a "Two" on a song you're going to perform.* But have you a crystal-clear vis-à-vis? And *why* you are singing to it or him or her? Is your marriage secure? Or is it shaky? Is the baby's arrival something you and your wife are using to save a failing marriage? Or is it a child who took a long time to get here—a baby you've both wanted for years? Is it *your* baby or is it one you've both adopted who hasn't arrived yet? Or isn't it a baby? Is it a job you're praying comes through for you, to free you from the straitened circumstances that've damaged your marriage? Or is it a pair of dice a second before you threw them? All of them could be workable substitutions. Shall I go on?

FR

Do you really do all that preparation for every song you sing?

DC

No. But if you start doing it you'll begin to exercise your imagination; get it to wake up and make its contribution to what you sing. In the end the job will get done unconsciously, just as each of us moves through our lives without giving any conscious attention to what our arms are doing. They know what to do because we're thinking, sentient human beings. Why should we be less than that when we sing? The wonderful thing about body language, apart from its extraordinary variety, is its universality. The gestures (curse the word) you use when you work have the opposite effect. They not only don't have a universal language, they betray that the song you're singing is nothing but a vocalization of the printed words and music.

FR

I understand. What I'm not so sure of is whether I can do it.

---

* The "Two" and the "Three" referred to in the dialogue are exercises explained in detail in *On Singing Onstage*, pages 137–163.

DC

Were you aware right then that you shrugged and threw out your arms in defeat immediately before you said, "What I'm not so sure of is whether I can do it"?

FR

No. Did I?

DC

You did. Your mouth said you weren't sure you could do it. The shrug and your arms said, "I give up! I can't!" Now, the point is that *they* knew what they wanted to say. Who told them? Not I. *You* did. And you were able to do that because your motor system responded to secret orders. How did William Schwenck Gilbert put it—in another context, of course? " . . . If they've a brain and cerebellum, too, they've got to leave that brain outside, And vote just as their leaders tell 'em to."* Your brain thought, "This is going to be very difficult," so when your mouth said you weren't sure, your brain, afraid to fail, took over and took orders from whoever those gremlins are. You shrugged, made the mental decision not to go for it, and said, as it shrugged, "I can't." (*Again, to the Class*) But he can and you can. We can because we do it all the time. And we do it with a good deal more eloquence than our mouths are capable of unless, of course, one of you is Bernard Shaw, Oscar Wilde, or Dorothy Parker. Remember, our bodies never lie. Unlike our mouths, we can always rely on them to speak the truth in their own unique fashion. If we leave our brains outside, mindlessness takes over and we move chaotically. Oh, we'll keep singing and even sensibly, but that's because we memorized someone else's words. But then, in all honesty, one could say that even our mouths are lying.

   FR worked on the problems covered in this dialogue until he came to realize that, in fact, much of his mind had been asleep when he sang. His last confession, when the light was clearly

---

* "When All Night Long" from Gilbert and Sullivan's *Iolanthe*.

visible at the end of the tunnel:

FR

What strikes me is how little attention I gave to a song. Oh, I learned it. Knew the words. Used all the technique I possessed to project the vocal line of the music so that its sound was the best I could make it. But the song as a living thing?—I never gave it a thought. The thing is that I used to like to . . . just sing. (*To* DC) You asked me a while back why I'd done it if not to make music. Well, I did make music in a way and, as I said, I liked it. But I never loved it. Never even enjoyed it. Never thought of it as art. Never felt that my job was to move people when I sang—to use the music and the words to achieve a purpose. (*To the Class*) And it's more than coming out from behind a curtain. I know it sounds pretentious, but it's about work. Just as painting, writing, composing are all about work. Sure, you're born with talents, but what's important is what you do with them. Well, I've run on long enough. Taken up too much time.

DC

No, you haven't. Your problems are the same as the next man's. Each of you works on what you need to do, but the great joy of doing it in a class is that, while you're working on your solutions, each one of us is out front thinking the old John Bradford observation only slightly altered: "There but for the grace of God, go I."

"Sweet Charity"

If My Friends Could See Me Now

Lyrics by Dorothy Fields

Music by Cy Coleman

Strut Tempo

162

high - est brow,___ which I must say is he,___ should pick the

low - est brow,___ which there's no doubt is me.___ What a

step up! Ho - ly cow!___ They'd nev - er be -

lieve it, if my friends could see me

now!___

"If My Friends Could See Me Now"

VERSE:
Tonight at eight (,) you should-a seen (,)
A chauffeur pull up in a rented limousine! (✓)
My neighbors burned (,) they like to die
When I tell them who is gettin' in
And goin' out is I (✓)

CHORUS:
If they could see me now, that little gang of mine (✓)
I'm eating fancy chow and drinking fancy wine (,)
I'd like those stumble bums to see for a fact (✓)
The kind of top-drawer, first-rate chums I attract
All I can say is, "Wowee! Look-a where I am. (✓)
Tonight I landed, Pow! Right in a pot of jam" ⌣
⌣ What a setup (✓) Holy cow! They'd never believe it,
If my friends could see me now (✓)
My little dusty group
Traipsin' 'round this million dollar chicken coop (✓)
I'd hear those thrift shop cats say (,)
"Brother, get her!
Draped on a bed-spread made from three kinds of fur" (✓)
To think the highest brow, which I must say is he,
Should pick the lowest brow, which there's no doubt is me (✓)
What a step up! Holy cow!
They'd never believe it,
If my friends (✓) could see me (✓) now!

"If My Friends Could See Me Now" from *Sweet Charity*, lyrics by Dorothy Fields, music by Cy Coleman. Copyright © 1965, 1969 Notable Music Co., Inc. and Lida Enterprises, Inc. International Copyright Secured. All Rights Reserved. All rights administered by WB Music Corp. Used by permission.

8

Up-Tempo

Referred to in the overall as *rhythm songs*, Up-Tempo songs are self-explanatory: Rhythm shares equal importance with the melody and may even preempt it. I have written at length on the reasons why Up-Tempo songs offer a cozy home for the performer whose calling-card is not his voice.* The nonsinger, liberated from the pain of hearing himself sing, is free to sell other wares when a sustained delivery of the melodic line is not integral to a professional rendering of a song. For the singer, Up-Tempo songs may sink from the weight of vocal heaviness.

As mentioned in the Swinging Ballad category, composers tend to leave their signatures on these songs. A Gershwin tune has its own recognizable "Fascinating Rhythm"; "I Get a Kick Out of You" is vintage Cole Porter; "Johnny One Note" and "Sing for Your Supper" are as Rodgers and Hart as "The Gentleman Is a Dope" and "Oklahoma!" are Rodgers and Hammerstein. Although contemporaneity is more overt in Marvin Hamlisch's "One (Singular Sensation)" than in Cy Coleman's "I'm a Brass Band," each song betrays its creator's distinguishing mark. So, too, Irving Berlin's "Blue Skies"; Jerome Kern's "Put Me to the Test"; Stephen Sondheim's "Live, Laugh, Love," and "Make the Most of Your Music"; Arthur Schwartz's "A Shine on Your Shoes"; Duke Ellington's "Satin Doll"; Frank Loesser's "Luck Be a Lady";

---

* See *On Performing*, Question 8, pages 72–75.

Harold Arlen's "Hooray for Love," "Between the Devil and the Deep Blue Sea" and "Ridin' on the Moon"; Jerry Herman's "Open a New Window," "It's Today," and, of course, "Hello, Dolly!"; Larry Grossman's "Rich Is"; Jule Styne's "Everything's Coming Up Roses" and Jerry Bock's "She Loves Me."

Indented, but no less significant, are two Up-Tempo groups of songs that bear mention:

1. The Up-Tempo Rhythm song whose rhythmic drive far exceeds the contribution of the melody to the song's unity. If Swinging Ballads allow the melodic line to retain its primacy, and Up-Tempo songs, as described above, maintain a fifty-fifty stand-off, this group has only one intention: to stimulate the listener with its insistent rhythmic patterns. When they are not working away, minimal melody remains. In this group may be found Gershwin's "I Got Rhythm"; Cole Porter's "Too Darn Hot"; Rodgers and Hart's "You Mustn't Kick It Around"; Marvin Hamlisch's "They're Playing Our Song"; Harold Arlen's "You Gotta Have Me Go With You"; Burton Lane's "There's a Great Day Coming Mañana"; Cy Coleman's "On the Other Side of the Tracks"; David Shire's "Two People in Love" and Andrew Lloyd Webber's title song for the score of *Jesus Christ Superstar.*

2. The Up-Tempo Double-Time song, whose truly driving rhythm accompanies a melody that, when that accompaniment is excised, sounds suspiciously like a ballad. The performer has only one defense: Ignore what is going on behind him and try to convince himself that he is, in fact, singing a ballad. In this group: Rube Bloom's "Day In Day Out"; Cole Porter's "Ridin' High"; Hugh Martin's "Love"; Lerner and Loewe's "I Love You This Morning," "Show Me," and "They Call the Wind Maria"; Lerner and Burton Lane's "Come Back to Me"; Frank Loesser's "Summertime Love"; Rodgers and Hart's "You Always Love the Same Girl"; and Bob Merrill's "Yes, My Heart."

Swinging Ballads and Up-Tempo songs, as categorical divisions, are often interchangeable. An instrumental arrangement can effect the changeover and even in the case of sung material, the line that separates them may be eradicable. Barbra Streisand's classic balladic treatment of "Happy Days Are Here Again" and, in my own studio, double-time arrangements of Rodgers and Hammerstein's "All at Once You Love Her" and Cole Porter's "I Am Loved" transform, to their advantage, stock Narrative Show

Ballads into fast-driving songs. The Swinging Ballad seduces the ear with the charm of its melody; the Up-Tempo song has only one intention: to excite. The American complexion that colors Up-Tempo songs is due to its jazz antecedence and, arguably, the general wit of the genre. These qualities, plus the significant contribution of the vocalist, make them required components of auditions, nightclub acts, recordings, and concerts. Rock and roll may be said to fall squarely within the defining margins of the category, but for young performers who are familiar only with that body of music and not on listening terms with the great standard repertoire, I recommend the work of the peerless Ella Fitzgerald, Mel Tormé, early Frank Sinatra, Cleo Laine, the late Sarah Vaughan, Lena Horne, and Carmen McRae.

THE SONG

I have chosen as a model Up-Tempo song, Cy Coleman and Dorothy Fields's "If My Friends Could See Me Now" from their score for *Sweet Charity*, a musical based on the Fellini film *Nights of Cabiria*. For this writer, Mr. Coleman is our most important—if not only—musical theater jazz composer. Trained as a serious pianist as a child (he was six years old when he gave his first Steinway and Town Hall recitals in New York City), he turned to jazz in his twenties and in the 1940s formed a successful trio. In 1953 he added composing to his credits, and four years later, with the supremely gifted Carolyn Leigh, he wrote the hit song "Witchcraft" followed by a string of standards: "You Fascinate Me So," "The Best Is Yet to Come," "When in Rome (I Do As the Romans Do)," and the lovely ballads "I Walk a Little Faster" and "It Amazes Me." With Miss Leigh as his partner, he composed *Wildcat*, his first Broadway musical, for Lucille Ball. The score included "Hey, Look Me Over," "What Takes My Fancy," "Give a Little Whistle" and the ballads "You've Come Home," "Angelina," and "You're Far Away From Home" (the last two beautiful Show Ballads, paired harmonically, were cut from the musical but are still published).

Wildcat was followed by the Sid Caesar vehicle *Little Me* with a score that included the insinuating "I've Got Your Number," the charming waltz "Real Live Girl," and the swinging "On the Other Side of the Tracks." His next show, *Sweet Charity*, the home score of our model song, began his affiliation with Dorothy Fields after the untimely death of Miss Leigh. Other hit musicals followed: *Seesaw*; and with Michael Stewart *Barnum* and *I Love My Wife*; and with Comden and Green *On the Twentieth Century*. At the time of this writing his *City of Angels*, written with David Zippel, tours, and *The Will Rogers Follies* is a Broadway hit. Like David Shire, Coleman is a composer and not a songsmith, and like Shire's, his music in no way recalls the work of Stephen Sondheim.

"If My Friends Could See Me Now," a "strut" number that was tailored to fit the dancing gifts of Gwen Verdon, works equally well when sung by a woman with a sense of humor who can "take stage" and "belt" out a song.* Like all Up-Tempo songs, it belongs to the performer. If she can sing, good. If she manifests a strong comic instinct, better yet. If she possesses both and can move with style, it's the best. She need not be an actor (although she may justifiably claim to be one) or a singer (although she may sing up a storm) or a dancer (although she may be the Queen of the Starlight Ballroom) or the hyphenate actor-singer-dancer (as classified by the casting agent). What she does need to have is that indefinable quality common to all great performers: a strong personality so markedly unique that nothing she performs is or ever can be more interesting than she is performing it.**

"If My Friends Could See Me Now" is scored in 4/4 time,† but it is more helpful to think of it in 2/2 or "cut time"—a time signature with two strong beats in each bar of music. The song is rooted in dance tempo—in this case, "strut tempo," a dance similar to the cakewalk. Like all songs associated with dancing, there is little to no room for rhythmic variations away from its dance parentage or even for ad-lib readings. The Verse is stark; it says what it has to say, champing at the bit as it races to get down to

---

* *Belting*: " . . .the practice adopted by "pop"singers (particularly women) of driving the chest register too high in the tonal range"—a quote from *The Dictionary of Vocal Terminology* by Cornelius L. Reid. From *The Random House Dictionary of the English Language*, Second Edition, Unabridged: "belt . . . to sing (a song) loudly and energetically (sometimes fol. by *out*."
** For younger readers: Barbra Streisand's first appearance on the stage in *I Can Get It For You Wholesale*, followed by the vehicular performance she gave in *Funny Girl*, describes this elusive quality. For older readers: Gwen Verdon's show-stopping debut in *Can Can*; Chita Rivera in *West Side Story* and the late Lenny Baker in *I Love My Wife*. For even older readers there is no reason to continue the list. Great performers appeared on Broadway with such a prodigality of composers, lyricists, librettists, actors, and playwrights that the name "golden age" of the theater has justifiably described the first half of this century.
† See *On Singing Onstage*, Rhythm, pages 29–31.

business at the top of the Chorus. So determined is it to get there that the Verse forfeits a Vamp. The Chorus arrives right on the heels of the last word of the Verse. It does pay its way, however. Miss Fields lays in exposition, sets down the performer's idiomatic way with words (solecisms appear at the top to establish character), and establishes the period style in which the song is written.

The Chorus is ABAB. Rather than a tacked-on mechanical finish, the last "8" contains a built-in Rideout. There are three published Chorus lyrics. To gain two Choruses, I have chosen the first, the first half of the second and the second half of the third Chorus. This is a personal choice. Away from the musical, the song can support only two Choruses and this selection seems the most valuable, but it is not written in stone. The title at the end of the first Chorus doubles as the first line of the second Chorus, thereby eliminating the need to sing the line twice.*

Young women who are not beautiful or pretty in the conventional rather than the cosmopolitan definition of these words, and who turn to the study of the dramatic and/or musical theater arts, are relegated to character or comedy roles as early as their prepubescent years. This is their painful destiny. That they may have no claim on or special talent to play either is beside the point. What is impressive are the multitudes of women who have a) played Desdemona's nurse and Nurse Preen in *The Man Who Came to Dinner*, b) played Bloody Mary in *South Pacific* or sung "Pickalittle" rather than "My White Knight" in *The Music Man* or c) danced Anybodys in *West Side Story*—for no other reason than the physical appearance that denies them the opportunity to play the girl who meets, loses, and regains the boy. An inflated number of Character and Comic Women whose rightful place in that pool may be considered moot is the result of this relegation.

THE DIALOGUE

RW is a comedienne who has a rightful hold on the title. She is genuinely funny. It is not that she does anything funny. There are no triple takes, pratfalls, and no reliance on vulgarity to achieve her ends. She thinks and is funny. A great clown once said that funny

---

* See the lead sheet and the phrased copy of the lyric.

men and women are "put together funny." Whatever defines it, RW has it.

DC has assigned "If My Friends Could See Me Now" because she can sing it and she is, in the true and literal meaning of the word, a performer.

RW

I saw this in the movie.

DC

I can't see where that'll be a problem.

RW

No problem at all. I just thought I'd mention that Bob Fosse's staging was great. And now I think I'll leave.

DC

Let's get serious. We decided to do the Verse—you can't do without it—and two Choruses. And though it'll be sung out of context, here again, as in the case of "Send in the Clowns" and "A Whole Lotta Sunlight," it might be of some help to you and to the Class if you'd fill in the circumstances that set up the song.

RW

Well, now, let's see if I can remember. Her name's Charity, but my boyfriend told me the picture was a remake of a Fellini movie, *Nights of Cabiria*, so her real name's Cabiria. Anyway, she's kind of tarty, not very bright, and she works in a dancehall. It sounds like my resumé. (*She sings a few bars of Rodgers and Hart's "Ten Cents a Dance." The Class reacts.*)

DC

Moving on.

RW

Yes. Well, I don't remember how, but a famous movie star picks her up on the street and takes her to his apartment. The decor's high-style Astaire, Rogers, Harlow, Garbo, Madonna, and French Renaissance. The rooms are a mile long by a mile wide. Lots of everything. She's knocked out by it all. He goes out and she sings . . . (*She nods to the pianist and, as if they had rehearsed it and before* DC *can stop her, she sings through the Verse. At the end of the first Chorus, she stops.*) I'm a little mixed up about how the second Chorus works. It's half of the second and half of the third Chorus, I think.

DC

Did the two of you rehearse that?

RW

No, but we're on the same wavelength. Was it okay? At least as far as I got?

DC

On the whole. (*To the pianist*) Better mark in the ritard on the downbeat of " . . . goin' out is I" at the end of the Verse. (*To* RW) That's the last two bars of the Verse. Up until then you're right in tempo, just as you sang it. As for when and where to breathe, that's up to you. The thing is, it moves. When and wherever you can grab a breath without a major disturbance to the lyric, do so and be grateful that you can. I'll mark your copy after Class if you like, but you should do that for yourself because you'll be the one who's singing the song. And don't forget, you're also the one who'll be moving throughout the vocal, so when in doubt, breathe!

RW

I always try to keep that habit in mind.

DC

Yes. This is the kind of song where possible loss of life takes precedence over what might otherwise be considered a sensible phrasing plan. You won't go so far as to breathe in the middle of a word, so beyond that, turning blue to achieve an effect will only turn you blue.

RW

Not to worry. About that second Chorus . . . ?

DC

As you know, there's a danger in going for two Choruses—something along the lines of leave them wanting more—but this song seems to demand it. And again, once it begins, it's a race to the finish. All that's necessary is to choose which of the three published lyrics you like. I think the first one is essential and I like the first half of the second and the second half of the third.

RW

Why?

DC

They allow you to remain general. You don't have to deal with anything specific that relates to the play. Also, the last line of the first Chorus is the same as the first line of the second. I suggest you combine them. One'll be doing double duty and you won't have to cope with a repeat line. Before the audience knows it's happened, you'll be off and away into the second Chorus.

RW

Great! I got it. My question today is: How much do I stage this? Or do I need to stage it at all?

DC

I don't think you should call up anyone to come over and choreograph something for you. Perhaps the Rideout'll need some staging, but for the rest—no.

RW

Whew! That's a relief.

DC

What it does need is a sense of place. That apartment has to be as real for you as this room you're standing in now. It's a room like none you've ever seen or known before except, as you said, in the movies. White piano, sweeping drapes, sexy lighting. I'd make sure I knew where every stick of furniture is; what three kinds of fur are on that marble floor; into which "wing" he exited so you could be alone to sing the song. You may even refer to him with a nod in that direction when it suits your purpose. " . . . To think the highest brow, which I must say is he . . . " comes to mind.

RW

May I just do a music reading today? I figure I'll be ahead if I get by that.

DC

Here we go.
(RW *sings through the Verse and two Choruses. There is a slight snag getting into the second Chorus* but it is smoothed over and the reading finishes without a hitch.)
Very good. Only one thing to say. In the copy, the *g*'s are inconsistently dropped or retained. (*He scans the music copy.*) In the Verse I see "gettin'" and "goin'" and in the Chorus there's "eating," "drinking," but—hold on, here's a "traipsin'." It isn't important one way or the other, but I think you should choose one or the other

---

* The reader may follow this on the lead sheet

and stick with it. Don't forget, when you're working on this at home, you have a narrative lyric here. Show us—don't tell us.*

A week later, RW is on stage for the first performance of the song. At the finish of the Verse, DC stops her.

DC

I hate to stop you. I'm sorry. I like the focus changes, but you're slow. The body language arrives late. Right on the downbeat o: each line. Sometimes even later. If we don't deal with it now it'l only get slower until you never will recapture those "lost" beats Let's see if you can move those "frames" faster. (*To* RW *and the Class*) Remember, it's imperative that midway in the line you begir to concern yourself with what you're *going* to sing and not witr what you're still singing. The song is not something you *react t* but a reaction to what you're *thinking*. Body language, if there is any, will be the result of *that* thinking. Since it's a reaction to those thoughts, it must *precede*, out of synch, what you're singing. When the reverse occurs—moving to what you hear yourself singing—I'l know your concern is only with the printed lines of the lyric and not with why you chose to sing them.

RW

I know all of that's true and fair, but God!, it's rough to do the spot changes and the physical stuff. Do it all together, I mean.

DC

A triple pirouette in the air is rough. Brain surgery is rough. This is not rough. Let's try what you were doing but this time . . . (*To the pianist*) . . . give her a break. Play it like a funeral march. (*To* RW) Now . . . your first frame was on " . . . A chauffeur pull up in a rented limousine." As I remember, you made a kind of Fonz-like move implying "Hey, get this!" Instead of that frame setting up the line, you waited to do it on " . . . pull up."** I'd like to see you do it

---

* See *On Singing Onstage*, The Narrative Lyric, pages 9-10.
** This is a common example of sluggish thinking. The performer waits until the active word in the sentence arrives (in this case, " . . . pull up") before he remembers to play what the line was about.

in the "Air" between " . . . Tonight at eight" and " . . . you should-a seen." The next move you made was on " . . . My neighbors burned!" You indicated with your thumb to your left, where I assume your neighbors live. Frankly, even timed well, it's not my favorite "gesture." Geography instead of attitude. But whatever you play, instead of dead-on " . . . burned," get it in the "Air" between " . . . limousine" and " . . . My neighbors."

RW

You make this sound so damned mathematical!

DC

Did your boyfriend also tell you that Fellini is on record for saying—in a different context, of course, but it's relevant here—"Art is the most subtle mathematical operation." Are you with me?

RW

You mean, did my boyfriend ever tell me? No. Did I hear you? Yes. Can I do it? I'll try.
>   (DC *nods to the pianist. He starts the Vamp.* RW *performs the Vamp with some difficulty because the tempo of the song has been brought way down. She manages to get through it and times the moves perfectly. She stops after* " . . . they like to die!"*)*
How was that? It felt great!

DC

It was fine. Only one correction. Remember, the focus change—the "to whom" you're singing—*always precedes the action and the sung line*. You've been playing the house on the first two lines. Then spot Left as you did (or Right—it makes no difference) *before* you start the move that indicates the location of " . . . My neighbors . . . " You cannot sing without having someone to sing to. The sequence will always be: focus, play, sing.

RW

We should have Class T-shirts with that printed on the front.

DC

How about "lower your spots and elevate your choices"?

RW

That one'd be better on a pillow.

DC

You win. Let's pick up the tempo and see if you can do it as well as you did in the dirge.

RW
(She nods to the pianist, performs the Vamp, again times the moves perfectly and arrives at the end of the Verse. She gets a hand.)
I've got it! By God! I've got it! I didn't think I'd do it but indeed I did!

DC

You certainly did. Does it make sense to you? After all, there's no law against what you did the first time. I doubt if anyone would've noticed there was anything wrong, but now it looks like your life is what you're singing about.

RW

It not only seems right, it feels right.

DC
(To RW *and the Class)*

This is nothing more or less than the "Three" exercise you all worked on in the second Technique Class.*

RW

But now I can see why you always say you don't want us to write a "Two" when we pick up a song. It's about body language and not about a long dialogue between me and—who was it I worked to? Oh, yes—my agent, Max.**

DC

Exactly. All you need to do is work through the song and use your thinking apparatus to propel the lyric forward rather than waiting for the lyric to prod you into thinking. (RW *starts to exit.*) Oh, and one more thing. Remember that petit-point pillow? Well, you don't have to elevate your choices, but your "spot" should be lower. You're playing too high. Bring your focus down.

RW

You'll do anything to kill my hand. (*She exits.*)

RW is on stage for her final performance.

DC

I've thought a great deal about the way "slow thinking" smears body language all over the vocal line. That was your problem last week, wasn't it?

RW

Among other things. But I think I've taken care of that.

DC

Before you sing, let me just take a moment to talk about the

* See *On Singing Onstage*, pages 159–63.
** See *On Singing Onstage*, pages 137–58.

purpose of the "Three" as it applies to performing. (*To* RW *and the Class*) What that technical exercise taught you—the "Three," that is—was the timing of when to drop what you're *thinking* in order to have enough time to set up what you're *going to sing*. Remember, while your mouth is still dealing with the lyric line, it's getting later than you think. Hanging on to yesterday's implicit cue until you've finished the entire sung line, *whether or not it creates body language*, will ensure that you'll be singing the next line without a reason to do so.

The trick, then, is to let your mouth finish the line while you run on ahead to create the *beginning of the life of the next implicit cue*. By the time the end of the sung line is on your lips—which is always just a moment away—you'll have laid in the preparation for the arrival of the new line. Now I know this is not easy to do—not until you learn how to do it. But then it becomes something that gets done without any strain for the simple reason that it's what you normally do in the course of living your life. I'd even risk suggesting that *everything we say in our lives is a "Three" because everything we say in our lives is born of a reason to say it*. What makes it difficult when you sing is that the flow of idea into language is dictated by the composer's time signature. (*To* RW) In "If My Friends Could See Me Now" the problem's more difficult because it's an Up-Tempo song. However, the technique remains the same—it just has to move faster. A matter of timing. But I don't have to tell you about timing. My dictionary defines it this way: "The act of adjusting one's tempo of speaking and moving for dramatic effect." Change *speaking* to *singing*, put it into the context of comedy, and . . . you have yourself another T-shirt. But now, we're due to see the whole performance. Am I right?

RW

I'll let you tell me when I've finished.
> (*She sings through the Verse and two Choruses. Under the circumstances, things go well.* DC *is convinced that if she sang it a second time they would go even more smoothly. The invented "business" is witty and the Class reacts favorably. When she finishes, there is silence out front.*)

Is anyone out there?

DC

I'm sorry. It was good. Quite good. I was just thinking about that Rideout. You sang half-notes straight through " . . . friends could see me . . . "

RW

I know it's obvious but . . .

DC

No, I liked it. I'm wondering how you can make those eight beats on that last word " . . . now" work for you. What you're doing is all right, but you're just standing there, arms out, selling it. We need something more eye filling. (*He thinks for a moment.*) Can you do that old vaudeville bit—go down on one knee, then down on the other, then up on one leg and then up on the other—all in four counts?

RW

You mean this? (*She tries it. It's messy but the Class is buying it.*) Wait a minute. Let me try it again. Jane Fonda, I'm not.

DC
(*To the pianist*)

Take it from " . . . They'd never believe it . . . " but let her have it alone. Come in for the rim shots after " . . . friends . . . could . . . see . . . me . . . " and get set for the four-bar Rideout. (*To* RW) On " . . . now"—wait four beats before you go into the knee bit. You can mark time or move back two steps and forward two steps and then get down fast on that knee. Oh, yes—start on your right foot for the steps and for the knee drop. Have you got all that?

RW

Yep. But can I practice that bit?
(DC *nods. She goes into the wing to work out the "business,"*

returns, crosses to Center stage, cues in the pianist and sings the last line of the song followed by the Rideout, performed as suggested. The Class gives her a hand.)
I think I can do it better.

DC

I'm not worried about that. All that's missing is the joy. It'll be fine when you get to it after singing through the whole song. But may we talk about some of the shtick you do in your performance?* You can cut holding up that imaginary wineglass on "I'm eating fancy chow and drinking fancy wine." In musicals when you need a glass they get you one. Save those sensory exercises for your acting teacher. We all know what a wineglass looks like. Anyway, that's not what you should be thinking because that's not what the line means. It's about the wonder of what's happening to you.

RW

You're right. I admit it's from the bottom of my barrel.

DC

And as a belated birthday present for me, would you cut pointing yourself out on the last line of the Verse: " . . . And goin' out is I"? Hand to chest for "I," hand out for "you," hand moving back and forth for "we"—whenever you busy yourself playing the pronouns—the meaning of the line goes by the board. We all know who "I" is. "I" is "you."

RW

You have the damndest way of picking out things I do that are really lousy.

DC

Well, I liked the jump in the air on " . . . Wowee! Look at where I

---

* *Shtick*: "[a] piece of business to gain a laugh." *The Random House Dictionary of the English Language*, Second Edition, Unabridged.

am!" (*To the Class*) All in all, I think she deserves a hand.

RW
(*Before they can respond. To* DC)

Don't say another word. Just let me have it. (DC *surrenders. She gets her hand. He stays mute.*)

CLASS

Is there any value in getting someone to stage this kind of song?

DC

You mean, choreograph it? None that I can think of. At an audition what she's done would show a choreographer she can move. This way she's not tied to a rigid presentation of the song. She can sing it like this anywhere she chooses or change it when the mood is on her or when better ideas occur to her. (*To* RW) You can cancel that call to Jerome Robbins.

RW

Damn! And I've already left a message on his machine. (*She exits before* DC *can rob her of the curtain line.*)

"By Jupiter"

Wait Till You See Her

Words by Lorenz Hart

Music by Richard Rodgers

184

185

"Wait Till You See Her"

CHORUS:
Wait till you see her see how she looks (✓)
Wait till you hear her laugh (✓)
Painters of paintings ‿ writers of books (✓)
Never could tell the half (✓)
Wait till you feel the warmth of her glance (✓)
Pensive and sweet and wise ‿ all of it lovely (✓)
All of it thrilling ‿ I'll never be willing to free her (✓)
When you see her ‿ you won't believe your eyes (✓)

VERSE:
My friends who knew me never would know me (✓)
They'd look right through me (,) above and below me
And ask (✓) "Who's that man? Who is that man?(✓)
That's not my light-hearted friend" (✓)
Meeting one girl was the start of the end (✓)
Love is a simple emotion (,)
A friend should comprehend (✓)
Wait till you feel the warmth of her glance (✓)
Pensive and sweet and wise ‿ all of it lovely (✓)
All of it thrilling ‿ I'll never be willing to free her (✓)
When you see her ‿ you won't believe ‿
‿ You couldn't conceive it (✓)
You won't believe your eyes (✓)

"Wait Till You See Her" from *By Jupiter*, lyrics by Lorenz Hart, music by Richard Rogers. Copyright © 1942 by Chappell & Co. Copyright renewed. International Copyright Secured. All Rights Reserved. Used by permission.

9

The Waltz

It is safe to assume that, in a manner of singing, man has sung as far back in time as Eden, and close on the heels of that Tarzan yelp, he danced. Since that primordial time dances have come and gone. Terpsichore may be inconstant, but she is an imaginative and giving muse. She gave to Spain, South America, and the Caribbean: the bolero, the tango, the samba, the mambo, the conga, the rhumba, the merengue, and the lambada. To America she gave the black bottom, the cakewalk, square-dancing, the Charleston, the boogie, the Big Apple, the turkey trot, and the Lindy Hop, the shag, the one- and the two-step, modern and tap dancing, the soft shoe, the twist, disco- break- and slam-dancing, and the mock dances created by composers and lyricists for instant play (if not replay): the Continental, the Yam, Ballin' the Jack, and the Piccolino. To the French she granted the gavotte, the minuet, and the ballet; to the Celts, the clog; to the English, the Lambeth Walk, and to the Bohemians, the polka. To the Viennese, she willed the Waltz, a dance step that has demonstrated phenomenal staying power. It is unique in the history of the dance, for no other dance tempo ever began in such disrepute and, by the strength of its case, ended in concert halls and opera houses and is with us still. Of one thing we can be sure: a Waltz is a waltz is a waltz. Capped or lowercased, there is no one who, capable of hearing one, can resist it. For that reason, I have given it its own category.

H.L. Mencken has said of it: "The waltz never quite goes out of fashion; it is always just around the corner . . . [it is] sneaking, insidious, disarming, lovely. It does its work, not like a college yell or an explosion in a munitions plant, but like the rustle of trees, the murmur of the illimitable sea, the sweet gurgle of a pretty girl . . . the waltz, in fact, is magnificently improper—the art of tone turned lubricious."* Ira Gershwin, a lyricist of good humor and fewer words, boiled it down to " . . . You for two-four, Me for three-four."

For this writer, the American Waltz king is indisputably Richard Rodgers. Consider: "The Most Beautiful Girl in the World," "Falling in Love With Love," "Do I Hear a Waltz?" "Nothing But You," "Lover," "Out of My Dreams," "Over and Over Again," "It's a Grand Night for Singing," "A Wonderful Guy," "This Nearly Was Mine," "Hello, Young Lovers," "Ten Minutes Ago," "My Favorite Things," "Oh, What a Beautiful Mornin'," and the glorious Waltzes that make up the overture to *Carousel*. Every composer has written them—some in profusion, as in the case of Mr. Rodgers, others less often. It is the three-quarter time signature that defines the category, and, as a feat of sorts, there is Stephen Sondheim's score for *A Little Night Music*, composed entirely in 3/4 time and its synonymous extensions: 6/4, 9/4, and 12/4.

Of interest: All Waltzes do not owe their allegiance to Vienna. Valses tristes and swing or jazz waltzes may share their three-quarter time signatures with the Viennese *oom-pah-pah*, but there is little else they have in common. Examples of Waltz Tristes: Lerner and Loewe's "I Still See Elisa" from their score for *Paint Your Wagon*; Burton Lane and Alan Jay Lerner's "Melinda" from *On a Clear Day You Can See Forever*, and Bock and Harnick's "Days Gone By" from *She Loves Me*. These waltzes give equal importance to the three beats in each bar of music (the *oom* is no stronger than the *pah-pah*'s within each bar) and by doing so add weight to both the melody and the lyric. Examples of Swing or Jazz Waltzes: Elmer Bernstein and Carolyn Leigh's "Walk Away" from *How Now, Dow Jones*; Norman Gimbel and Jean (Toots) Thielemans's "Bluesette";

---

* From *H. L. Mencken on Music* by Louis Cheslock, published by Schirmer Books.

the charming "I'm All Smiles" from Michael Leonard and Herbert Martin's score for *The Yearling*; and Jerry Jeff Walker's "Mr. Bojangles," sung by the late Sammy Davis, Jr. These songs have a kick to them, due to a hint in the accompaniment of a "hiccup" after the downbeat in each bar, that invests the Swing Waltz with a captivating friskiness.

Waltzes are not easy to sing. Probably no other time signature sets up a similar degree of conflict between the conductor and the vocalist. The reason? Sung Waltzes have an alarming tendency to slow up without the performer's conscious awareness that it is happening. To guard against the tendency, make certain that when there is a breath to be taken at the end of a line it will be at the expense of *what has just been sung* and not *what is about to be sung*. Get off the note sooner rather than later and you will arrive at the downbeat (the "oom"), which is on the immediate horizon, on time. Lose a fraction of a second sitting on that last word and you will be late. As each inspiration of breath occurs, late becomes later, and before eight bars have gone into history you will be imperceptibly (to you) behind the pianist/orchestra, and the Waltz will begin to sag. Following close on: notes from irate conductors and accompanists.

It is important to remember that, like the songs in Category 12, Waltzes have their origin in the dance and even when they are sung seek performances that are not nailed to the floor.* This would not be true of *valses tristes*, in which the script advances at a stately tempo that, coincidentally, happens to be in 3/4 time. But Viennese Waltzes and Swing or Jazz Waltzes "move," and a leaden performance puts the lie to what the Waltz is all about.

THE SONG

I have chosen Richard Rodgers and Lorenz Hart's Waltz "Wait Till You See Her" from *By Jupiter*.** The Verse is to be sung. The forty-bar Chorus is pure Rodgers, and Hart's lyric demonstrates again his talent for finding ever-new words to sing about the old word "love." Rodgers gives the lyric of the Verse its deserved prominence by scoring a simple line built almost consistently on

* See Category 12, Catchall, relating to dance songs sung.
** The song was dropped from the show for reasons no one seems to have recorded. However, the song, by virtue of its quality, survived the assassination.

intervals of chromatic seconds. The "Air" that sweeps the Verse into the Chorus is all any Viennese Waltz could ask for.

The song-form: ABAC and straightforward; the Chorus is in Rodgers's personal style that in his best tunes seems always to make a song sound inevitable. The lavish melody of the Refrain is supported by another of Hart's paeans to the perfect girl.* In the second half of the Chorus, a rising scale moves up to a vocal climax on the word "free," followed by an eight-bar extension that nails down, by means of four dotted half notes, a reprise (in the final four bars) of the original theme of the title at the top of the Chorus. The accompanying lyric is vintage Hartian humor (" . . . When you see her, you won't believe your eyes"). Altogether, a joy to sing.

THE DIALOGUE

DC assigns the song to a young Leading Man whose voice absolutely categorizes him as a singer. There are any number of Waltzes whose melodic lines are not demanding. "Wait Till You See Her" is not one of them. It asks for and should be sung by a singer who can shape a lavish musical phrase and on " . . . I'll never be willing to free her," climb the scale unintimidated by its height (an F).

BL enters. His particulars: just passed through that dolorous event, his thirtieth birthday—a pain for him but a blessing for the casting agents. No longer a Juvenile, he has begun the move into Young Leading Man—a less crowded section of the casting pool. The musical theater is historically distaff heavy. Women far outnumber men on the roster of great stars. When a Leading Man comes along who can sing, act, and move skillfully, his chances of employment are considerably enhanced. Because BL is an attractive man, those who audition him will cross their fingers and sit forward on their seats when he enters. Four bars into the sung song will further bolster their interest. As for his acting skills and physical style—he is working on them.

BL's first music reading is no surprise. The song is sung with ease. The Class may be guilty of downgrading singers who are

* "The Girl Friend," "The Most Beautiful Girl in the World," "You Are Too Beautiful," "Thou Swell," "The Lady Is a Tramp" (complimentary by way of what the lady is not), "I Married an Angel," and "(You Are) From Another World."

guilty of producing only arid, impersonal, albeit musical, statements, but when they hear a music reading in which no performance is expected, sound has its day. The reaction to BL is a total surrender that barely camouflages green-eyed envy.

DC

Well, you know the song and you sing it as well as I knew you would. There's no doubt we've all just heard a beautiful song sung beautifully.

BL

Actually, I think I could go up a key. That high F is no problem. (*The Class boos.*)

DC

Fine. But perhaps it'd be better to see if we can get in a key change within the body of the song. We'll see.* For now, I'd like to try something. You've just sung the song as printed—in the classic Verse-Chorus tradition. Let's try a Chorus-Verse-Chorus and see how it works out. We'll start at the top of the Chorus—"Wait till you see her, see how she looks"—but this time try it in ad-lib. Move it along in speech rhythms and keep the ad-lib going up to the end of " . . . Never could tell the half." (DC *asks the pianist for a sting coming out of an ad-lib Vamp and demonstrates the first sixteen bars of the Chorus in ad-lib.*) Now, as a transition out of the ad-lib, let's have a rubato spread on " . . . Wait till you feel the . . ." and, then, right on "warmth," you and . . . (DC *nods to the pianist.*) . . . hit the waltz as written.

BL

I like that. What happens at the end of the first Chorus? I mean, how do we get back into the Verse?

---

* The following section will be easier to follow if the reader refers to the lead sheet. The song is essentially scored as written—only the sequence has been altered.

DC

No problem. After you finish ". . . When you see her," the pianist will slide into a sting and you'll be free again. Take a "beat" and, in ad-lib, continue on with ". . . you won't believe your eyes." You'll be out of the Chorus and into the Verse without sounding like "Oh, Lord, here comes the Verse." We'll see how we slip back into the reprise of the Chorus, or some part of it, when we get there. All of this sounds more complicated than it'll sing. (*To* BL *and the pianist*) On that last line of the first Chorus: ". . . you won't believe your eyes," don't go for an "ending" because we'll be going on. You'll feel that when you sing it. The ad-lib should continue right on into ". . . My friends who knew me," etc. You'll be Versifying before anyone out front knows it happened. A painless reprise.(*The pianist follows as* DC *sings it.*)

BL

Then the Verse is free all the way?

DC

Yes. There's one thing that we can talk about. I have this feeling that somewhere in the second half of that first Chorus the lyric needs a shift of gears. It's been speaking about your feeling for the ". . . her" referred to in the title, but finally all that ecstatic praise becomes redundant. It isn't Hart's fault, but I think you'll have a problem varying that unmodified joy. To forestall any sag in the attention of the audience, somewhere around the finish line in the first Chorus (". . . When you see her"), stop all that raving about her—in your head, I mean—and introduce into your thinking the *why* of the song: the behavior of your friends that puzzles you. Shouldn't they be happy for you? And if not, why not? Have they never been in love? Here is the confusion that justifies continuing into the conversational ad-lib of the Verse in order to explain what's on your mind—why you were impelled to sing the song in the first place.

BL

I think I understand. But why is a straight-out singing of the song not enough? Doesn't he want everyone to know how great the girl is?

DC

It's enough if all that's at stake is a straight-out singing of the song, and in your case this would be no hardship for us—you sing it beautifully. But I worry that when one is only concerned with beautiful singing, you risk the possibility that someone may sing it better than you do. More beautifully than you do. After all, beauty of tone is measurable. If the competition is just a vocal one, it more rightly belongs at the Metropolitan Opera auditions. In the theater, there are other imperatives. I don't want to disabuse you of the value of a well-sung song, but there is the well-performed song to consider. As Stanislavski has said, ". . . as a means of extending your imaginative powers you will have to invent . . . ['given circumstances']. . . . Always answer for yourself the given questions: 'Where, when, for what reason or purpose is this?'" In the theater a song is not only sung, it is sung *because* . . . and only the limits of your imagination restrict the dramatic impact of what you sing.

> *(Convinced, at least for the moment,* BL *sings the second half of the first Chorus, adds the ritard on ". . . you won't believe your eyes," and, after the sting, stays in ad-lib and moves into the Verse.* DC *stops him halfway through the Verse.)*

Perfect. But you can work on that ad-lib at home. What we need now is to get us back into the Chorus reprise at the end of the Verse. I don't see the need to start at the top of the second Chorus, do you? We don't have a new lyric and redundancy was the original motive for rearranging the song. (*To the pianist*) Now for that four-bar build on the last downbeat of the Verse: ". . . comprehend." That's where we can modulate into the key of F and mark the build "marcato." What I'd like to hear is the sound of a mighty waltz being kept at bay when those chromatic chords start their climb into the new key. (DC *speak/sings and "beats" out a broad oom-pah-pah, oom-pah-pah, oom-pah-pah, oom-pah-pah. To* BL *and the pianist*) And now, cut the first sixteen bars and come in on ". . . Wait till you feel the warmth of her glance," but stretch it out in a sexy rubato. A Puccini-like hold on ". . . feel" wouldn't be amiss because you'll be back in Vienna on ". . . *warmth* of her glance," and from then on, it's full steam ahead down the straightaway.

BL

And the Rideout? Do I do it as written?

DC

I like the idea of an extension. (*He thinks for a moment.*) How about
. . . (*He sings.*)
    You won't believe,
    You couldn't conceive it,
    No! You won't believe your eyes . . . ?*
        (*The pianist has guessed his intentions and follows along.*)

BL

I think I'd better go home, get this all clear in my head and not
waste any more of the Class's time. (*He smiles.*) Gee, I thought I
had this number down cold before I got up today. (*He exits.*)

DC
(*To the Class*)
Remember that, although a song may be sacred, there is nothing
sacred about its sheet music.** If you think of sheet music as the
bare bones of the song, an arrangement may be said to be the
fleshing out of that skeleton. It can be rightfully maintained that
every song we hear on stages, in clubs, on television, on the radio,
and on LP's and CD's is an arrangement. Only the imagination and
the taste of the performer and the arranger define the extent of
what is allowable. At its most creative, the arrangement is not a
destruction but a heightened translation of the song as printed.
(This does not apply to vocal music heard in the concert hall. The
composer's specific instructions are printed on the published pages
of these songs. The art of the lieder singer lies within and despite
these constrictions).

---

*This extension is written into the lead sheet.
** See *On Singing Onstage*, Sheet Music, pages 3-15, and pages 21-31, for a further
discussion of the published copy of a song.

It is a week later. BL is back on stage. The changes have been incorporated and BL and the Class are agreed that they work.

DC

Now let's deal with the key change we talked about last week. (*He turns to the pianist.*) That "fill" coming out of the Verse? Were you able to use it to modulate up a major second out of the home key of E flat to F Major?
>(*The pianist has solved the necessary chord changes and, as he plays them,* BL *follows the new "fill" and comes in on "* . . . *Wait till you feel the warmth of her glance" in F Major—the higher key he requested the week before. It works. Although the lyric is the same as before, now there is the distraction of the new and brighter key to justify the reprise.*)

BL

I like it a lot. May I stay up on those F's for the last line and the Rideout: "No! You won't believe your eyes!"?

A VOICE FROM THE REAR OF THE CLASS

Go for it, man!
>(BL *goes for it and the Class gives him a hand.*)

DC

Will we see a performance today?

BL

Well . . . (*He thinks it over.*) . . . I could give it a try.
>(*He walks away for a moment, then comes back to Center stage and, after a few moments, nods to the pianist, arrives at a Center focus on time and sings the first sixteen bars of the Chorus.*)

DC
(*Stopping him*)

Your instincts are good—this *is* a house number—but the execution of the focus changes is sloppy. We've gone through this before with AB's performance of "I Got It Bad."

BL

There's so much to remember. I was trying to play the song and I guess the eyes began their old rolling habits.

DC

Your eyes won't roll when your thinking is sane. Their job is to seek out the *to whom* you're singing—a recognition of the *presence of the theater*—the same theater that first impelled you to start singing when you came out. Let's do this by the numbers. If we're agreed that house numbers should be announced at the top—after all, you *are* singing to everyone; *everyone* is there—why play to a Center spot through the entire first line? Travel with that focus.

BL

I did travel, didn't I?

DC

No, you didn't. The first word " . . . Wait" can be thrown to Center* but then start relating to the Left and Right—not seeing anyone in particular and everyone in general. And keep it going right through until the finish of " . . . Wait till you hear her laugh."
    (BL *tries it.*)
Not bad. It's a little stiff. Why don't you stop singing it and try speaking the words instead—just tell us about it.
    (*The pianist bows out and* BL *speaks out front, spotting as* DC *has suggested. It is perfectly performed.*)

---

*The focus of a song that starts, for no reason, at some arbitrary spot in the theater, or room, looks haphazard from out front. There is a certain neatness in throwing the first word to a Center spot and moving right on with a "travel."

BL

It's always so damned simple. Why the hell do I screw it up? Let me try singing it this time. (*He does. It is not as smooth as a moment ago.*) Don't even say a word. (*He nods to the pianist and tries again.*) That felt better.

DC

Well-executed focus always feels good because it simulates life. It's what you'd do if you recognized that it's the audience to whom you're addressing yourself. But let's go on. This "general focusing" I call "traveling" doesn't work for long. It tends to thin out and diminish the importance of what you're saying. A good rule: *Keep it down to no more than two lines of a lyric.* From there on your options will be the two laterals—spotting to the Left or the Right and, of course, the power "spot": Center, where key lines, punch lines and the first mention of the title should be directed.

BL

What about the Rideout?

DC

More often than not it, too, goes Center, but there are exceptions. It would depend on the lyric. Sometimes it can be played to the house. The importance of titles lies only in the *first* reference to them. Repeats are nothing more than stage waits—no more valuable than "fill lines"—and should be covered* with anything that gives the audience something to *look at* since a repeat line gives them nothing to *listen to*. (*To* BL *and the Class*) A general focus— what we've been calling "traveling"—keeps objective what you're singing because its object is to tell everyone the facts of the lyric.** This song, "Wait Till You See Her," is already lumbered with an insistent objectivity. The "*You*" and the "*Her*" in the title are a dead giveaway. You're going to be telling everyone about someone other

---

* By "covered" I mean body language. The first title is not only Centered but should be delivered like a punchline—no movement at all—a "freeze."
** See *On Singing Onstage*, pages 101-111.

than yourself. Generalized focus achieves this for you. But, at the same time, if your choices of what you play are not committed to a strong subjectivity, you'll wash out on the stage. Important here, then, is to let your mouth do the *telling* while you busy yourself *showing* the audience how you feel about the lady. Great performing, like everything that lives on a stage, has one end (with many means), and that is how to hold the eye of the audience. Unlike plays, in which the Director manipulates the focus of the audience's attention by the intelligent use of lighting, staging, positioning of the players, and the speed allowed entrances and exits, and film, in which the camera does the instructing, singing inherits no outside aid: *You* are the what must be seen and heard and *you* are the single agent to whom attention must be paid. (*The Class has been taking notes.* DC *turns back to* BL.) Is this clear?

BL

It's in my head. All I have to do is remember to do it.

DC

That has to do with practice, and the need to practice technique is a given in all the arts. Learning how to do anything needs practicing. But let's continue. We now know that we can't keep traveling beyond " . . . Never could tell the half." So, wherever your eyes end up—and I wouldn't "stage" this— move them to the opposite Lateral Spot (Left or Right). Now you're particularizing your focus by working to one member of the audience (or so it will appear from out front) and singing " . . . Wait till you feel the warmth of her glance." Then switch to the other Lateral Spot (Right or Left) and sing " . . . Pensive and sweet and wise."

BL

And come back to Center for " . . . All of it lovely, all of it thrilling, I'll never be willing to free her." Right?

DC

You've got it. Moving along and, in a sense, comparison shopping.

You have four focus choices available to you. A Center spot, Left and Right Laterals, and a general focus targeted to everyone. Remember that performing in all other venues allows for unrestricted spotting. The *to whom* is anyone, anywhere. At an audition, the performer works to an almost empty theater or room. Busy or confusing focus changes can be misread. I think a general focus is good here for " . . . When you see her you won't believe your eyes." It's a line that belongs to everyone, don't you think?

BL

Especially coming from the previous line " . . . All of it lovely, all of it thrilling, I'll never be willing to free her." It gives me somewhere to go.

DC

Exactly. And now, still in ad-lib, we're into the Verse. I'd go back to Center and stay there all the way through the end of the first " . . . Who is that man?" Can you tell me why?

BL

Well, as you said, it's the "why" I'm singing the song. It's the power stuff—the hook that gets me out of those one-note raves in the Chorus. But why get off the Center spot after the first " . . . Who is that man?"?

DC

Because you have a repeat of it. Remember, a repeat line is deadweight. The first time you say it, it is born of your confusion and that's a money line, but I'd bring on some body language—perhaps frustration?—along with a general focus into the theater at large to "spike" the repeat line.

BL

I'm beginning to get the hang of this. I go back to Center for the punch: " . . . That's not my light-hearted friend."

(DC *nods.*)

. . . then a Lateral—Left or Right—on " . . . Meeting one girl was the start of the end," another Lateral—Right or Left—on " . . . Love is a simple emotion" and . . .

DC *and* BL
(*Together*)

Center for the punch: " . . . A friend should comprehend."
(*The Class applauds.*)

BL

We ought to do an act.

DC

Later. Now we're rounding third and heading for home plate. I think it was Voltaire who said something about "the secret of being boring is to tell everything," so why don't I block it and we can get to the Rideout faster?

BL

It's all yours.

DC

The "house" gets the reprise of " . . . Wait till you feel the warmth of her glance, pensive and sweet and wise. All of it lovely, all of it thrilling, I'll never be willing to free her." Wherever you end up, move to the other Lateral (Right or Left) for " . . . When you see her you won't believe" . . . then a switch to the opposite Lateral (Left or Right) for " . . . You couldn't conceive it" and back to . . .

BL
(*Can't resist it*)
Center for "You won't believe you eyes!"

DC

On that string of high F's you asked for a week ago.

BL

Well, I marked it all while you were feeding me, so now all I have to do is get it into the act.

DC

And don't forget, all of this has to be invisible. Whenever the listener is aware of the technique, it's a sure sign the execution was poor. The next time you're up, I'd like to see the performance.

BL
(*Exiting*)

That makes two of us!

It is a week later. BL is on stage again.

DC
(*To quiet* BL's *evident nervousness*)

Look, this is a Class, not an opening night. And it's the first time you're performing the song. Why not think of this as the end of the first week of rehearsal. There's still enough time to fix whatever doesn't work.

BL

It's the expectations.

DC

Of what? Failure?

BL

Well, yes, I guess so. It's just that I expect I'll screw up everything

I've rehearsed at home.

DC

You must know something we don't know. Why don't you stop worrying about what will happen and deal with now. As I keep saying, "Now" is where all songs take place. Philip Larkin wrote that " . . . all too eager for the future, we make bad habits of expectations."

BL

Do you have a quote for every emergency?

DC

No, but Samuel Butler did say that " . . . appropriate things are meant to be appropriated."

THE CLASS

But it isn't unreasonable, is it? I mean, to feel shaky the first time each of us is going to show our performance?

DC

Unreasonable to feel shaky? No. But talking about it is only a ploy to protect your work from possible rejection. We all know that script, don't we? Better to put that energy into concentration. The more successful you are, the more you'll know whether what you worked on at home—works.

(BL *sings the song.* DC *refrains from interrupting him. The focus plotting has worked out well—with only a few fluffs. To* BL's *credit, he has managed to dissemble them and keep going.* DC *begins his comments on the performance.*)

On the whole, you're to be congratulated. Considering all you have to juggle, things worked out very well indeed. The singing is still gorgeous. Maybe not as pure as it was in that first music reading, but that was all you had on your mind then. As for the technique of focusing into the theater, by and large you should feel proud of yourself. When there was an error, you covered it and no one, least of all those out front, would've known an error had been made. (*To the Class*) Remember, focus choices are not handed down from the Mount. There are many ways to sing any line of any song and different plottings can help to keep a performance fresh. (*To* BL) Do you really like this girl?

BL

Why . . . yes. Didn't that come across?

DC

No more so than you might feel about your new car.

BL

I don't have an easy time showing my real emotions.

DC

Aren't you in the wrong business? Maybe a switch to politics?

BL

No, I'm serious.

DC

So am I. Perhaps this will help. When you read through this lyric—and each of you should be letter perfect with what a song *says*, especially if you plan to perform it—you begin to see some clues that can be helpful to you. To begin with, in this case, what is *he* like? Do you know him? More important, do you recognize any of him in you? For, after all, *you are the song*. Is he a cold man? Closed off? Or is he a man who's more in touch with his feelings?

BL

Oh, he feels, all right!

DC

Good. How about his ability to put those feelings into words? On a scale of one to ten, how would you rate him?

BL

Pretty damn high, I'd say, from the way he talks about the girl. He knows about paintings, he reads books, he speaks of her laugh and her look. Not too many guys I know describe their wives or lovers as " . . . pensive and sweet and wise." And he uses words like "lovely" and "thrilling" and you know he's used them before and without any embarrassment. And, also, his friends are just like him, which is why he can't figure out why they don't understand what he's going through.

DC

For a man who has trouble showing his real emotions, that's a helluva speech you just gave! How about bringing some of that understanding of who he is, the joy he feels in this relationship, into your performance? I'd like to add one more observation about the lyric. Mr. Hart has an affection for verbs. There's one in almost every key line of the song. Let's see. (*He picks up a copy of the sheet music.*) Starting from the top of the Chorus, what have we got? Well, there's "see . . . hear . . . tell . . . feel . . . free . . . believe," and in the Verse "knew . . . know . . . look through . . . ask . . . comprehend," and in the Rideout we've another "believe" and a "conceive it." If verbs are the active elements in a sentence, here's a man of action. Not a man given to passive contemplation. I'd say he's on a roll!

BL
(*He has been listening attentively.*)

God! I wish I could get past singing a song the minute I pick up a copy of it. I'd save myself a lot of time and energy.

DC

And have a lot more fun singing! A man who looks like you and makes such sumptuous sounds when he sings can afford to put those assets aside and worry about them later. You're doing yourself a disservice. There's so much more to singing than supporting breath, placing vowels where they belong, and obeying technical rules—even the ones I teach. I'd rate it right up there, just below orgasm. And you don't even need a partner. Well . . . almost. A great teacher once told me, "Never go out on a stage and say (silently) to the audience, 'I have this great song I want to sing.'" Not that there's anything wrong with the sentence—only that it's missing the key word: "I have this great song I want to sing for *you*."

BL

I'll bring this back. Thank you.

DC

Just start the journey. Why not make a good habit? The future will come in any event, expectations notwithstanding.

(BL *exits.*)

"She Loves Me"

Tonight At Eight

Lyrics by Sheldon Harnick

Music by Jerry Bock

A Nervous Allegretto

ten more hours to go._____ It
ten more hours to go._____ I'll

may be a mis - take, but that's the chance I have to take and if it
know when this is done, if some-thing's end - ed or be - gun and if it

goes all right, who knows, I might pro -

pose to - night at eight.

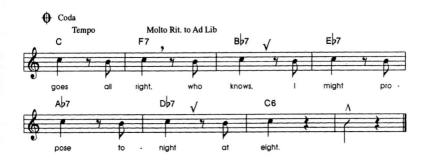

goes all right, who knows, I might pro -

pose to - night at eight.

"Tonight at Eight"

CHORUS 1:
I'm nervous and upset (✓)
Because this girl I've never met (✓)
I get to meet tonight at eight (✓)
I'm taking her to dinner at a charming old café
But who can eat (,) tonight at eight (✓)
It's early in the morning
And our date is not till eight o'clock tonight
And yet already I can see
What a nightmare this whole day will be (✓)
I haven't slept a wink
I only think of our approaching tête-à-tête
Tonight at eight (✓)
I feel a combination of depression and elation
What a state to wait 'til eight (✓)
Three more minutes
Two more seconds (,)
Ten more hours to go (✓)
It may be a mistake
But that's the chance I'll have to take (,)
And if it goes all right (,)
Who knows (✓) I might propose
Tonight at eight

CHORUS 2:
I wish I knew exactly how I'll act
And what will happen when we dine
Tonight at eight (✓)
I know I'll drop the silverware
But will I spill the water or the wine
Tonight at eight (✓)
Tonight I'll walk right up and sit right down
Beside the smartest girl in town
And then it's anybody's guess (✓)
More and more I'm breathing less and less (✓)
In my imagination
I can hear our conversation taking shape
Tonight at eight (✓)

I'll sit there saying (**,**) absolutely nothing
Or I'll jabber like an ape
Tonight at eight (✓)
Two more minutes
Three more seconds
Ten more hours to go (✓)
I'll know when this is done
If something's ended or begun
And if it goes all right (**,**)
Who knows (✓)
I might propose
Tonight (✓) at eight (✓)

"Tonight at Eight" from *She Loves Me*, lyrics by Sheldon Harnick, music by Jerry Bock. Copyright © 1963 by Alley Music Corp. Trio Music Co., Inc. Copyright renewed 1981 by Jerry Bock Enterprises and Mayerling Prods. Ltd. International Copyright Secured. All Rights Reserved. Used by permission.

Patter Song

The following description of the Patter Song is excerpted from *The Concise Oxford Dictionary of Music*:

> Comic song, prevalent in opera, which is a rapid iteration of words, the music merely being lightly supportive. Examples exist in Haydn, Mozart, and Rossini operas; there are many in the Gilbert and Sullivan operettas [they are] usually solos, but *Ruddigore* has a patter-trio.

Although Rossini died in 1868 and Gilbert and Sullivan ended their collaboration in 1896, the Patter Song thrives on musical theater stages and in the Pop Music scene, where as "rap" it continues to hold sway.

The above definition is adequate but I would add that

1. The lyric and its fluent delivery take primacy over the "light supportive music." (The music of the Patter Song may sometimes be more than a light support of the lyric. See below re: Stephen Sondheim.)

2. Rhythm, as such, does not add anything but speed to the proceedings. The Patter Song moves fast but rarely, if ever, swings.

Required of the performer: the ability to think and convert thought into a swift, continuous verbal response coupled with an evident pleasure in being able to do so.

That Gilbert and Sullivan held the patent on these songs throughout the latter half of the nineteenth century is well known.

"When I, Good Friends, Was Call'd to the Bar" from *Trial By Jury*, "My Name Is John Wellington Wells" from *The Sorcerer*, "I Am the Captain of the Pinafore" from *H.M.S. Pinafore*, "Model of a Modern Major General" from *The Pirates of Penzance*, "When You're Lying Awake" from *Iolanthe*, "I've Got a Little List" from *The Mikado*, and "In Enterprise of Martial Kind" from *The Gondoliers*—are Patter Songs the world has been humming, if not singing, for over a century.

In our time, Stephen Sondheim is their heir. Among his masterpieces: "I'm Calm," "Pretty Little Picture," and "Everybody Ought to Have a Maid" from *A Funny Thing Happened on the Way to the Forum*; "It's the Little Things You Do Together," "Getting Married Today," and "Another Hundred People" from *Company*; "Kiss Me," "A Little Priest," and "Pirelli's Miracle Elixir" from *Sweeney Todd*; "Everybody Says Don't" from *Anyone Can Whistle*; "Chrysanthemum Tea" and "Please Hello" from *Pacific Overtures*; "Bobby and Jackie and Jack" and "Franklin Shepard, Inc." from *Merrily We Roll Along*; "Color and Light," "Everybody Loves Louis," and "Putting It Together," all from *Sunday in the Park With George*; "On the Steps of the Palace" from *Into the Woods*; "A Weekend in the Country" and, in part, "It Would Have Been Wonderful," "Now," and "The Miller's Son" from *A Little Night Music*; and, lastly, "How I Saved Roosevelt" from *Assassins*. With Richard Rodgers, Sondheim collaborated on *Do I Hear a Waltz?* in which "What Do We Do? We Fly" may be considered a Patter Song, and with Leonard Bernstein, so would "Gee, Officer Krupke!" and "America" from *West Side Story*.

It is recommended that any performer, regardless of his intention or ability to perform these songs, read through Mr. Sondheim's Patter Songs to discover his genius not only for the elision and alliteration that allow his words to move at top speed, but for putting together words that never before had come together. (From *Into the Woods*: " . . . He was robbing me, raping me, rooting through my rutabaga, Raiding my arugula and ripping up the rampion . . . .") And each of these put to the service of the script; each song to be sung when it must be and, most important, why and where it must be.

Sondheim is not alone. Cole Porter could turn out triple-time tongue-twisters: "Let's Not Talk About Love" sung by the late Danny Kaye from Porter's *Let's Face It*, and from *Kiss Me, Kate*:

"Where Is the Life That Late I Led?" "I've Come to Wive It Wealthily in Padua," and "Too Darn Hot"; George and Ira Gershwin's "The Babbitt and the Bromide" and much of their scores for *Of Thee I Sing* and *Let 'Em Eat Cake* are pastiche songs in the style of Gilbert and Sullivan; Kurt Weill with Ira Gershwin wrote "Tschaikowsky (And other Russians)" for Mr. Kaye's Broadway debut in *Lady in the Dark*. The late, gifted Sylvia Fine, Mr. Kaye's wife, was one of the most fluent of Patterers, and for her husband she wrote two classics: "Anatole of Paris" and, with Max Leibman, "Maniac Depressive Presents" (Lobby Number). Not to be excluded are Leonard Bernstein's "I Can Cook Too" from *On the Town*; Jule Styne and Comden and Green's "Drop That Name" from *Bells Are Ringing* and the same writers' "Adventure" from *Do Re Mi*; Wright and Forrest's "Rhymes Have I" and "Not Since Nineveh" from *Kismet*; Lerner and Loewe's "Why Can't the English?" and "A Hymn to Him" from *My Fair Lady* and from *Brigadoon*: "My Mother's Weddin' Day" and "The Love of My Life"; Cy Coleman's "Deep Down Inside" and the title song from *Little Me* (both with Carolyn Leigh) and (with Michael Stewart) "Prince of Humbug" from *Barnum*; Jerry Bock and Sheldon Harnick's "Twelve Days to Christmas" from *She Loves Me*.

THE SONG

"Tonight at Eight," the assigned Patter Song, is from the last-named score. The musical was written in 1963 and is arguably one of the loveliest works written for the musical theater in the last thirty-odd years. There is not a false note to be found in it. Bock's talent for creating analogous music and Harnick's gift for simple purity in his lyrics tend to subjugate their scores to the requirements of the time, the place, and the sociopolitical-economic profile of the scripts they choose—for example: the vernacular of *The Body Beautiful*; the Judaic wash over *Fiddler on the Roof*, and the more upscale intonation of *The Rothschilds*; the jazzy period sounds of New York in *Fiorello!* and *Tenderloin*. Unlike Stephen Sondheim, whose dazzling mark is on everything he writes, Bock and Harnick's signature is eclipsed by a determination to stay within the organic musical margins of the material. Anyone lucky enough to sing their scores experiences the unique sensation of music, lyrics, character, and story coming together in a unity rarely encountered in the musical theater. *She Loves Me* is a favorite of mine because in many ways it recalls two of Jerome Kern's finest scores: *The Cat and the Fiddle* and *Music in the Air*.

Patter Song songs are content to be what they are: rapid-fire verbal fireworks. "Tonight at Eight" is rarer because it is more. The speed of the song and the fluency of its language are not arbitrary. They are there to dramatize and musicalize a state of hysteria. Sondheim's "I'm Calm" from *Forum*, written the year before, achieves this stunning effect. So, too, does Weill and Brecht's *"Ruf Aus Der Gruft"* ("Call From the Grave") from *The Threepenny Opera*.

The song's time signature is 2/4, which announces at the very start the character's nervous state. The twelve bars, beginning with the 25th bar of the Chorus (there is no Verse) that slow up the Niagara of words with a series of quarter notes, is sheer show business.* This theme is repeated, with a subtle variation, in the lyric:

Three more minutes, two more seconds,
Ten more hours to go . . .

which is altered to:

Two more minutes, three more seconds
Ten more hours to go . . .

suggesting that the first Chorus should take one second under a minute to get through. I have tried it and it does—another example of Bock and Harnick's determination to stick to the facts.

THE DIALOGUE

MM is a gifted comic performer—a triple threater with a voice that beguiles the ear with its natural production, a sense of humor, and a body able to do everything and anything he asks of it. He has trained in Paris with Étienne Décroux and Marcel Marceau, but boasts of never having set foot inside the studio of a singing teacher. "Tonight at Eight" will give him an opportunity to combine patter with his gift for mime, oxymoron notwithstanding.

DC

This is a wonderful song, don't you think? Especially for you.

* See *On Singing Onstage*, 2/4 time signature, page 29.

MM

Oh, yes! I think my problem is going to be editing myself. Everything I'll put in I'll probably end up taking out or way down. I mean, this is fertile territory!

DC

Don't worry about that. We can always make less of too much. It's pumping up too little when too little is all there is that's troublesome. But how about the song? The key we chose? The tempo? Let's deal with first things first and hear you sing it.

MM

The printed key was a little low. I asked the pianist to move it up. Is that all right?

DC

Not too high, I hope. Let's see. It's printed in C. I think no higher than D Major should do it. Otherwise it'll sound shrill, or worse, operatic on the last eight bars of each Chorus. The man is nervous enough without sounding like a strangled chicken.

MM

D should be fine. Now about that nervous man I'm supposed to be . . .

DC

Sing. We'll worry about everything else after we nail the song.
(MM *sings through the two Choruses of "Tonight at Eight."*
Just as DC *and the Class expected, he is letter-perfect.*)
Very nice indeed. Just one suggestion. I think Bock and Harnick's arrangement of it in *She Loves Me* is a good notion. They don't bring the rhythm in until the top of the fifth bar on the word " . . . meet." Before that, the phrases are short and clipped. The first one: " . . . I'm nervous and upset" is in ad-lib, then take a breath

(whether or not you need one), and go on to " . . . Because this girl I've never met." Take another breath and then full speed ahead.*
From there on there's no stopping him.

MM

That fits in nicely with the "business" I planned. Now about that "nervous" question. How nervous is nervous?

DC

As we've said, I don't like to talk about a performance before I see it. Let's just say that he isn't so nervous as to seem afflicted but nervous enough to be panicky about the prospect of a dinner date with the young lady. About the where or when to breathe: There was one spot where you sent out what, I hope, was an unconscious piece of misinformation. When you breathed between " . . . already I can see" and " . . . What a nightmare this whole day will be," I thought you meant that the date was for eight o'clock and already he could see. Was he blind before eight o'clock? (*The Class laughs.*) No, I'm quite serious. Elide those two lines.

MM

That was a mistake. I knew it was wrong as soon as I sang it. It's one of the long phrases, but I'm sure I can handle it.

DC

Good. Now let's talk about your diction. You'll have to move your mouth and your tongue more when you sing. Tire your face. One does a lot of lipreading in the theater, despite of or even because of all that amplification, so articulate. Take pleasure in the words. Finish them, especially when they end with a consonant. If they please you, they'll please us. Here's an example of the need to tell us what the song *says* as well as what you *mean* by what it says. Sing it again and don't forget the ad-libbed first lines at the top before you move into tempo.

* The reader may follow this on the lead sheet.

(MM *sings the song again. Following* DC's *suggestion,* MM
*makes the words sound almost tasty. Some characterization has
begun to slip in.*)

You should try to restrain yourself in a music reading. Just sing the
song and make it phrase-worthy. Keep the performance at arms
length. Time enough for that when you can give it your full
concentration.

MM

I know. It's hard to keep the guy at bay.

DC

Well, we'll see him the next time you're on stage. Until then, be
sure you memorize the lyric until it's imprinted on your mind. Go
up on it while you're working the song and you might as well just
walk off.

Some days later, MM is back on stage. The Class, accustomed to
seeing his work as an experience set apart from the usual, is
especially alert. He nods to the pianist from Center stage, comes
front in the middle of the Vamp, and, working focus changes
relative to a house number, performs "Tonight at Eight."* There is
much to commend it and much to discuss. The Class applauds the
work and him.

MM

It's getting through the first time's the hard one. I could feel all of
you staring at me in the dark like a pack of . . . well, never mind. I
got through it. What did you think?

DC

For a first time, I thought a lot of it.

---

* See Category 9, "Wait Till You See Her," for blocking focus choices for a house number,
pages 196–201.

MM

. . . was what?

DC

No. I'm serious. I thought a lot of good things about it. But to begin with, I can understand why you were concerned about the man's nervous condition. But the concern is the root cause for the trouble you're having. The man looks hysterical—certifiable. The thing is, you're *doing* "nervous." Here's a song that demands a state of un-nervousness so that you're able to project its illusion. I'm thinking about those belly-wop dives the great clown divers do in an aquacade and how lethal they'd be if the men didn't know what they were doing. I'm not even sure I understand the purpose of all those twitches and flutters and tremors. Is this a song about a man with a tic? If it is, he should be talking about a date with a neurologist. And sooner than tonight at eight.

MM

I can fix that. I was pushing. "First time" nervousness.

DC

Well, if that's the case, why not use *that* nervousness since it's already there?

MM

I'll pull it way down. How about the shtick here and there and everywhere?

DC

I'm always uncomfortable when someone asks me that question, and I'll tell you why. Because it can only be answered with "I liked this and I liked that." Now, my liking something is fine as long as you know that it's what *I* like and what *I* didn't like. And what I didn't like may very well be something someone else likes. In a nutshell, that's the problem with what you call "shtick." It's all about my tastes as opposed to yours or someone else's.

MM

But isn't that what all study is about?

DC

No, not at all. You study a subject to learn how to do it. The marketplace judges it, for better or for worse, and in good time. I'm here to tell you what you'd tell yourself if, when you're working, you could stand back and see its effect. Did it play? Was it well executed? Would different choices have been more valuable?

MM

But I like your taste.

DC

That's nice to hear but I'd rather you cultivated your own standards. Mine are mine.

MM

I understand. But how can I begin to cultivate mine if certain standards aren't set for me? I really would like to know what you thought.

DC

This is going to sound like I'm at a candy store counter saying "I'll have three of those" and "two of those" and "oh, yes, four of them, please."

MM

Well, for me, those pieces of business are like candies. I work hard enough making them.

DC

I'll be serious then. There are some lovely things I liked more than a lot. So here come the "I like's." I liked playing, in opposition, the crazed joy on the word "depression" and the drop into the sad clown face that set up "elation." I liked holding up three fingers before " . . . three more minutes" and then getting confused and holding up four fingers just before " . . . two more seconds," and the "take" after that. I liked, too, the offbeat reading of " . . . I know I'll drop the silverware but will I spill the water or the wine?" Instead of the obvious worry about committing a social gaffe, you were more interested in trying to figure out which one it would be. Yes, I liked that. I liked feeling your forehead and then taking your pulse in the "Air" after " . . . More and more I'm breathing less and less."

MM

You were certainly paying attention. What about the "I didn't like's"?

DC

I didn't like both endings surrendering to the idea of proposing to the lady. It gives the first Chorus an "ending" and robs you of a sufficient reason to go on.

MM

But he wants to marry her, doesn't he?

DC

We can talk about that later. Let's stick with the "I didn't likes" for now. About the piece of business where you check your temperature and your pulse. I think it would work better for you if you did them in reverse—pulse first and then feel your forehead for the temperature "frame." It'll help you move smoothly into tapping your hand against your head for " . . . In my imagination I can see our conversation taking shape." That way you'll be there instead of going from your head to your hand, holding your wrist, and going all the way back to your head again.

MM

That'll make it a lot easier to get it all in without smearing over that line.

DC

That's another thing. You have the title, more often than not, as a safety to play through. You tend to think you've only got the line, without the title, to work in. It makes "Tonight at eight," each time you sing it, sound like a parenthesis at the end of each line you sing. Do you follow me?

MM

Yes, I know. It's my eagerness to set up the new line. I guess I have more time than I need. I sure get to say the title often enough. I'll just keep playing through them—or almost through them, anyway.

DC

Another thing to remember that'll keep you from flying through the roof: This song is no more rapid than the rhythms in which you speak. If you just talked it and the pianist joined you at some point, you'd discover your speech rhythms are no faster than what he's playing when you sing it. Don't let that jumpy accompaniment drive you up the wall. It's enough that you have to deal with the hyper state you're in. Believe me, you have more time than you think to do what you have to do. And, oh, yes, you're working too wide and high with your hands. It makes it almost impossible to see you. My eye keeps being drawn too far to the right and left and above your head. A good idea when you practice the performance is to place yourself in an imaginary corridor where the walls are no wider than the width of your body and the ceiling no higher than your chest. It'll help you to remember to bring all the shtick, as you call it, down and in. That ceiling and the imaginary walls won't let you go too wide and high. Once you're aware of the size of what they need to be, you can always widen the walls and raise the ceiling. Now, of course, this doesn't apply when you touch your forehead or, for that matter, your ears or your nose, you understand.

MM

I never heard you mention that trick before but I think it should help a lot. The thing is I tend to do too much, as I said the other day. Then I spend the rest of my time shaping it and bringing it down. What I wanted to find out today was what you thought of the whole performance generally. I can go home now and work on this and try it again next week. Thanks for the "I likes." I'll think about the "I don't likes."

DC

That's the idea. (*To* MM *and the Class*) We've been talking about "shtick" or "business." My dictionary defines it this way: "a movement or a gesture, especially a minor one, used by an actor to give expressiveness, drama, detail, etc., to a scene or to help portray a character." It should be pointed out that when MM works from character, the physical language—his *exterior* life, no matter the comedic intention—is true because it's supported by an *interior* life. When it's "business" for the sake of "business," it becomes a busyness that upstages and erases the essential "him." At that moment, the shtick is all there is and we get down to what "I like" and what "you like." He stops *being* as soon as he starts *doing*. And then he looks less the man and more the mime. Now, mime is not to be belittled, but it's another ball game. It portrays, in gesture and movement, a character, an idea, even a story, but always in the abstract. The man behind the mime is invisible. (*To* MM) There is nothing wrong with this, but in the theater we need to know the real man—to know *you*. We must know who you are and the circumstances in which you find yourself. There is no metaphor allowable. Abstraction is anathema. (*To the Class*) Now, I know that many of you watch MM and wish you could do what he does. But just as you work to free yourselves of physical self-consciousness, so must he work to give substance to his extraordinary ability to physicalize text. Without that basis in truth, the activity becomes mere decoration for decoration's sake. Without real pertinence, the more polished the externalized "shtick" appears, the more MM remains invisible. (*To* MM *again*) You have to keep in the forefront of your mind who you are and why you're singing this song to us. When you lose sight of these essentials, you'll fall back on "business" because you do it so well. But after a bit, it's fatiguing to watch—like a trick repeated over and over again. I want you to be so alive to the possible danger of meeting that girl tonight at eight that I see not only *you* under those circumstances—circumstances we all know only too well—but so engaged am I that, in my mind's eye, I see *me*, in the same bind, as well.

MM

Whew! I'm glad I've got that down on my tape. I'll see you all next week.
(*The Class applauds him as he exits. The hand is deserved.* MM*'s work is rich in invention and he has the courage to play it full out—no matter the risk.*)

MM's final performance of "Tonight at Eight" is put on stage the following week. He has worked hard. There is a new man performing up there. DC praises him.

DC

Very good, indeed. Only two things are left to speak about.

MM

I knew I wouldn't get off scot-free.

DC

They're not major points but they're worth mentioning. I think we could fix up that Rideout. If you remember, we spoke about this the other day. While you were doing it, it occurred to me that you were flying too high as you were nearing the finish line. You only have that one sting at the end of the song, which means the song is over after the sting. It'll be hard as the devil to land that plane, get out of it, and walk into the terminal all in one beat.

MM

I'm glad you brought that up because I do feel like an idiot with just one chord to ride me out on the last word.

DC
(*To the pianist*)

Keep the tempo going right through " . . . I'll know when this is done, if something's ended or begun and if it goes all right . . ." Then, right there, start a ritard and follow him as he slowly, and then more slowly, stutters out " . . . Who knows . . . I might . . . propose tonight . . . at eight." Instead of that rim shot at the end, change it to a pathetic, *piano* sting. Like a little sigh. You can even pedal it so that it lingers in the air. (*To* MM) The first Chorus ended on a "high." Don't change that on the second time around. Stay excited and eager right up until that ritard. Then, somewhere at the end of the phrase " . . . if it goes all right," slowly begin to realize what her accepting you would mean: marriage, kids, trapped, tied down. Keep slowing down as these revelations occur to you. By then you should be not quite sure it's such a good idea. Even the dinner date seems risky. The final " . . . Tonight at eight" will be followed by that sad sting you'll hear instead of the rim shot. You can use the sting for reaction. Maybe a slow-to-arrive but, nevertheless, sneaky, lecherous smile will work.

MM

Great. I like it. And then I can just step out of the song without feeling I'm still a foot off the floor. It'll cool me down a lot, too.

DC

Let's try it. Even if it's off the top of your head. First take the music reading so you get used to that ritard instead of the old way of riding it out in tempo.
(MM *and the pianist work through the new "last '8'" music reading two or three times to set the timing of the ritard.*)

MM
(*Crossing back to Center stage. To* DC)

Where shall we take it from?

DC

Where is it easiest for you without going all the way back to the top?

MM

How about from " . . . In my imagination I can hear our conversation taking shape. . ."? The last half of the second Chorus.

DC

Fine. Don't rush right into it. Take a few moments of preparation to collect yourself and to figure out where you've been and where you're going.
> (MM *does so and then sings through the last half of the song and, in the last "8," begins the slow realization that she might say "Yes." The ritard becomes an organic inevitability. Then, rather than placing the sly smile on the sting, he begins his transition on " . . . propose tonight at . . ." and, a split-second after the last word " . . . eight," timed to the sting, he covers his mouth like an impish schoolboy. It works. The heat of the song has cooled down and getting out of the song presents no problem. He is pleased with the new ending.*)

MM

It felt good. Real good.

DC

It looked even better than that. Before you sit down for a deserved break, I just want to caution you. As you heard, there was a good deal of laughter throughout the performance of the song. When you hear it, don't play into it. Do the song! Singing what you have to say is not the same as speaking it. When you're doing a routine in a club or playing a comedy on the stage, you can time off the laughter you get. If a line or a piece of business gets a laugh, you can hold back the next thing you have to say. But when you sing, there's an orchestra or a pianist with you and both he or it—and you—are victims of the song's time signature. Because you cannot stop singing to wait for your laugh—or to wait for it to subside—the temptation is often there to start pressing. Before you know it, you've stopped playing the song and you've begun to go for the laughs. The obvious danger here is that what got you the laugh in the first place was the truth of why you were singing the song that, in turn, made you do what you were doing. Now you've surrendered cause to effect—playing for a reaction from the audience.

MM

I know what you mean. It's hard to go for something, hear them laughing, and not allow that to screw up your thinking.

DC

The thing is, all audiences are different. One night you get it and the next time it'll lay there. What you can trust is the material. What you cannot depend on is how they'll react to it. The sure sign of an amateur is the one who, having gotten a smile, goes for a laugh. A laugh? Then let's try for a boff. A boff? How about a hand? But, more often than not, all it ever was meant to evoke was the smile. Press harder and you will lose everything. Comedy is a serious business, one you can never be sure of.

MM

I guess that's something I should remember every time I get a little too sure of myself.

DC

You're not guilty of any of that kind of behavior. Not as yet. I just thought it was worth mentioning when someone like you, who works in comedy, is on stage. This is, after all, a class and not an entertainment, but when someone performs as well as you do, it's hard to remember that we're not in a theater. For all I know, you would never be guilty of that kind of "Shriner" behavior.

Oh, I don't know about that. Once, when I was a kid, I put a lamp shade on my head and . . . (*He looks at* DC *and decides to quit while he's ahead.* MM *exits.*)

"Funny Lady"

How Lucky Can You Get

Words by Fred Ebb

Music by John Kander

Ragtime

Ba - do - di - o - di - o - di   o - di - o - do— mmm.—— Ba- do - di - o - di - o - di

o - di - o - do— mmm   1.Sat - in on my shoul - der and a   smile on my lips,——
                        2.Wrap it up and charge it, that's my   fa - vor - ite phrase,——

How luck - y can you get?   Mon - ey in my pock - et, right at
How luck - y can you get?   When I see the chauf - feur, think I'll

my fin - ger tips.——   How luck - y can you get?
give him a raise.——   How luck - y can you get?

(2nd x)

Ev - 'ry night a par - ty where the fun nev - er ends.—— You could
Week - ends in the coun - try with a bar - on, of course,—— and a

230

Life's   a   bed   of   ros-es squirt-in'   per-fume   on   me.____ You   can

spare   me   the   blues.____   I   don't   sing   in   that   key!____

And   if

there's   a   man   who'd   leave   me,   I'm   de-light-   ed   to   say,____   I

have-n't   run   in-to   him   yet.   Gee!   Whee!

Wow!   How   luck-y____   can   you____

get?!!!____

"How Lucky Can You Get?"

CHORUS 1:
Ba-do-di-o-di-o-di-o-di-o-do (✓)
Ba-do-di-o-di-o-di-o-di-o-do (✓)
Satin on my shoulder and a smile on my lips (✓)
How lucky can you get (✓)
Money in my pocket right at my fingertips (✓)
How lucky can you get (✓)
Ev'ry night a party where the fun never ends ⌣
⌣ You could circle the globe with my circle of friends (✓)
Someone I am crazy for is crazy for me
I'm his personal pet (✓)
Wow, how lucky can you get (✓)

CHORUS 2:
Wrap it up and charge it, that's my favorite phrase (✓)
How lucky can you get (✓)
When I see the chauffeur think I'll give him a raise (✓)
How lucky can you get (✓)
Weekends in the country with a baron (,) of course ⌣
⌣ And a wardrobe to choke Missus Astor's pet horse (✓)
Makin' merry music with the one that I love
We're a perfect duet (✓)
Gee, how lucky can you
Whee, how lucky can you
Wow, how lucky can you get (✓)
Hey there gorgeous big success (✓)
What's your secret (,) just lucky I guess (✓)
Life's a bed of roses squirtin' perfume on me ⌣
⌣ You can spare me the blues (,)
I don't sing in that key (✓)
And if there's a man who'd leave me ⌣
⌣ I'm delighted to say (,)
I haven't run into him yet (✓)
Gee (,) Whee (,) Wow ⌣
⌣ How lucky (✓) can you get (✓)

"How Lucky Can You Get?" from *Funny Lady*, lyrics by Fred Ebb, music by John Kander. Copyright © 1975 Screen Gems-E.M.I. Music, Inc. International Copyright Secured. All Rights Reserved. Used by permission.

11

Showstopper

If a Roxy Rideout* guarantees a "hand," the Showstopper is its song equivalent. Designed to score from the first note of the Vamp through and until the last note of the Chorus has sung and played itself out, everything is there to support purpose. Tempo is only one of many elements that assures this intended effect, but, slow or fast, there is an implosive energy that lies below the surface. Add an extended Rideout and what was a sure thing is made doubly so.

John Kander and Fred Ebb appear to have taken possession of this category, but not without a fight. Disregarding their challengers for a moment, a list of Kander and Ebb songs that are exemplars of the form would have to include: the anthem "New York, New York" from the film of the same name; "Sing Happy" from *Flora, the Red Menace*; "Nowadays" and "And All That Jazz" from *Chicago*; "City Lights" from *The Act*; "Cabaret," the title tune of the musical, and from the film of the same name: "Money, Money, Money" and "Maybe Next Time"; "Colored Lights" and "All the Children in a Row" from *The Rink*; "Home" and "Yes" from *70 Girls 70* and . . .

Re: the challengers—all first magnitude. Among them: Lerner and Loewe's "The Rain in Spain" and "The Ascot Gavotte" (with

* See Introduction, page 15.

the Beaton costumes and the final spoken "Move your bloomin' arse!!!"); Charles Strouse's title tune and "But Alive" from *Applause*; Frank Loesser's "Adelaide's Lament" and "Take Back Your Mink" from *Guys and Dolls*; Jule Styne's "Don't Rain On My Parade" from *Funny Girl* and, with Stephen Sondheim, "Everything's Coming Up Roses," and, of course, "Rose's Turn," the eleven o'clock number as well as a Showstopper from his masterpiece *Gypsy*; Stephen Sondheim's "I'm Still Here," "Broadway Baby," "Who's That Woman?" "The Right Girl,"and "The Story of Lucy and Jessie"—all from *Follies*—and the same composer's "You Could Drive a Person Crazy," "Side By Side By Side," and "What Would We Do Without You?" from *Company*; Andrew Lloyd Webber's "Buenos Aires" from *Evita*.

There are mock Showstoppers that stop a show by virtue of their performance and/or staging of the song. These songs may bring a house down, but separated from the performer and/or the production values, the song will lose what was not inherent—for example: the songs of Irving Berlin, the Gershwins and Jerome Kern when they were sung and danced by Fred Astaire and Ginger Rogers. On the stage, Gwen Verdon worked her magic on "A Little Brains, A Little Talent" and "Whatever Lola Wants" in Richard Adler and Jerry Ross's *Damn Yankees* and in Cy Coleman and Dorothy Fields's *Sweet Charity*: "I'm a Brass Band" and "If My Friends Could See Me Now."* The loss of the performer in these Showstoppers can be expected not to kill the songs but to cut them down to size. Whoever sings and dances Jule Styne's "All I Need Is the Girl" in a production of *Gypsy* inherits a great show tune and Jerome Robbins's breathtaking staging. The combination of the two is a guaranteed Showstopper, but out of context and deprived of the choreography, it retains its excellence but the Swinging Ballad or the Up-Tempo category (depending on the speed of the delivery) more correctly defines it.

Finally, there are songs that stop shows by virtue of the production values superimposed on them or by the canny construction of the arrangements. The addition of a Roxy Rideout can be expected to entice an audience into overreaction; shorn of the Rideout, the song would have passed unnoticed.** In

---

* The model song for Category 8, Up-Tempo.
** See Introduction, pages 15–16, on Rideouts.

these instances the "build" is not organic to the songs but to their outward appearance on the stage and/or to the mechanical aid delivered by the orchestrator and state-of-the-art sound amplification. Contemporary stars in concert performances rely on these effects. The point is, when a song is performed on a stage or in an "act" with nothing going for it but the naked song and its clothed singer, it may be betrayed or revealed as something less than it appeared to be—a Showstopper—when it was clever packaging coupled with a brilliant performance or just plain feathers that created the fuss.

THE SONG

As befits their hold on the title, I have chosen John Kander and Fred Ebb's "How Lucky Can You Get?" from their score for the film of *Funny Lady*. On screen, Barbra Streisand sings it in the simplest possible performance of the song. Had she sung it in the theater in the same manner, it would still rightfully belong in this category, which implies that the song, on film or onstage, calls for no added pizzazz to corroborate its showstopping status. What it does require is a voice and the performing skill to play and project the Janus-faced lyric.

Built on one four-bar phrase that jumps a fourth to reiterate the theme over and over again in partnership with climbing key changes (therein lies its excitement), the insistent melody adds a fervor that supports the dissembling lyric. The tune comes packaged with Kander and Ebb's fondness for a repeating Vamp, this time a variant "doo break" scored to be sung on meaningless syllables that establishes, from the top, the song's ragtime tempo. There is an eight-bar Interlude during which the lyric reverses focus and becomes internalized, but the main theme (with a slight variation) returns in its original key accompanied by an extended, full-throated Rideout. Everything about "How Lucky Can You Get?" is crafty. The performance must be outwardly straightforward but internally dense. The tension created by these oppositional poles creates the combustive energy that makes this showstopping song, when it is well performed, a Showstopper.

THE DIALOGUE

SK is a singer. Everything about her voice and its "sound" advertises this. She claims to have been born singing; instead of a squall announcing her first breath it was an open, resonated tone. The Class and I believe her. Further claims: SK has never had or felt the need of a singing lesson; she just sings and achieves instinctively what others work for years to accomplish. Her voice is rich, the bottom range full and rounded, the middle range moves up to a C sharp and defies nature by staying within a chest resonance. Above that, and with no discernible break, she "mixes" head and chest and on a clear day, soars up to an F natural.*

SK is handsome in that use of the word that attempts to fill the space between beauty and the absence of it. Because the Class is concerned, at the very least, with singing on stage, she is the target of blatant envy on the part of those actors who are struggling to master an art that is forever doomed to lie a hairbreadth beyond their grasp. For DC, she is a rare treat; he can assign anything within those margins allowed her by the unyielding laws of the casting call.

DC

Did you know this song?

SK

Of it. I'd heard it. I saw the film and I'm a Streisand fan.

DC

You're not going to let that get to you, are you?

SK

Once it might've. But I think I'm free of that now. This Class has

---

* The descriptive words "chest" and "head" that, for most of us, differentiate the range and sound of the "belt" singer from the "head" range of the "legit" soprano are considered misnomers by those in the know. I use them only because they conjure up, on the instant, the identity of each group.

helped me a lot to understand that a song may be sung by anyone provided she can sing it. Come to think of it, no law stops you from trying even if you can't. No, Miss Streisand has her innings and I plan to have mine.

DC

Why don't you sing through it. Phrase it as you feel it should be phrased and then we can talk about it after we've heard it.
    (SK *sings the "doo-break" at the top of the song, but before it ends,* DC *stops her.*)
You don't need those eight bars as they appear in the published copy. Cut the last four and sing the first four bars that don't have any lyric following the "ba-do-di-o-di-o-di-o-di-o-do" break. Sing the phrase twice, as written, and move right into " . . . Satin on my shoulder."

SK

That's a break for me. I was wondering how the devil I'd fill eight bars of that. There must've been a voice-over group singing those last four bars. They sounded like a vocal arrangement when I read it.

DC

I don't recall the scene specifically but that's probably so. But let's move on.
    (*She sings the song straight through.* * *Her voice is an ideal match for the demands of the song. An added talent for "going" with the period musical joke is also evident.*)
Beautiful. The song appears to have been published as it was sung in the film. Those long pockets of "Air" after the first Chorus and the bluesy reprise of the first eight bars before the start of the Interlude beginning with " . . . Hey there, gorgeous . . . " aren't required here. Your cuts are exactly right. Very good work indeed.

---

* The reader may follow the lead and lyric sheets on pages 229-231 and 232. They are the finished version SK will sing and not the song as published.

SK

That one cut had me a little worried. Without it I thought maybe the E flat key for the " . . . Hey there, gorgeous . . . " section might be throwing me too high. How did the F natural sound on " . . . *Big* success" and " . . . *Just luck*y, I guess . . . "?

DC
(*After the catcalls from the Class have subsided.*)

If you've a top F as good as that, flaunt it. Can you rely on it?

SK

I think so. Certainly when I'm a little nervous. Everything seems to be too low then.

DC

Do you want to quit here for today or would you like to show us a first performance?

SK

Why not? If I postpone it it's only going to be more of the same. I mean, wondering if what I'm planning is working out all right.
(*She crosses to Center.* SK, *like all natural-born singers, does not find Center a distressing place, nor has she ever known the problem of the actor-singer who has to invent somewhere, a country to go to, in order to sing. She is there already. After cuing in the pianist,* SK *focuses Center midway through the Vamp, looks at the audience left and right of her as the "doo-break" begins. Throughout the break there is an icy bleakness on her as she spots, generally, and continues playing to the house into the Chorus: "Satin on my shoulder and a smile on my lips." The coldness remains as she spots easily to Center for the first title: " . . . How lucky can you get?"*)

DC

Very good work for a first time. We don't have to deal with the singing of the song. I knew from the music reading there'd be no problem there. Let's jump into the performance and talk about what you're playing and doing.

SK

That "doo-break" at the top has me crazy. What do you do with all those "ba-do-di-o's"?

DC

Well, to begin with, they're not "ba-do-di-o's" because if all they are are "ba-do-di-o's" they sure as the devil will drive you crazy. We spoke about that when FR had those "woh, woh, woh's" in "Baby, Baby, Baby." (*To* SK *and the Class*) Granted that "doo breaks," humming, and la-dee-da's are nonsense syllables, they make their own kind of sense when an attitude justifies singing them. It is the attitude that gives them their comprehensibility if not, as yet, their language. (*To* SK) After the break, you elected to play icy cold, but I'm afraid that by doing so you painted yourself into a corner with nowhere to go and the "ba-do-di-o's" to prove it. We're left with no one to root for—the man who done her wrong or the ungrateful lady. But did he do her wrong? Every line in the lyric attests to his good and giving nature.

SK

Yes, but . . .

DC

I know. But the lyric is the truth. Remember, whatever you choose to sing, you *sing it because it is the truth*. We may lie when we speak, but when we sing we're in a state of soliloquy and then we may be said to be speaking/singing to the gods. No need anymore to lie. We're free, at last, to tell the truth. And the truth is that the man gave you wealth, smiles (at least on your lips), clothes, parties, a social set in which to move, charge accounts, a chauffeured car, baronial weekends, someone you love who adores you, and, at the end, an admission that you've never met a man—which would include him—who would choose to leave you. Hey, now! How lucky can you get!?

SK

But isn't the whole song putting up a front? That all of that means nothing because she doesn't care a damn for him?

DC

Where does it say that? I must've missed it.

SK
(She scans her music, searching through the lyric.)

Uh . . . well, I mean it's obvious.

DC

Not from the lyric.

SK

How about " . . . You can spare me the blues. I don't sing in that key"?

DC

As I recall, that line occurs in the very last eight bars after a full Chorus has been sung plus an Interlude and the first two bars of the last eight. If you proceed, staying always in the present (where all songs are sung), the line isn't even on or in your mind at the top of the song. The extraordinary journey this lyric affords you is that after this paradisiacal listing of what conspicuous consumption and heaven consist of, suddenly you reveal that you don't allow yourself the luxury of indulging in the "blues." But you don't want to get to it until it occurs to you, at that moment in the script, to speak about it. Only then, when you're impelled to tell them that paradise has mountains and valleys . . .

SK
(*Interrupting*)

I see. I'm never any wiser than they are. I'm telling everyone the truth until it's more than I can stomach—until I manage to get out the real truth that heaven is a hard place to live in when you don't give a damn for the guy who took you there.

DC

Perfectly put. But this is too difficult to try for today. I think you should take it home and start again to work on it. (*To the Class*) Are there any questions?

CLASS

Is this something of a rarity? I mean we usually sing songs that come right out with it. This lyric goes out of its way to fool us, to beat around the bush.

DC

Not that rare. Many of the Weill-Brecht songs in *The Threepenny Opera*—I'm thinking in particular of the lovely tango Jenny and Macheath sing, all dripping with honey but hiding their venal relationship. And there's Sondheim and Rodgers's "Here We Are Again" from *Do I Hear a Waltz?*, in which the singer appears to be singing to another person and only at the very end do we learn we've been fooled: She's singing to herself. And there are many more that don't come readily to mind.

SK

It presents a kind of neat problem. I mean saying one thing and meaning another.

DC

But you're not doing that. Not consciously. For most of the song you're saying and meaning the truth, and the truth is that you have everything and you consider yourself lucky that you have us there to tell it to. When you're shifting gears into the last "8," yes, another truth pushes its way to the surface, but even then it's only an oblique reference you permit yourself. What is it you say? Ah, yes " . . . You can spare me the blues, I don't sing in that key." But then, you dissemble the pain of the confession and move quickly into self-advertisement—namely, " . . . And if there's a man who'd leave me, I'm delighted to say, I haven't run into him yet." From there on you're *gee*-ing and *wow*-ing and *whee*-ing about how lucky you are, yet again.

SK

I see what you mean. I think I made the usual mistake—being smarter than the person singing the song.

DC

But you *are* the person singing the song.

SK

I know. But that's my problem. I like to sing so much that, before I came here, all I ever did was sing the song and get a bang out of singing it well. Now I've learned there's more to it than that. I have to know what I'm singing about. This time I think I've gone too far the other way.

DC

I see. But there is a difference. You never sang the song before you came here. You sang its melody. And by the way, there's nothing wrong with that when you sing as well as you do. But the real joy— the art of singing—is the art of creating a life out of which a song is born. I like to call it the "inevitability factor" that lies in wait at the end of a Vamp. Inevitable, that is, that at the instant when you start to sing, the death of the Vamp invokes the birth of the song.

SK

But didn't I do that?

DC

In a partial way, you did. You got away from the melody and looked at the lyric and said to yourself, "Ah-ha, this lady's got all this great stuff in her life and underneath she's really miserable." But just as the actor may not take sides in the play, the performer may not take sides when he sings his songs. We tell it how it is. Judgments are made by the audience. If you join them, you've joined the *reactors* to the script. *You are its teller.*

SK

So what I did was to put my own moral judgments on the lady. I can see why I had no place to go. I was stuck with it from the start all the way to the end. I knew something was wrong. I couldn't get out of that one rut. Even when I wanted to move, I didn't know what to do because, instead of thinking about what I meant, I was only thinking about what a bastard he was. And that had absolutely nothing to do with what I was singing. Oh, well, back to the drawing board. (*She exits but a week later* SK *is back on stage.*)

DC

How did it go? Was it easier for you to find your performance this time?

SK

That remains to be seen. Last week was very helpful. I think I was working harder than I needed to. And I like letting a little bit of a bigger truth slip in when I ride into that last eight. It's like playing the trump card.

DC

Enough. As I always say, I'd rather see and hear it than hear about it. (*She sings through the song.* DC *allows her to finish without interruption. The Class applauds the work.*)
Well, that was more like it. How did you feel?

SK

A lot easier. Things felt like they were flowing. Did they look it?

DC

All in all, yes. But can we go through it quickly and straighten out the timing of some of the "business"? To begin with, I liked the playful reading of the "doo-break," but why do you wait right up until the downbeat of " . . . Satin" and then race to cross your arms over your chest and touch your shoulders? It looks rushed and even a little stagey. Stay at zero for the first two bars of the Vamp, then move your hands out and up to that position all through the repeat of the "doo-break." You'll arrive early enough to set the line. Anyway, the move isn't that important. You're singing " . . . Satin on my shoulders," so really all you're doing is no more than a charade. Timing the move will give it its style. What's important is how she feels about the dress. Try it.
(SK *nods the pianist in and sings through the "doo-break" and into and through the first line of the Chorus. After the second try she has it. This time even her arms leave her shoulders in the middle of the line to frame " . . . and a smile on my lips.")*
Fine. Do you see now how late you were?

SK

Oh, yes. You can feel it when it's pointed out to you. You really do have to get ahead of yourself and not be swept up by the fun of just singing the song. Dammit, it's work.

DC

Once the coordination begins to work for you, the muscles of your mind take over and it becomes a kind of second nature. BL and I talked about this during his performance of "Wait Till You See Her." And it's worth remembering that the work becomes less and less a conscious effort. Like anything, the longer you do it the more it becomes habitual and, in the end, you'll even have fun "just singing the song." But you're well on your way. Let's get back to the performance and that dance step you're doing on " . . . Ev'ry night a party where the fun never ends." I liked it, but I think it's a better idea to start it on the repeat of the title two bars sooner. We've heard the title—it's only a fill line from here on. The same goes for the promenade to the Left at the end of the first Chorus. Don't wait. Spot Left and start your stroll as you sing " . . . Wow, how lucky can you get?" By the time you reach Left stage you'll have sung the title, walked through the "Air" fill, and be ready for " . . . Wrap it up and charge it," etc. By the way, you won't get a hand for walking. You'll need energy, a sense of purpose, and some arm activity to make that promenade work for you. And to keep the eye of the audience off your feet.

SK
(*Taking notes*)

Not so fast! (*She scribbles quickly.*) Okay. There must be more.

DC

Just a few other suggestions. Instead of telling us about giving the chauffeur that raise, why not get the idea or, better yet, just at the last moment remember you forgot to tell him. Try doing it coyly or maybe reprise the pixie who sang the "doo-break" in the Vamp. Going on, sometimes you stay too long preening on the "wardrobe" line. And another place you might think of going for a different color would be on " . . . Makin' merry music with the one that I love, We're a perfect duet"—perhaps you could take a moment to recall the scent of the perfume you wear at night. I mean, don't think it's dancing you're talking about.

SK

Yes! Yes! That's good! I like anything that gets me away from raving about how great my life is.

DC

But that's the point. When it's all you're thinking about, all we get is a commentary. There's nothing active going for you. What you need is a *subjective* subtext to balance the *objective* lyric you're singing. We *hear* about your life—especially when you sing it so well. What we have to *see* is how all that luxury affects you. Without that, the song is nothing but a news report you could sing to us, unseen, from the wings.* For now, work on this at home. Especially the timing of what you're doing. When you become more and more alert, you'll discover an added bonus: richer, more eloquent, and, better still, more personal body language. When I see you next, we can clean up the Interlude and the Rideout.

SK

I forgot my tape machine and now I'll have to decipher these scribbles when I get home. But I do think this is going to be a great song for me when I finally get it all set.

DC

Agreed. The mechanics are like learning how to drive. At first you think, "I'll never coordinate all the things I have to remember." Then suddenly you're doing them with no strain whatever, and with time left over to chat with someone in the car. It's always the same solution to the same problem—knowing what you're *going* to say rather than playing what you *hear* yourself saying.

SK

I understand. I'll be back.

Again, it is a week later, but before SK begins her final "fix," DC addresses the Class.

---

* See *On Singing Onstage*, pages 8–9 on subjective and objective lyrics.

DC

I recalled two other songs that say one thing but speak another script that hides behind and between the lines. Let's see . . . there's a wonderful song of Kander and Ebb's that I recommend to the women as well as to the men. It's called "I Don't Remember You" from their score for *The Happy Time*—a lovely melody that embellishes a two-faced lyric. Also, by Burton Lane and E. Y. Harburg, a tune called "There's a Great Day Coming Mañana" from *Hold on to Your Hats*. It's a sly pie-in-the-sky listing of what lies ahead when and if tomorrow ever comes. When other songs occur to me I'll pass them on, but for now, let's get back to our lucky lady. (*To* SK) How're we doing?

SK

Well . . . better, I think.

DC

As I recall, we were going to pack it away today after we shaped the "Hey there, gorgeous" section, the last "8" and froze the Rideout. Am I right?

SK

Yes. First, though, can we clear up when and where I do that promenade walk?

DC

You were at stage Left in time for the top of the second Chorus. I'd stay there all the way through until the end of the second "8" after the chauffeur gets his raise—including the title.* For one thing, a lateral walk seems ill-taken when you get there and then come right back. Was the trip necessary? I don't mean that you've decided to surrender your preferred home in Center, only that it should look like the theater on the Left of you drew you to them to

* Again, this section is more easily understood if the reader keeps the lead and/or lyric sheet in front of him.

add importance to the tale. Usually, we'd elect to come home*
while you were singing the repeat title, but I like the idea of staying
put and luxuriating in how lucky you are to have that young
chauffeur around. Use the title, then, as a subjective comment on
the services he renders.

SK

Oh, I like that.

DC

But as soon as " . . . get" is on your lips, spot Center and saunter
back for "Weekends in the country," etc. Stay Center for the next
line—I think it's the one about your wardrobe choking Mrs. Astor's
pet horse. Right?

SK

But why not move on to the Right for that line?

DC

For one, it's what I was talking about a moment ago. You just
arrived at Center. It looks hurried from out front if you leave that
soon. Also, have you kept the idea of inhaling the scent of
remembered perfume just before " . . . Makin' merry music . . . "?

SK

Yes. I liked that bit.

DC

Well, then, you'd never have enough time to do the "business" if
you were moving to the Right in the "Air" just before you began
that line. You only have a dotted quarter rest. Better to stay where
you are. There you have all of " . . . Gee, how lucky can you,

* See Introduction, page 13.

Whee, how lucky can you, Wow, how lucky can you get?" to spot Right and sachet over to that side of the stage.

SK

How far should I go on that promenade?

DC

I always think one or two steps is all that's needed. For one thing, you don't want to give up the strength you command when you stand in Center, so when you do move away, in the back of your mind you're always thinking, "When can I get back?" Also, a couple of steps shows you can "work" the stage. Remember, every time you move to the Left or Right on the stage—or in a room—you're thinning out the power you'd have had if you'd remained in Center. When you're standing at Left or Right more than half the audience is not in your line of sight. A good idea, when you're on either lateral side, is to play straight in front of you (small "c" center) or to that part of the theater or the room that doesn't have you. So, when you're standing on the Right, either "c" and/or to the Left. And if you're on the Left side, play to "c" and/or spot to the Right. Is all this clear? If not, I'll hop up and show you what I mean.

SK

I think I've got it. Sit. Be comfortable.

DC

Thank you. Let's get back, then. You're stage Right at the end of the second Chorus, ready for the return cross back to Center for the " . . . Hey there, gorgeous" section. Am I right?

SK

Yes. Center's where I do the mirror "business" and talk to my image. It feels good. I mean, I think you'll like it.

DC

I know I will. But what I wanted to say is, don't return to Center to *put* the mirror there. The mirror *is* there. You know it's there. It's *your* mirror. If you remember, we talked about the need to know exactly where you are when the geography of the song is significant. I think it came up when RW was working on "If My Friends Could See Me Now." *Where* the mirror is, then, is *why* you walk back from Right to Center. You want to check out the way you look and, more important, have a chat with yourself. Can we pick it up from the end of the first Chorus?

(DC *tells the pianist to play a free bar and then play the two-bar fill before* " . . . Hey there . . . " SK *spots Center and moves back from stage Right to sing the Interlude.*)

Very good. Try it again. It's a little jerky. And, oh, yes, would you reverse the "business" you're doing? Don't fix your hair on the last line: " . . . Just lucky, I guess." Your hands are way too high to get them down in the "Air" before " . . . Life's a bed of roses," etc. If I remember correctly, it was the first of a series of moves. I liked them. Just reverse the order: Deal with your hair first, then the neckline of your dress, and end the "business" down at your hips. In that way your arms'll be down in the neighborhood they need to be in for the last "8."

SK

You know, it felt odd when I was doing it. Having to get them down so fast, I mean. When do we get to know these things for ourselves?

DC

Stanislavski has said, " . . . first do your work correctly and only later will you be able to render it more beautiful or lustrous." In the beginning, *correctly* means that you must put some of your thinking onto what you're doing. How it feels. Is it true? Does it work—and from my own point of view, is style served? Only when all of that is part of your accumulated knowledge will you be able to trust that it is beautiful, because it's been created by you to achieve maximum effect with a minimum amount of visible labor.

SK

I can't wait.

DC

One last thing. Leave the mirror while you're still singing the last word of the Interlude, " . . . Just lucky, I *guess.*" You're waiting too long before you move on. Spot to Left or Right for " . . . Life's a bed of roses squirtin' perfume on me," then to the opposite Lateral for " . . . You can spare me the blues. I don't sing in that key!" And, finally, to the house, generally, for the next two lines before the Rideout begins on "Gee! Whee! Wow! How lucky can you get!"

SK

That's pretty much what I planned. May I try that whole section? (*To the pianist*) Take it from the same place before the Interlude.
    (*He plays the "fill" and* SK *crosses from Right to Center to perform the mirror soliloquy. The execution is seamless. The last "8" goes as* DC *suggested. When the Rideout has sung itself out, the Class applauds.*)

DC

First-rate work! And it'll only get better the more you work it. Don't forget, you're still *doing* it on a conscious level, but when it's your own—when you *are* it—the performance will only become more and more, well . . . lustrous. One thing about the Rideout. This is a song whose very structure begs for a "hand." And you'll get it every time. Every time save one. You have to know, in advance, that you won't get it at an audition. It will seem like a mighty silence when that last note has sung itself out. Don't run scared. Start an inner descent as you hold the last note so you're not way up in the atmosphere at the very end with nowhere to go but a quick fall. Were there a "hand," you'd ride it to get out of the song, but as I've said elsewhere, they just don't behave that way when you're job seeking. So don't be caught asking for one. Come out of it as gracefully as you can: cooling, cooling, cooling as you hold that last note, and when it's sung itself out, all you'll have to do is step back into the real world with nothing of the song left on you. That way you'll forestall any discomfort and the ball will be in their court. You've done wonderful work for yourself and for the Class. That applause was real.

SK

I know. I felt it. Thanks, kids.

DC

What did Ira Gershwin write? Ah, yes—" . . . Applause, Applause! Vociferous applause from orchestra to gallery could mean a raise in salary. The manager, he audits our plaudits!"

SK

From Mr. G's mouth to the ear of God!

"Mexican Hayride"

Girls

Words and Music by Cole Porter

old gyp - sy proph - e - sied when I was three_____ and
what did she tell_____ this lit - tle lamb?_____ That,
one day, a la - dy kil - ler I would be_____ and
now, well, I cer - tain - ly am._____ Yes,
now when I dash a - long the bou - le - vard_____ in
top hat, white tie and glove_____ I'm
al - ways es - cort - ed by a bod - y guard_____ con -

254

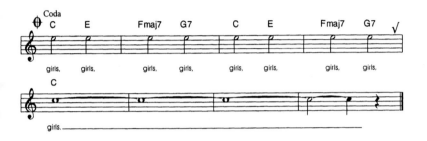

"Girls"

VERSE:
An old gypsy prophesied when I was three
And what did she tell this little lamb (✓)
That one day a lady-killer I would be
And now (,) well I certainly am (✓)
Yes now when I dash along the boulevard
In top hat, white tie and glove (✓)
I'm always escorted by a bodyguard
Consisting entirely of ⌣

CHORUS:
⌣ Girls (✓) to the right of me
Girls (✓) to the left of me
Girls in front of me, girls behind (✓)
Girls all over me (,)
I don't mind ⌣
⌣ Oh (✓) what a rogue am I
So much in vogue am I (✓)
Simply smothered in kisses and curls
By the girls, girls, girls, girls, girls
Girls (✓) miles and miles of them
Girls (✓) piles and piles of them
Girls for playthings and girls for show (✓)
Girls on top of me, girls below ⌣
⌣ Hey (✓) life's a fantasy
Say (,) I'm the man t' see
If you're looking to have a few whirls (✓)
With the girls, girls, girls, girls,
Girls, girls, girls, girls (✓) girls (✓)

"Girls" from *Mexican Hayride*, music and lyrics by Cole Porter. Copyright © 1944 by Chappell & Co., Inc. Copyright renewed, Assigned to John F. Wharton, Trustee of the Cole Porter Musical & Literary Property Trusts. International Copyright Secured. All Rights Reserved, Chappell & Co., Inc. Publisher. Used by permission.

12

Catchall

The Catchall category attempts to deal with loose ends: Narrative, Comedy and Dance songs. Each of these can find a home in any one of the preceding groups, but distinguishing characteristics suggest their right to a home of their own. What is important to remember is that if all songs are meant to be sung, all songs are not meant to be sung by everyone. This category consists of songs that come to life only when they are performed by those with the special skills required to give them life.

Narrative Songs

I have written about the indiscriminate use of the Narrative song.* To reprise: It should be taken up tenderly. Very few performers with whom I have worked are blessed with the gift for making a story interesting. The Narrative song is nothing more than that—a story set to music. Since this category has the distinction of being vocal music that is far better seen than heard, stunning vocal ability is not an imperative, nor is interpretive skill, if by the latter one implies a gift for ferreting out the psychological underpinning that lurks beneath the surface of a text. But if interpretation describes that special talent for sheer storytelling—

* See *On Singing Onstage*, pages 3-17.

for being able to *do* the tale as well as *tell* it—Narrative songs present the ideal window in which to advertise that know-how. For those who have seen the late Danny Kaye "work" the Frank Loesser score for *Hans Christian Andersen** and the songs of his wife, Sylvia Fine, nothing further need be said. Performers who do not possess this special expertise are advised to stay away. Narrative songs are ruthless exposers of inadequacy.

I would not care to guess whether the number of those who can write them or, more germane to this volume, can perform them has diminished the need for them, but it is a fact that they are virtually extinct in the musical theater. The French have always been partial to them. Jacques Brel's "Au Suivant" and "Jef"; Charles Aznavour's "Le Cabotin"; Michel Emer's "L'Accordioniste," and Marguerite Monnot's "Les Blouses Blanches" (both sung by Piaf) are all classics. In England, Noel Coward wrote and sang them by the score; "Bar on the Piccola Marina" and "Alice Is at It Again" come to mind. Sadly, although these artists and their songs are available on recordings, the loss of their visual power robs them of their raison d'etre. Country-Western, in America, favors the "Ballad of . . ." and Narrative songs maintain a kind of currency in the contemporary music marketplace—for example, Randy Newman's "Davy, the Fat Boy," the late Harry Chapin's "Taxi," Jerry Jeff Walker's "Mr. Bojangles," and Jimmy Webb's "MacArthur Park." In each case these songs recall the artists who sang and sing them—substantiation for the assertion that in or out of the musical theater: If you can't do them, don't sing them.

Theater songs representative of the category include:

> Frank Loesser: "Thumbelina," "The Ugly Duckling," "Inchworm," and "The King's New Clothes" from *Hans Christian Andersen*. Stephen Sondheim: "Pretty Little Picture" from *A Funny Thing Happened on the Way to the Forum*, "On the Steps of the Palace" from *Into the Woods*, and "The Story of Lucy and Jessie" from *Follies*. Wright and Forrest: "The Olive Tree" and "Gesticulate" from *Kismet*. The Gershwins: "The Babbitt and the Bromide" (also at home in the Patter Song category) from *Funny Face*, "Mischa, Jascha, Toscha, Sascha," "The Jolly Tar and the Milkmaid" from the film *A*

---

* The film is on videocassette.

Damsel in Distress. Kurt Weill: "The Saga of Jenny" and "The Princess of Pure Delight" from *Lady in the Dark*. Noel Coward: "Uncle Harry" and "Chase Me Charlie." Harold Arlen: "Tess's Torch Song." Jerry Bock: "Tango Tragique" and "A Trip to the Library" from *She Loves Me*. Cole Porter: "Kate the Great" from *Anything Goes*, "Katie Went to Haiti" from *Dubarry Was A Lady*, "The Tale of the Oyster" from *Fifty Million Frenchmen* and "Mister and Missus Fitch" from *The Gay Divorce*. Richard Rodgers: "Johnny One Note" from *Babes in Arms* and "She Could Shake the Maracas" from *Too Many Girls*. Burton Lane: "On the S.S. Bernard Cohn" from *On a Clear Day You Can See Forever*. Harvey Schmidt: "Melisande" from *110 in the Shade*.

A case may be made for a subdivision of the Narrative song—namely, the Biography song. The performer of a Narrative lyric shuttles between subjective and objective readings predicated on his need to *be* the Narrator and *play* the narrative. The Biography lyric remains subjective for obvious reasons: The performer relates the facts of his life rather than a tale he tells. In this group:

The "I am . . ." songs of Gilbert and Sullivan. Frederick Loewe: "C'est Moi" from *Camelot*. Hugh Martin: "I'm the First Girl" from *Look, Ma, I'm Dancin'*. Leonard Bernstein: "I Can Cook Too" from *On the Town*. Richard Rodgers: "Elizabeth the Queen" ("I'm Elizabeth the Virgin Queen, Don't Laugh") from *The Garrick Gaities*. Cole Porter: "Dainty Quainty Me" from *Seven Lively Arts*. Cy Coleman: "The Buddy System" from *City of Angels*. David Shire: "Miss Byrd" and "Life Story" from *Closer Than Ever*.

Comedy Songs

As commonplace as "Thank you, we'll call you" in the mechanical dialogue of an audition is "Have you got a funny song?"* The problem here is twofold:

1. There are no published funny songs that those who audition performers have not heard and heard again—and again. Even if the

---

* See *On Performing*, Question 6, pages 65-70.

lyric was the best of Ogden Nash in partnership with Neil Simon and Larry Gelbart, it would blunt after the hundredth hearing. Admittedly this is true for over-forty audiences and auditioners, but Bobby Short, Steve Ross, Michael Feinstein, and other cabaret artists sing and play show tunes in their original versions, and their success with younger listeners implies that, for them, a wheeze may not always indicate asthma.

2. The idea that a request for a comedy song will engender a comic performance is simplistic. It is absurd to suppose that, given a funny lyric, a performer will transmute into a comedian. The awful truth is that we are not all of us funny. I do not make a plea here for deep introspective self-analysis, but the beginner—as well as the more advanced artist—should try to maintain some degree of objectivity about what he can and cannot do. This objectivity is difficult to bring to bear. In my own experience, I cannot recall anyone willing to confess that he could not do a funny song—if only he had one. I exempt those who work the nightclub, cabaret, and late-night television circuits from this personal observation. Stiff competition in those venues inevitably separates the wheat from the chaff. At auditions in the musical theater it is not a funny song they want to hear but a comedic gift they are out to find. The true comic instinct can make funny anything from our national anthem to the Happy Birthday song if the singer has an amusing slant on how to do it.* This is not to sell short a first-rate piece of "special material," but there is just not that much of it around. Having said this, a list of suggested Comedy songs follows:

- Cole Porter: "Let's Do It," "It's De-Lovely," "Brush Up Your Shakespeare," "By the Mississinewah" (a duet), "Find Me a Primitive Man," "Friendship" (a duet), "The Great Indoors," "I Sleep Easier Now," "I've a Shooting Box in Scotland," "The Laziest Gal in Town," "Most Gentlemen Don't Like Love," "Nobody's Chasing Me," "The Physician," "My Cozy Little Corner in the Ritz," "Please Don't Monkey With Broadway," "They All Fall in Love," "Two Little Babes in the Wood,"

---

* As I have mentioned in *On Performing*, an example of this theory put to the test: "Sweet Georgia Brown" sung by Mel Brooks and Anne Bancroft in *To Be or Not To Be*—in Polish.

"Well, Did You Evah!" and "When I Was a Little Cuckoo."*

• Rodgers and Hart: "To Keep My Love Alive," "In the Flower Garden of My Heart," "That Terrific Rainbow," "Zip," "Everything I've Got," "Bewitched, Bothered, and Bewildered," "He and She," "What Can You Do With a Man?" and "Too Good for the Average Man."

• Ira with George Gershwin: "Aren't You Kind of Glad We Did?" "Blah, Blah, Blah," "Stiff Upper Lip," "By Strauss," "Could You Use Me?" and "Boy! What Love Has Done to Me!"

• Ira with Vernon Duke: "I Can't Get Started With You," "He Hasn't a Thing Except Me," and "Island in the West Indies."

• Vernon Duke with Sammy Cahn: "Good Little Girls."

• Burton Lane with Alan Lerner: "Wait Till We're Sixty-Five."

• Burton Lane with E. Y. Harburg: "When the Idle Poor Become the Idle Rich," "The Begat," and "When I'm Not Near the Girl I Love."

• E. Y. Harburg with Harold Arlen: "Buds Won't Bud," "If I Only Had a (Brain) a (Heart) the (Nerve)," "Let's Take a Walk Around the Block," "Push the Button," "Napoleon," and "I Don't Think I'll End It All Today."

• Cy Coleman with Carolyn Leigh: "Real Live Girl," "Dimples," and "Le Grand Boom-Boom."

• Cy Coleman with Dorothy Fields: "Big Spender," "Welcome to Holiday Inn," and "I'm a Brass Band."

• Jerry Herman: "Bosom Buddies," "Gooch's Song," and "The Man in the Moon."

• Noel Coward: "Chase Me Charlie," "Mrs.Worthington," "Mad Dogs and Englishmen," "The Stately Homes of England," "Nina," "That Is the End of the News," "Three White Feathers," "I've Been to a Marvelous Party," and "Why Do the Wrong People Travel?"**

• Kander and Ebb: "Home," "If You Could See Her (The

* It is suggested that in the case of many of Cole Porter's and Lorenz Hart's lyrics, reference to Robert Kimball's *The Complete Lyrics of Cole Porter* and *The Complete Lyrics of Lorenz Hart* may unearth third and fourth Choruses whose lyrics are not as well known as those in the published copies of their songs.
** If Narrative songs are not for everyone to sing and Comedy songs are ill-advised material for the humorless, Noel Coward's songs carry the extra burden of their Mayfair idiom.

Gorilla Song)," "Class," and "The Grass Is Always Greener."

• Leonard Bernstein with Comden and Green: "One Hundred Easy Ways to Lose a Man," "Wrong Note Rag," and "Come Up to My Place."

• Leonard Bernstein with Stephen Sondheim: "America," "Gee, Officer Krupke!" (not a solo).

• Stephen Sondheim with Richard Rodgers: "What Do We Do? We Fly."

• Stephen Sondheim on his own: "Come Play Wiz Me," "Everybody Ought to Have Maid" (not a solo, but with some lyric jockeying it may be sung as one), "Comedy Tonight," "That Dirty Old Man," "You Could Drive a Person Crazy," "Buddy's Blues," and "Agony."

• Stephen Sondheim with Jule Styne: "Mister Goldstone, I Love You," "If Momma Was Married," and "You Gotta Have a Gimmick."

• Jule Styne with Bob Merrill: "His Love Makes Me Beautiful" and "Sadie, Sadie"

And. . . .

One final word of caution: The late actor Edmund Gwenn was noted for his work in serious as well as comic roles. It is reported that, on his death bed, when he was asked what it was like, he replied, "Dying is easy, comedy is hard."

Dance Songs

Self-explanatory: first the song is sung and then danced or at least the performer indicates in eight, sixteen, or thirty-two bars that what he has just sung about can be corroborated. Even more than the ability to sing, act, tell a tale, and/or be amusing, dancing cannot be feigned. An afterthought: The word "dance" in the title of a song does not necessarily mean it is denied the nondancer. There are many theater and film songs about dancing that do not demand a demonstration. In these instances, the burden of the lyric will determine whether the vocal should be or need not be accompanied by a dance. The songs that follow sing, dance, and speak for themselves:

Jerome Kern: "Pick Yourself Up," "Never Gonna Dance," and

"I Won't Dance." Irving Berlin: "Top Hat, White Tie and Tails," "A Couple of Swells," "My Walking Stick," "Stepping Out With My Baby," "Something to Dance About," and "You're Easy to Dance With." Cole Porter: "Rap Tap On Wood," "A Little Rumba Numba," "Be a Clown," "Can-Can," "Too Darn Hot," and "Now You Has Jazz." Jerry Herman: "Tap Your Troubles Away." Harry Warren: "My One and Only Highland Fling," "Shoes With Wings On," and "I Wanna Be a Dancin' Man." Jule Styne: "Papa, Won't You Dance With Me?" and "All I Need Is the Girl." Morgan Lewis and Nancy Hamilton: "The Old Soft Shoe." Billy Goldenberg: "I Love to Dance (Like They Used to Dance)."

There are songs in which precedent suggests a display of dancing along with a vocal performance because they are associated with dancers who introduced them on the stage or on film. On second reading and separated from the memory of their signature performance, they may not require it. Again, the lyric can be trusted to grant or withhold permission.

THE SONG

I have chosen Cole Porter's "Girls" although it is not, in the classic sense, a dance number. Nowhere in the lyric is there an allusion to dancing, and since it could be considered a hybrid cross between a Comedy and a Dance song, it may be sung by a dancer/singer or an actor who can move. It was introduced by the late Bobby Clark, a roustabout clown with painted-on eyeglasses who smoked a cigar that had a life of its own. He created his own "props" and, like W. C. Fields, worked with the skill of an acrobat. "Girls" is illustrative of Cole Porter's distinguishing mark: urbane wit and a marriage of the sacred to the profane. The song is from the musical *Mexican Hayride* in which Bobby Clark appeared with June Havoc. The score included "I Love You," "It Must Be Fun to Be You" (cut but still published) and one of his "shopping list" songs: "There Must Be Someone for Me."*

---

* Sometimes referred to as "laundry list" songs made famous by Mr. Porter's way with stacking up, line upon line, glittering lists to define: "You're the Top," "Let's Do It," "A Picture of Me Without You," "Please Don't Monkey With Broadway," "But in the Morning, No," "Fresh As a Daisy," "Farming," "Let's Not Talk About Love," "Be a Clown," "Cherry Pies Ought to Be You," and "Can-Can."

The Verse refers to a prophesying gypsy who gives out advice. It is a distinguishing Porter theme. The advice may come from "mother" or "grandmother"—it does so in many of his Verses—but it is Porter's voice we hear.* The Chorus (ABAB) is the stock thirty-two bars; the second half a carbon-copy reprise of the first sixteen bars. Another Porter trademark: there is not an excess syllable to clutter up the lyric.**

THE DIALOGUE

DC assigns the song to a dancer who can sing. This sentence, simple as it may appear, describes, if not a latter-day phenomenon, one that is unique to the last forty-odd years in the American musical theater. During the first four decades of this century choreographers were Dance Directors, choreography was billed as staging or routining, and tap dancing was its dance language. Dancers danced and singers sang, and the wall that separated them was never scaled. When they came together in Chorus ensembles they were listed in the Playbill as Dancing Girls, Dancing Boys, Singing Girls, and Singing Boys, and, until recently, they were known in the trade as "gypsies," a term that described their nomadic movement from one show to the next. The designation can be traced back to mid-Victorian stages in England. In Arthur Wing Pinero's play, *Trelawny of the Wells*, the character of Sir William Gower refers to Edmund Kean as "that splendid gypsy." The word, used as a pejorative, appears more than once: Actors are "a vagabond class" whose lesser talents are "gypsies" who are "garish" and "dissolute." In our time the word came to identify solely the Chorus dancer who, moving from show to show, was often hired and rehired by choreographers less out of nepotism than a need for dancers who were familiar with their particular style of dance routining. No longer a pejorative, the word is disappearing from the theater vocabulary due not only to the extraordinary expertise of present-day dancers but to the necessity

---

* See "Most Gentlemen Don't Like Love," "My Mother Would Love You," "Ace in the Hole." Lorenz Hart employed the same device in "A Little Birdie Told Me So," "The Heart Is Quicker Than the Eye," and in one of his earliest lyrics: "He Was the Last Rose of Summer."

** The printed lyric on page 256 includes a reprise not printed in the published copy of the song. It is not by Cole Porter and may not, under any circumstances, be performed in amateur or professional productions or appear in print anywhere but on the pages of this volume.

for dancers (and singers) to hold onto a job that pays their bills. Gone is the gypsies' blithe and carefree sense of the sheer pleasure of being in a musical. Like workers everywhere, they work to eat.

Since *Oklahoma!*—the Rodgers and Hammerstein watershed musical that, overnight, changed musical theater forever—the dancer and the singer, like the actor, have hyphenated. From that fateful third month of the year 1943 when *Oklahoma!* premiered, Dancing Girls and Dancing Boys were legitimatized: the more respectful "Singing Ensemble" and "Dancing Ensemble" or, simply, "Dancers" and "Singers" defined them in the theater program. The wall that separated them was first scaled by the few, and then, like all walls, was at last torn down. Today's Chorus singers are classically trained and dancers are ballet schooled as well as jazz and tap proficient. Both groups have homogenized into all-round artists. Illustrative of this phenomenon is the impressive percentage of understudies for leading roles ("white" contract performers) who are drawn from the ranks of Chorus singers and dancers ("pink" contract holders). One has only to recall *A Chorus Line* to understand the dramatic transformation of the actor, the singer, and the dancer into the actor/singer/dancer.

AC is one of this breed—a dancer who can sing anything from "I Got Rhythm" to "Bess, You Is My Woman Now" and more than competently play a scene from an August Wilson play. Beyond that, he possesses great personal charm, a quality that softens the self-conscious machismo of Mr. Porter's "Girls."

Before moving on to AC's music reading and subsequent performance, it should be noted that much of the work concerns movement either staged or danced. Description can be a tedious business.

DC

Well, there shouldn't be any problem with this number. All you have to do is be brilliant.

AC

That's how I saw it. I said to myself, "Now, man, there's no problem here. You take a cup of Kelly, add a smidge of Sammy D., a couple of grains of Gregory H., mix it all together, pour on some

Honi Coles and what have you got? Brilliant."

                                    DC

That's what I meant. No problem.

                                    AC

Before we get to B for brilliant, how about starting with A for ad-lib? I mean, the Verse.

                                    DC

Stick close to Porter's version and stay in tempo. Those syncopations in the Verse would lose their punch if you fooled with them.

                                    AC

So it's cut time straight through?

                                    DC

Yes. Like "Tonight at Eight," this song starts out in high and is hell-bent to stay there.

                                    AC

Talking about singing what's written, I thought I'd keep it in the printed key of C. I could go higher but there'll be a lot of moving around, so I don't see any point in knocking myself out.

                                    DC

Agreed. But first let's hear it. The Class doesn't know what we're talking about.
    (AC *sings through the Verse and two Choruses.* The Class*

---

* It is sung as printed in the accompanying lead sheet.

registers their pleasure in hearing a song so obviously cut to fit
the performer.)
Very good.

AC

You know, I think I've got myself a song here that has no subtext. It means what it says 'cause what it says is what it means. The man's lethal.

DC

I don't know about that. I've said it many times—there are no exceptions to the rule: Anything and everything we say has a supporting subtext. Right off the top of my head I could ask you a simple question that'd prove the point. Who was this gypsy who prophesied when you were only three years old that you'd be so irresistible to women?

AC

He's just kidding. There was no gypsy. He's making that up.

DC

Why?

AC

Whaddya mean, why?

DC

Why? Why doesn't he start the song with the line about walking down the boulevard dressed up to kill?

AC

I dunno. I guess he's trying to impress everybody with his . . . well . . . his sex appeal. He doesn't want to sound too full of himself so he dreams up that gypsy bit.

DC

Voilà, subtext. Words are smoke screens. If there wasn't that continual flow of jokes made at your own expense you'd turn off every woman in the audience. They dissemble whatever it is you're covering, whether or not what you say about your conquests is true.

AC

I see what you mean. In fact, that was worrying me when I first read through it. I thought, "How the devil am I going to sing this and keep the women on my side?"

DC

You were right to worry. And for that very reason. The point is that you can't sing this song straight.

AC

What I was leading up to was that I have an idea for staging it that now, when I come to think of it, has its own subtext.

DC

Good. But first let's clean up your music reading. I think the last line of the Verse should ritard in order to stop you from dashing headlong into the Chorus.

AC

You mean on " . . . consisting entirely of . . ."?

DC

Yes. Try it. I think you'll see what I mean.
        (AC *sings from " . . . Yes, now when I dash along the boule-*

vard," etc. *through to the end of the Verse.*)
It's a little messy. (*To* AC *and the pianist*) You can't stop tempo in the middle of a bar. It's impossible to accompany or conduct it. There'd be anarchy in the pit. It has to happen on the downbeat of the bar—in this case on the syllable " . . . sist." And get ready because the rhythm comes right back on the downbeat of the last word, " . . . of" followed by those three rim shots you played. (*To* AC) As soon as that ad-lib begins you're on your own. There'll be two fermatas or "holds" on " . . . tire . . . ly," just before " . . . of" to keep the Chorus at bay.* Then the three beats and from there on through to the end you're in tempo all the way.

AC

Let me try that. (*To the pianist*) Can we take it from the same place—" . . . Yes, now when I dash along . . . "?
   (*The pianist gives him two free bars and* AC *sings through the second half of the Verse.*)
How was that?

DC

Perfect for me. How was it for you?

AC

Fine. Now I don't have worry about him . . . (*Indicating the pianist with a nod*) . . . being with me for the downbeat of the Chorus.

PIANIST

And I don't have to worry about when he's going to get around to singing it!

DC

Both of you will always know you're together on that last bar of the Verse. Otherwise, there's nothing of great importance to be

---

* See *On Singing Onstage*, Analysis of a Lyric, pages 15-17.

discussed. Breath marks and glottals will fall into place pretty much where you'd expect them to. I should point out that the song works the more squarely you sing it. There's no room for any kind of jazzy, off beat phrasing. It's all going to be about what you do with it. (*To* AC *and the Class*) When a song is scored in a dance tempo—in this case, a two-step—that tempo has a tyrannical hold on the vocal. If it's a waltz, a waltz is what you must sing. You can't argue with it. Those three beats in each bar are as relentless as the coming of tomorrow. A dance song sung and a dance song danced have that in common: They're always performed in tempo. (*To* AC) Having said that, let's go on to a couple of places in the Chorus that you ought to watch out for.* To begin with, don't hold either the " . . . Oh" or the " . . . Hey!" at the top of the second half of each Chorus. In both cases elide it to the line before. In the first Chorus, don't breathe after " . . . what a rogue am I." Keep singing right through " . . . So much in vogue am I" and then breathe before " . . . Simply smothered," etc. It's the same in the second Chorus after " . . . Hey!" That breath'll get you through to " . . . whirls." Breathe deeply again because it's going to have to last you through all the " . . . Girls" up to but not including the last one. And, oh, yes, I'd like to add two more bars of " . . . Girls." What does that make? (*He counts on his fingers.*) Eight. Then get a good breath for the last " . . . girl"—you'll need it for the Rideout— which makes it nine. Nine girls all together!

AC

I should be so lucky!

DC

Do you want to go for it now?

AC

Nope. I'd rather go over it at home. I've got the tape and while I freeze what we covered today I can work out that idea I told you about.

---

* Again, the reader should refer to the lead sheet to better understand the following exchange.

A week has passed. AC is in costume. He wears a shirt and a tie, gray slacks, and a jacket.

AC

I dressed for this.
> (*The Class laughs. His usual mode of dress is California Melrose Avenue mod.*)

DC

Show business asks sacrifices of all of us.

AC

Ain't it the truth. But the song kind of calls for it. Something about "top hat, white tie and glove" got me a little nervous about showing up in stuff out of my own closet.

DC

You mean you borrowed that outfit?

AC

You think I got enough bread to buy period clothes? (*He looks down at himself.*) Hey! You know, I feel pretty good in this getup.

DC

I hate to be the bearer of bad news, but you look great. Before you jump in, may we see the Verse? Try and hold off on the Chorus.
> (AC *nods the pianist in, comes front and after checking into Center for the first word of the Verse, " . . . An," he plays the house on the opening line: " . . . An old gypsy prophesied when I was three." He spots Left to make more specific " . . . And what did she tell this lamb?" Then to the Right for " . . . That, one day, a lady killer I would be" and, finally, straight front for " . . . And now, well, I certainly am!" He returns to a general house focus for " . . . Yes, now when I dash along the*

boulevard in top hat, white tie and glove" and returns to Center for the last line " . . . I'm always escorted by a bodyguard consisting entirely of girls. ")

DC

First rate! Of course, there are always many options, but you've made neat and clean choices that aren't confusing. But we have to talk about the body language. I like the idea of using dance rather than realistic physical language in the second half of the Verse, especially since I imagine you'll be doing it from then on until the end of the song. But before that, in the first half of the Verse, you're still you. Quicken the speed of your thinking. You're slower than a snail. You wait too long to frame " . . . And what did she tell this little lamb?" The move arrives right on the downbeat. Start it slowly as soon as you hear yourself saying the last word of the first line: " . . . three." Try it for me.

(AC *sings, to the House, "An old gypsy prophesied when I was three" and slowly moves his arms out in the "Air" before he continues singing " . . . And what did she tell this little lamb?")*

How did that feel?

AC

Nice 'n' easy. I don't know why I still have a problem with that. Hell, after all, I *am* a dancer.

DC

But that's the reason why. Dancers deal only in numbers, in counts. That means that dancing is, by definition, *on* the beat. And that's how it'll be when you get to the staged stuff on " . . . top hat, white tie and glove." Until then, you aren't dancing. At least not in the strict sense of the word. You're *you* giving out information we have to hear. If you don't time it the way all of us ordinary folk use our bodies when we speak, it'll begin to look "stagey" too soon. We'll be seduced into watching you move instead of listening to you sing. And we want to hear those first eight bars or we won't understand the rest of the song. Does that make sense?

AC

Sure. I understand. But on " . . . top hat, white tie and glove" I begin working *on* the beat?

DC

Exactly. Because you're no longer you the man; you've become you the dancer—and a dancer moves according to the rules, by the numbers, on the beat. And you want us to see the dancing. It's part of your performance of the song. The script'll be heard almost unconsciously, but we'll be watching what you're doing. The cake is still important, mind you, but the icing is what'll sell it.

AC's plan for the staging of "Girls" is amusing. Essentially it is danced with four invisible girls. To establish the illusion he keeps his arms in the "arm-in-arm" position indicating that two girls are on either side of him and all five are performing a "routine." The girl on his left, on the outside, is irritatingly inept, and this is indicated throughout the performance by a series of withering "takes," "burns," and "skulls" he directs exclusively to her.* In the second Chorus, to his evident horror, "miles and miles" of girls seem to be coming at him especially when they turn into "piles and piles" of them. The horror, however, turns into ecstasy when they become playthings on top of him and he executes a small but pleasureful reaction immediately after singing about the "girls below." The Rideout is performed in "stock" Rockette fashion. As he sings the last—the ninth—"Girl" he throws a murderous glance at the end girl as they "kick off" into the wings. DC joins the Class in a round of applause. A perspiring AC reenters from the wing. He is clearly pleased with their reaction.

---

* The three words have a show business connotation. Two of them, "takes" and "burns," are in *The Random House Dictionary of the English Language.* "'Take,' a visual and mental response to something, typically manifested in a stare expressing total [wonderment]." (There are single and double takes—DC.) A "slow burn" is defined as " . . . a gradual building up of anger, as opposed to an immediate outburst." (*Burn* with or without the modifying *slow* is immediate but slow in execution—DC.) A "take" that wipes away all expression from the face is called a "skull." The etymological origin of the word probably refers to both the featureless skeleton of a human skull and to the blank, painted-on face of the circus clown.

DC

It's just about perfect. Beautifully thought out and elegantly danced. Can you tell us how you got the idea for the slow girl on your left?

AC

You won't believe this, but not a day after you assigned the song I was watching an old movie at my girlfriend's place. It was *Idiot's Delight* with Clark Gable playing a hoofer in an act with a group of girl tap dancers. They're trapped in this hotel in the Alps with a handful of oddballs right at the very beginning of the Second World War. Well, one evening they do a number from their act and they're terrible. They're supposed to be. And I thought, What a great idea to do "Girls" that way. It was a lot of fun working out how to play off them, since in my case they were all invisible. Oh, yes, I cut the group down to four, two on each arm. As soon as I got the idea for the one girl not being very good, it all fell into place. It's still a little shaky.

DC

It's the first time. What's important is that you know it works. You heard the Class. (*To the Class*) It worked? (*Shouts of "Bravo"*) It worked.

AC

What really knocks me out is that this is the first time I've ever done this kind of thing. I'm always choreographed by someone else. I thought I couldn't dream up a time step, never mind a whole number.

DC

You should be proud of yourself. You looked great. Oh, and by the way, you ought to give considerable attention to the jacket, the pants, the shirt, and the tie as a working addition to your wardrobe.

AC

Are you kidding, man? I got friends. You want to bring my life to a—how do the papers put it?—an untimely end?

DC

Take off the tie. You're too damn good to die young.

1000 Umbrellas

by Andy Partridge and Colin Moulding

Slow Jazz Waltz

eyes when you fell out with me now I'm___ crawl - ing the wall pa - per_

___ that's look - ing___ more___ like a road - map to

mis - e - ry oh oh mis - e - ry___

How can you smile and fore - cast

weath- er's get-ting bet-ter and you'll soon for- get her if you let the sun- shine come

through.___ How can you smile and fore - cast

weath- er's get-ting bet- ter if you nev- er let a girl rain all o- ver_

___ you.___ And

just when I___ throught that my vis - ta was gold - en in___

280

"1000 Umbrellas"

One thousand umbrellas upturned
Couldn't catch all the rain that drained out of my head (✓)
When you said we were over and over I cried (✓)
Till I floated downstream to a town they call misery (✓)
Oh oh misery (✓) misery oh oh misery (✓)
And one million teacups I bet couldn't hold all the wet (✓)
That fell out of my eyes when you fell out with me (✓)
Now I'm crawling the wallpaper that's looking more like a
    roadmap to misery (✓) oh oh misery (✓)
How can you smile and forecast weather's getting better (,)
And you'll soon forget her if you let the sunshine come
    through (✓)
How can you smile and forecast weather's getting better (,)
If you never let a girl rain all over you (✓)
And just when I thought that my vista was golden in hue (✓)
One thousand umbrellas opened to spoil the view (✓)
So with a mop and a bucket I'll just say forget her (✓)
And carry on sweeping up where I've been weeping (✓)
The jesters will creep in to strike down the newly crowned
    monarch of misery (✓) oh oh misery (✓)
How can you smile and forecast weather's getting better (,)
And you'll soon forget her if you let the sunshine come
    through (✓)
How can you smile and forecast weather's getting better (,)
If you never let a girl rain all over you (✓)
Just when I thought that my skies were a June-July blue (✓)
One thousand umbrellas opened (✓)
Two thousand umbrellas opened (✓)
Ten thousand umbrellas opened (✓)
    To spoil the view (✓)

"1000 Umbrellas" by Andy Partridge and Colin Moulding. Copyright © 1986 by
Virgin Music (Publisher) Ltd. International Copyright Secured. All Rights
Reserved. Used by permission.

13

Contemporary

It is not unreasonable to suppose that when time was so young that there was no need for the word "history," tribal communication was effected through primitive quasi-spoken languages and sung and danced song. The victors of predatory wars inevitably took home not only the spoils of war, but coopted the indigenous, insular speech of the vanquished and their music as well. Ineluctably, this subsumption created nations out of ever accreting communities whose spoken languages may be said to have developed from a relatively small root system. The disparate sounds of music, resistant to surrender, remained separate and distinguishable. A country's mappable boundaries and languages may alter and evolve, but its particular musical profile is immutable. We do not need guess-work to distinguish between what is recognizably French, Italian, English, Spanish, German or Russian music. Austria is Mozart, Brahms, and Strauss. Brazil is Villa-Lobos, Milton Nascimento, and Jobim. Scandinavia is Sibelius, Nielsen, and Grieg. The tango recalls Argentina, the Portuguese wail the Fado, and the sitar defines India as exclusively as the five-note pentatonic scale identifies the Orient.

From fin de siècle seventeenth century down to this very day an identifiable American music has been created out of a convergence of disparate melodies and rhythms brought to these shores by waves of immigrants along with their baggage. Colonial hymns,

Civil War and First and Second World War songs, hillbilly hoedowns, Western folk tunes, soulful Talmudic threnodies, Mexican mariachis, black gospel music and spirituals, jazz: the folk music of America with its rhythmic and melodic origins in the plantations of the South and its true roots in the memories of African slaves, and, finally, the subsequent classical contributions of Leonard Bernstein, Aaron Copland, Roy Harris, Morton Gould, Charles Ives, David Diamond, Samuel Barber, Gian Carlo Menotti, among others, who mined these sounds of music in a salmagundi of symphonic, concert, lyric theater and ballet scores.

Fin de siècle twentieth century maintains open lines of communication that allow for the rapid introduction of a wide variety of sounds. Not so long ago the traveler, moving at the pace of Hannibal crossing the Alps, could only experience native music at its source. Today, we sit easy in our easy chairs, stack our CD's and hear it all. The world-wide recording network is accommodating to all the music of the world if not the spheres, and tomorrow even those as yet unknown celestial melodies may well be the music we will be hearing, humming, singing, and buying. In this country we absorb alien music with a speed that only hunger for change or boredom with the old can explain. Reggae from Jamaica; calypso from Trinidad; protest music from Africa; the English hit parade beginning with the Beatles; the French chansons of Trenet, Brel, Chevalier and Piaf; Jobim's bassa novas from Brazil; rock and roll from our own blues and folk material; and the sometime nettlesome "rap"—all find their way onto Billboard's charts and bring more and more richness and variety to an already saturated marketplace.

For as long as I can remember, music has been defined as "classical" (or "serious") or "popular" (frivolous?)—rarely "good" or "bad." Both categories are loose, ill-chosen appellations. Music described as "classical" purports to be formally and artistically more sophisticated and enduring, but Gershwin's concert pieces and *Porgy and Bess* endure; so, too, the operas of Offenbach and Strauss. They may be banished to the realm of the "semi-classical" (semi-frivolous?) fare heard at "pops concerts" (a venue that straddles both musical shores), but they do not forfeit their places in the repertories of concert halls and opera houses everywhere. Coming from the other direction, the Swingle Singers swing through their arrangements of Bach in jazz clubs; Bill Evans and his trio play Granados, Scriabin, Fauré, and Chopin accompanied by a symphony orchestra; Miles Davis trumpets Rodrigo's "Concierto de Aranjuez" for guitar, and Duke Ellington's music may be heard in traditional high-churches. In return, jazz has been embraced by composers as classic as Ravel, Poulenc, Milhaud, Prokofiev, Krenek, Ives, Copland and Bernstein. Clearly, music may be "classical" and "popular."

Musical theater, too, is Janus-faced. One can attend Sondheim's *Sweeney Todd* and *A Little Night Music*, Cole Porter's *Kiss Me, Kate* and Rodgers and Hammerstein's *Oklahoma!* and *Carousel* in the opera house; Jerome Robbins has choreographed Jerome Kern's lovely "I'm Old-Fashioned," and Gershwin's "Who Cares?" is danced to choreography by George Ballanchine. A suite'd *West Side Story* and the overture to *Candide* are staples of the concert hall, and the Cleveland Symphony once commissioned a score from Jerome Kern comprising themes from his score for *Showboat*. Classical singers as far back as Caruso, McCormack and Tibbett and as current as Farrell, Horne, Sutherland, Te Kanawa, Stratas, Pavarotti, Domingo, Carreras and Hampson, among others, have crossed over into the "pop" fields to reap what harvests they could. True, their programming stays within the standard song repertoire, but Caruso recorded "Over There," McCormack sang "Mother Machree," and Tibbett introduced Harold Arlen's "Last Night When We Were Young." Homogenization as yet has not enlisted rock and roll; it is still singularly "popular," although enthusiasts even now have begun to define its more elevated forms as "classical" rock.

It is not my intention here to write at length about rock music in all its styles and variations, but to ignore it—and its ancillary cousins: Country-Western, Pop, Rhythm and Blues, Punk and Post-Punk, Reggae, Gospel and the hybrid Blues-Gospel connection, Soul, Rap and the Brazilian invasion—would be to turn an unreasonably deaf ear to a major voice of the music of our time. It would be easy and even truthful to take refuge in the confining scope of a volume concerned solely with the musical theater and its performing techniques, since Contemporary music, in all its guises, is not often heard in theater precincts. When it has risked the deeper waters it either fails or is a pale facsimile of the real thing.

There have been exceptions. Theater pieces devoted to Gospel music continue in a limited but consistent flow. Sung by black casts and delivered in pure and true renderings, they are restrictive for all the right reasons. Contemporary, too, are *The Wiz* and *Dreamgirls*, both successful musical pieces, but less remembered for their words and music, and in the case of the latter, more for the memorable features created for it by the late Michael Bennett. A watered-down "rock" sound and sensibility informs *Hair, Godspell, Jesus Christ Superstar, Evita, Starlight Express* and a fraction of the music for *Cats*. Their scores are not without merit but Broadway remains, on the whole, uninterested and even invulnerable to outside contemporaneous sounds. I believe that future rock forays into theater precincts must not be counted out. Close your ears to it, ignore it if you can—rock and roll in all its guises will not go away. For most young people, it is the music of their lives and times. They cannot be expected to call the show tune their own, much as it still lingers in the air.*

I have always held to the opinion that anyone who attends a teacher in order to learn how to sing and/or perform rock and roll opposes my theory that if you have to learn how, you should not sing it at all. Since it is not my purpose here to editorialize further, there are the following, less prejudiced, words to be said:

1. The indistinct margins of the Contemporary song when rock and roll is implied are so ambiguous that precise definition is impossible. Hard rock? Soft rock? Folk rock? Jazz rock? Punk rock? Funk rock? Classic rock? Acid rock? Roots rock? Art rock? California rock? Grunge rock? Metal? Hard metal? When a Contemporary song is requested for a musical theater audition, a rock-and-roll song is seldom, if ever, what they want to hear. It is more than likely a tacit euphemism for "Don't sing a show tune."

2. The choice of a rock-and-roll song is most often made after hearing it on a recording. The danger here is threefold:

a) By virtue of its power, the sustained sonic boom must dwarf or, worse, totally submerge the vocal statement. As for the lyric, unless its printed version accompanies the recording,

---

* Most show tunes are unknown to the younger members in my classes, but, once heard, their unqualified affection for them reaffirms the power of this music to enchant. "I like a Gershwin tune, How About You?" is not only a lyric; it is an on-going question whose answer, from one generation to the next, appears to be an unqualified "Yes, I like it too." *Crazy for You*, with a rickety, jerry-built libretto that supports the Gershwin score of *Girl Crazy* along with a handful of other Gershwin standards, is a Broadway hit.

only the writer knows.

b) With too few exceptions, top-rated performers are instrumentalists who sing. (The guitar has been, and still is, the preferred self-accompanying instrument.) Measured by musical theater standards, their vocal gifts are inadequate. On the other hand, when I had the opportunity to teach many of the performers who played major roles in *Jesus Christ Superstar*, I found that those who survived the vocal strain were classically trained singers who knew how best to deal with the soaring, searing range of the "pure" rock sound required by the score. On the rare occasion when a star performer parts with his electronic partners (his instrument, synthesizers, and sound tracks of advanced musical sophistication) and ventures onto a legitimate stage, as in the case of Sting in a recent revival of Weill and Brecht's *The Threepenny Opera*, the career move is lamentably mis-taken. It is only fair to add that, in his natural habitat on recordings and on the concert stage, he is a man of distinction.

c) Since rock and roll lives its primary life on vinyl, tape, and CD's, it reaches the ear of the public in a sophisticated, if manipulated, guise. Even when a song is singled out and performed on MTV, special effects and rapid-cut choreography merchandise the song. When performer/groups produce a concert tour, these special effects are appended to the sung material along with lasers, lights, electronic inflation of decibel units, backup groups, and sets as lavish as anything Ziegfeld dreamed of. Take the trimmings away and what do you have? Whatever it is that remains must be considered of minimal value to a performer at an audition who will be working on a bare stage or in an empty room with an out-of-tune piano and the bare song.

3. *Performing* styles, as they relate to the musical theater, are alien to the performance of rock music, which has its own style— one that is more relevant to excitation than to interpretation. Its *vocal* style is its very stylelessness, since purity of sound, good diction, and a manifest knowledge of phrasing would impugn the performer's right to sing it. This is not to say that Michael Jackson (whose gift for vitalizing what he sings with elegant dance patterns cannot be faulted), Bruce Springsteen, Mick Jagger, Aretha Franklin, and Bonnie Raitt, among others, are not performers of quality nor that they should be denied the right to cross over—only that they would be required, somewhere in midstream, to swap horses. Madonna has appeared on Broadway in David Mamet's play *Speed-the-Plow* and in films, but as yet has not risked the deeper waters of the musical stage. Miss Ronstadt appeared in *La Bohème* Off-Broadway, but with less than positive results.

Let it be said, then, that hard rock may be disregarded as source material for a musical theater audition. Beyond rock lies softer rock and music defined by the acronym MOR (middle of the road). Here, in open country, the choice of what to sing where, is yours and, again, as long as it is not a show tune, it may be anything else. "Anything else" is admittedly nonspecific because the phrase invokes a vast library of music that ranges from "classic" jazz standards like Irving Berlin's "Puttin' on the Ritz" (given a bit of body English in 1986 by Taco), moving on to the pop standards: "What Are You Doing the Rest of Your Life?" and "Come in From the Rain," passing through the standard "Both Sides Now," on to Tammy Wynette's "Stand By Your Man," across the "Bridge Over Troubled Waters," under "The Wind Beneath My Wings," into Billy Joel's "New York State of Mind," and busting out all over into Stevie Wonder's "You Are the Sunshine of My Life."

MOR music is not only many things but a combination of the many. There is Blues and there is Rhythm and Blues; there is New Wave, New Age, Country-Western, New Wave Country-Western, Jazz, Jazz-Rock, Art Rock, and on and on. The same may be said of those who sing their own songs. Prince is generally described as a Hard Rock singer/composer, yet he may appeal to a wider audience who would not be, by choice, in his corner but after attending a film he has scored—as in the case of *Batman*—happily purchase the CD of his background score. The sexually powerful Bruce Springsteen is a rock-and-roll artist who evolved from the fresh-air currency that illuminated the words and music of the Beatles. By investing his hard-driving songs with current, nonrevolutionary socio/political statements, he attracts young audiences whose parents were and are drawn to the softer textures of Paul Simon's songs that similarly sing of injustice.

The benign social commentary of Josh White's and Harry Belafonte's Folk songs of the thirties, forties, and fifties, like the times, evolved into the less benign social lyrics of Bob Dylan and Joan Baez. They in turn brought on the middle-class protest songs of Randy Newman that by the eighties and nineties had hardened into the brutal, unsparing angst of Tracy Chapman's Folk Rock inner-city commentaries.

Country-Western as a genre sound, too, has grown up, up, and away. The laments of Willie Nelson, Hank Williams, Patsy Cline, and Loretta Lynn created a truly sophisticated New Age Country-Western by cross-breeding the Blues with the old innocent purity. Along with a dash of Pop and Texas Country sound, a second generation was born: Lyle Lovett, K. D. Lang, K. T. Oslin, and Randy Travis, among others.

The emergence on the Pop musical charts of Rap, Gospel, and Brazilian music has not prevented these genres, early on, from similarly coupling and spawning hybrid sounds. In the sense that Rap is exclusive unto itself, it does not yield much of a harvest for the musical theater performer. Aside from its often overt sexual scripts, it sings (speaks) of the very special parochial world of urban unrest and social strife. It has been referred to as a "newspaper" for the underprivileged black teenager who does not read the daily news. 2 Live Crew's problems with the censor would eliminate it—not from the theater, perhaps, but as possible audition material. As of this writing, it appears to be limited to night clubs where its combustive language is of interest to special-interest audiences.

Gospel does come in the separate wrappings of the sacred and the profane. Set apart from the unforgettable Mahalia Jackson's allegiance to the pure and traditional and Marion Williams's present-day recordings of the gospel vernacular, Gospel has enriched the musical theater in *The Gospel at Colonus* and *Your Arm's Too Short to Box With God*, and it can be heard as a fractional part of the scores of *Raisin* and *Purlie*. It has also evolved and broadened into Gospel Blues and its parallel descendant, Soul, best rendered by Aretha Franklin.* Like the spiritual, it is recommended only to the black performer. This is not to imply that the white performer is unable or forbidden to sing it—only that custom creates its own kind of racist exclusivity. Like Rap, the Brazilian invasion is what it is, and when what it is is not germane to an audition for a Broadway musical, it should be left to those native throats who sing it as expertly as Jobim, Milton Nascimento,

---

* Recommended: Inez Andrews, Bessie Griffin, and Albertina Walker, all of whom walk the line both on and in between what Jon Pareles, *The New York Times*'s music critic, calls "Sunday morning church music and the Saturday night devil's music of the Blues."

Djavan, Ivan Lins, Gilberto Gil, and Gaetano Veloso, among others.

Finally, when a Contemporary song is requested at an audition for the musical theater, the rules of "what to sing" remain the same as they are for a "show tune."* The performer will always need material that

1. *Is musically and vocally stageworthy.* Musical worth is not a question of market value. Composers of Contemporary theater scores are no less interested in vocal power and range than their more traditional colleagues. If, as is often the case, the sole purpose of a song is to excite by repetition of a rhythmic theme, the performer will not have an opportunity to demonstrate the singing skills that are intrinsic to the musical theater.

2. *Has something to sing about.* Just as the composer and the lyricist are concerned with how well the performer can *sing*, the librettist and the director are parochially interested in what he can *do*. A lyric that goes nowhere cannot be expected to take the performer anywhere. On a recording, intelligibility need not be an integral element of a performance. This unfortunate aspect of the Contemporary song may or may not be disadvantageous. It is important, however, that the performer familiarize himself with a copy of the lyric to determine whether intelligibility was or was not disadvantageous—before the moment of choice.

3. *Retains a certain verticality when it is sung on a stage (or in a room) under the harsh conditions of an audition.* A song "works" in the theater because of its construction and its ability to "stand" on its own with the aid of, among many things, a theatrical performance. On a recording, neither verticality nor horizontality are imperatives—what is aural is all. On a stage, what is heard shares equal importance with what is seen, and what is seen is attention-getting to the degree that the song's component parts (words and music) are able to support, in the manner of a gantry, an ear- and eye-filling performance. No performance worth attending can be said to "work" unless it moves, rocketlike, up and through the fourth wall driven by its intention to grab and hold the attention of the listener. Not unreasonably, club acts and concert performances are not that distant from the requirements of the theater when the choice of "what to sing" must be made. Songs and their

---

* See *On Singing Onstage*, pages 50–53, on choice of material for an audition.

performances must carry their weight in both venues.

In conclusion: The successful recording of a Contemporary song and/or its performance on a concert stage is less a performance of the song than an advertisement of the performer. This need not be negative praise, but it is not the goal of a song intended for the musical theater stage. Whether a voice is superb, all right, or no more than necessary, dramatic projection gives a song its theatrical validity. I have seen an artist stop a show with very little vocal gift but with stunning interpretive skills, and I have heard a singer do the same with a voice so superb that sheer tonal beauty caused the audience almost to forget to breathe. In both cases these miracles were the result of the union of the artist, a pianist or an orchestra, and, of course, the music and words, the eternal dyad, that brought them together.

It can be seen that the Contemporary song, as a defining category, is inclusive of a broad spectrum of popular music. Like clothes, gourmet cuisines, and hairstyles, it is always changing, and it is always a case of *chacun à son goût*. John Rockwell has written in *The New York Times*: " . . . some of us will always want hot dance music, others weepy ballads, still others clever novelty numbers. Most of us want all these things at one time or another. When something new comes along, like rock in the 50's or rap in the 80's, it doesn't or shouldn't constrict our range of choice by eliminating anything else. It should merely increase our opportunities for musical pleasure." We are all in agreement with Mr. Rockwell, but whereas in the previous twelve categories choice was the child of this writer's knowledge of pop and musical theater music, a model Contemporary song was not easily made. From the start, I have tried to stay away from extremes. It is safe to say that a song sung by Milli Vanilli is too "pop" and simplistic, Midnight Oil too political, the Sugar Cubes and the Red Hot Chili Peppers too nonvocal, the Jesus and Mary Chain too special, Joe Satriani too instrumental, the Smithereens too primitive, Violent Femmes too unmusical, Kate Bush too precious—music that is so all-inclusive of so many styles makes difficult the choice of one. Omitted are songs played and sung by their composers because, as a general rule, these performers are not concerned with broad musical statements that require a demanding vocal range.

THE SONG

All this having been said, I have selected "One Thousand Umbrellas" from the repertoire of XTC, an avant-garde English group. XTC, whose work is considered to be substantial and enduring by those who should know, is Andy Partridge, Colin Moulding, and Dave Gregory. Their recordings have never made a major noise, perhaps because their music, although eclectic, is difficult to classify. There is a hint of the Beatles, grown up, in their best songs: "Battle For a Rainy Day," "Season Cycle," and the sample song. Its subject matter is as old as time—a distant descendant of "Frankie and Johnnie."* Even the metaphor of rain to describe the singer's despair is old hat—namely, Harold Arlen's "Stormy Weather," Alec Wilder's "Rain, Rain (Don't Go 'Way)," Jimmy Van Heusen's "Here's That Rainy Day," and Burt Bacharach's "Raindrops Keep Fallin' on My Head", among many— further proof that popular music still sings the same old songs decked out in clothes that currency is barely able to disguise. The tempo, a jazz waltz, is upbeat and in direct contrast to the bluesy "I-love-her-but-she-doesn't-love me" lyric; the words are an unconscious echo of Edith Sitwell's symbolist "Façade": " . . . rain that drained out of my head," " . . . now I'm crawling the wallpaper that's looking more like a roadmap to misery oh oh misery," " . . . the jesters will creep in to strike down the newly crowned monarch of misery"—verbal imagery less absurdist than Dame Edith's, but intriguing and fun to sing. Despite, and possibly because of, the derivative tone of the piece, "One Thousand Umbrellas," with its funny-sad lyric and enticing arrangement, accomplishes what all good songs seem to achieve—a new twist to prove the essential validity of the old. I have printed the words as they appear in the accompanying folder of their *Skylarking* CD without punctuation. The song is AABA with a second Chorus reprise shortened by a cut of the first "8" the second time around. There is a mechanical Rideout attached to the end of the second Chorus, but an amusing rewrite of the title keeps the song buoyant through to its end.

Songs that sing of lost love are historically delivered by women,

---

* "Frankie and Johnnie"'s first appearance is shrouded in darkness. Both the music and the words are anonymously written and the incident upon which the lyric is based is said to be a true one that occurred as early as 1850. The song is reputed to have been sung at the siege of Vicksburg.

but the old Tin Pan Alley laws that determined which sex may sing what song have begun to dissolve—sometimes with radical and egregious overkill. "One Thousand Umbrellas," by virtue of its lyric, should be performed by a white, black, Latino, or Oriental man who is old enough to know what he's talking about.

THE DIALOGUE

FB is from Lubbock, Texas. He announces it before he is asked. For him it is a badge he still wears with honor regardless of the money he has paid out to rid himself of an almost ineradicable dialect. It is a case of Alan Lerner's statement (with one replaced word): "A Texan's way of speaking absolutely classifies him." (The following dialogue ignores the orthography of a Texas drawl. DC assumes the reader is familiar with its sound.) It is DC's effort to accommodate the old FB by assigning a song that will feel as comfortable as a pair of old boots. FB is not unaware of the gesture.

FB

I sure hope my speech teacher never hears me do this number.

DC

Think of it as a part you're playing. There's always the possibility that you'll get rid of that accent and along'll come a musical of *Stagecoach* or *Red River*. After all, they've made one out of *Jekyll and Hyde*, *Shogun*, and *Kiss of the Spider Woman*. And *Shenandoah*'s already checked in. You never know.

FB

They better not do that to me! Before I'm done I'm gonna go to that ball and pass myself off as Professor Higgins. But how'd you ever hear of this song? I know the group, but I didn't know the song.

DC

Is that respect I hear in your voice or do I detect just a hint of condescension?

FB

No. No. Respect, man! XTC is not your run-of-the-mill rock group. I just hadn't gotten around to picking up their latest.

DC

Well, there you are. I'm one up on you. (*To* FB *and the Class*) It isn't surprising that this song can only be heard on a recording. Like so many contemporary songs, it has no theater or film affiliation. But it's a good song. A swinging song. (*To* FB) Don't you agree?

FB

Oh, yes. I like it. A lot. It's what you call a jazz waltz, I think.

DC

Or a swing waltz. I'm proud of you. You identified it. Have you learned it?

FB

Yep, but I'm having a helluva time breathing when I need to. There's not much room in those long lines, is there?

DC

Well, let's limp our way through it. Breathe when you can—wherever it causes the least damage—and I'll keep my ears open to see if you're on the ball.
    (FB *gets a four-bar swing waltz Vamp and sings through the two Choruses.* DC *permits him to finish so that the Class may hear the complete song. To* FB *and the Class*)
This is the kind of song and lyric that in the past was more commonly sung by women. This time it's a "*she* done *him* wrong" script. And the images, too, are decidedly male-oriented. Here's a "misery" song that doesn't work if a girl changes the pronouns and tries it on for size. Her dependence on him would be considered intolerable today. However, his dependence on her is somehow

condolent—and for the women listening even gratifying. (*To* FB) What saves it from mawkishness are those images I mentioned— " . . . one million teacups I bet couldn't hold all the wet that fell out of my eyes," and " . . . Now I'm crawling the wallpaper that's looking more like a roadmap to misery," and " . . . if you never let a girl rain all over you" and, of course, the title of the song—" . . . one thousand umbrellas." Wonderful stuff, eh?

FB

Yep. My favorite's " . . . the jesters will creep in to strike down the newly crowned monarch of misery." It's got a neat flow to it.

DC

If you remember, when BL sang "Wait Till You See Her," we spoke about the phrasing difficulties built into the singing of a waltz. Three beats to a bar have a way of making you feel you've been shortchanged of that one extra beat (the fourth one) you're used to in almost all the other songs you sing. By the way, both songs have extended Rideouts. In the Rodgers waltz it's more a part of the whole. In this song, the Rideout—at least, musically—is tacked on. But you do have a lyric change. And it's even amusing. By the way, is your tape machine on? (FB *nods.*) All right, then.* In the first sixteen bars—not counting the repeat on " . . . misery, oh oh misery"—I suggest you grab a breath after " . . . drained out of my head," after " . . . I cried," and after the first and second " . . . misery." The repeat naturally has a breath following it because the "Air" allows it. Got that?

FB

Not so fast. (*He scribbles rapidly.*)

DC

I thought you said you were taping this?

---

* The reader will find this easier to follow if he refers to the lead and lyric sheets.

FB

Damn! I forgot. I'm not used to that newfangled stuff.

DC

Put away your pencil and relax. The second section, almost a reprise of the first, is pretty much the same ground plan. Breathe after " . . . hold all the wet" and after " . . . when you fell out with me." But hold off on the next breath until after " . . . a roadmap to misery." Again, you can breathe after " . . . oh oh misery" before moving into the Bridge. Are you still with me?

FB

If it's on my tape, I am.

DC

The thing to worry about in both Bridges is the breath you take after " . . . if you let the sunshine come through." Get off that last word, grab a breath, and go right on with " . . . How can you smile," etc. You'll need it. Once you've passed " . . . if you never let a girl rain all over you," there's plenty of time to breathe.

FB

You won't believe it, but I understand all this.

DC

Well, that makes two of us. The Class is fast asleep. I've cut one of the "8s"—actually its sixteen bars, but you know what I mean—to shorten the number. So we're back to the original phrasing plan for the second go-around. Breathe after " . . . forget her," after " . . . weeping," after " . . . monarch of misery," and, as before, after the " . . . oh oh misery," and finally after " . . . let the sunshine come through." We've covered the second Bridge—we're riding down the home stretch now. The obvious . . . (FB *joins him.*) . . . After

" . . . One thousand umbrellas opened," after " . . . Two thousand umbrellas opened . . ."

FB

Let me have this one, okay?

DC

It's all yours.

FB

After " . . . Ten thousand umbrellas opened" 'cause I need a breath for the Rideout, so I take a breath before " . . . to spoil the view."

DC

You got it!

FB

I better cut outta here while I can and work on this at home. Oh, one thing. . . . You said I could drop my g's, right?

DC

Don't drop them. Murder them!
(FB *exits—a happy man.*)

A week later. FB is on stage. He takes a music reading. The phrasing is laid in as planned. DC congratulates him.

FB

I had a great idea for this number. I thought I'd sing it sitting on a stool. It'd be more like me. Nice and easy. D'you know what I mean?

DC

Yes. You mean you thought you'd sing it sitting on a stool—that it'd be more like you. Nice and easy. Sorry, but no stool. I've a theory that anyone can be a star if you sit him down and give him back his lap. In the early days of television there was a rash of popular comedy revue-type shows. Each week there'd be a guest, and when it was a pop singer, he always sang his songs sitting on a stool. There must have been a run on the damn things. Judy on a stool. Ella on a stool. Peggy on a stool. Frank on a stool. Tony on a stool. And then the host joined the guest and *he* sat on a stool and they sang duets on stools. And you know something? They did look better sitting down. Why? Well, after all, when you sit and sing, half your body is cancelled out. No need for it to do anything. Better yet, it's the half that's farthest from the mind. Life is suddenly so simple.

FB

I guess that means no stool. The thing is, you're always telling me I do too much. When I play back my tape at home I can hear you saying "Don't do that." *Don't* do that. Don't *do* that. Don't do *that*, either.

DC

That's not doing too much. That's choosing to do something that doesn't pay its way. Whenever someone says, "I was afraid to do too much," I figure it's a cop-out.

FB

How do you mean?

DC

It eliminates the risk factor; an excuse to get away with nothing. After all, what *is* too much? And how do we know what would have been too much if you forbid anything to happen? So let's get rid of the stool and get rid of worrying about how much is too much.

Let's stand up, take the rap for yourself, and sing the song.

(FB *crosses to Center. He waits and plays generally into the theater. DC is again struck by the unselfconsciousness of his casual, "comfortable-with-himself" manner. He presents himself naturally without having to lean on the mechanical techniques that others rely on to achieve similar results. After a moment or two, he nods the pianist in, times the Vamp neatly, and launches into "One Thousand Umbrellas." After the first Bridge is "crossed," DC stops him. FB, disbelieving, takes a moment to come back to the real world.*)

I see why you were worried about doing too much. But it's the wrong kind of "too much." You've elected to pull out all the emotional stops and the song is drowned in an excess of "feeling." The music is locked out. But it's the music that supplies the emotion. That's the composer's task. The audience will "feel" because music speaks directly to their emotional lives. Rest assured of that. They "feel"—you "do." Do the song and work to educe the feelings you need from them in order to score. To move them. To move them to cry or laugh or whatever you will. That's the pleasure and the joy you'll experience from performing. Its very purpose, in fact. You're not up there to give *you* a good time but to make it your business to see to it that the *audience* has a good time. Could it be that you're personalizing this too much? (FB *does not respond.*) Are you all right?

FB
(*With effort*)

I'm okay. Anything else?

DC
(*Senses when to change the subject*)

I know I said the drawl is somewhat applicable, but I think it's keeping the lyric from getting out. We don't hear it. It might help if you put the words outside your mouth, as if they were lines in a cartoon. You know what I mean—inside a balloon. Perhaps the mushy sound is due to the first problem—overemotionalizing the text.

FB
(*Coming out of it*)

You always say "draw on your own experience." I guess I drew too close to the cutting edge.

DC

If you remember, last week you said it was a swing waltz. The melody and the rhythm put the lie to personal tragedy. Also, the song's subjective. We've talked a great deal about the need to objectivize this kind of lyric. The words are full of "I," "I," "I," and "me," "me," "me." It's time to take *them* into consideration. The jazz waltz should be of great help to you. It's sprightly and "up." This isn't a man in mourning for a lost love. He's a street philosopher. The point he's making is, "You've got to get involved. You can't stay apart, isolated. Living means coupling and maybe uncoupling. How can you recognize the good times if you haven't allowed yourself to experience the bad?"

FB

I just got off on the wrong track. Let me bring this back. It'll be a lot easier from here on in.

DC

I know it will be. The song looks great on you. All you need is the right outfit to sing it in. You went to that ball too soon. (*To the pianist*) I think you're playing this a shade fast. He's having trouble getting through the Bridge. There are a lot of words to get out. (*To* FB *and the Class*) A good rule to remember: When you have a song that moves like this, pull out the most difficult line. In this case it would be " . . . weather's getting better and you'll soon forget her if you let the sunshine come through" or " . . . weather's getting better if you never let a girl rain over you." Sing it at a tempo that's not only comfortable for you but one the audience will understand. Now then, that'll be the tempo for the entire song—right from the top. When you first start the song it may seem a bit slow but when you get to that busy line you'll be glad you chose the tempo you chose. Are you all with me?

THE CLASS

That would be true for rhythm songs particularly?

DC

Yes, but not all rhythm songs present this problem. I'm speaking here about complicated, busy lyrics that aren't easy to hear when the set tempo is just too fast to allow intelligible articulation. "I Got Rhythm" is fast, but the script is spare. Ballads and blues are slow movers by definition and wouldn't pose the problem. (*To* FB) Don't forget, even you hadn't heard the song before. Give the audience a break. They'll be hearing it for the first time. Furthermore, you don't want to go too fast in this song because, as you rightly felt, the man is in some pain. But what I like about him is that he hasn't gone under. What happened to him was rough, but he still has a sense of humor and the wonderful ability to say the old words in a new way. *One thousand* umbrellas? *Two thousand* umbrellas? *Ten thousand* umbrellas!? Come on! He's not counted out yet. Not by a long shot.

FB

I think I'll listen to this when I get home and use it for a life lesson. (*He exits.*)

FB's last performance is a good deal less self-involved, but a patina of his painful personal experience lingers and gives the song a distinctive and touching quality. The Class responds with its usual enthusiasm when they know a fellow classmate has done his best work.

DC

Splendid work! Just one suggestion. Some of the melody is sloppy. Especially in the line " . . . Now I'm crawling the wallpaper that's looking more like a roadmap to misery." (*To the pianist*) Can you give him a finger tape?* (*To* FB) Is your tape machine on?

FB
(*Fumbling with the switch*)

Now it is. (*He and the Class are silent as the pianist plays through the entire song, recording just the melody, note to note.*)

DC

There now. You've got the number by the numbers. No more need to fake.

FB

Thanks. I think one of the things that helped me this time was working the song at home in front of a mirror.

DC
(*Mock horror*)

Don't tell me that. I don't want to hear about it.

FB

Why? What's wrong?

DC

Nothing's wrong. It's just not the way I work. If I did that when I sang I'd get off on myself trying to do the performance and, at the same time, watching me do it. I work to experience, and I figure they'll watch if what I'm doing and saying is true and interesting.

CLASS

But it seemed to work for him, didn't it?

* See Introduction, page 14.

DC

Everyone has their own methods, I suppose.

FB

I think I tried it to get out of myself. Get away from last week's mess when I was up here.

DC

My point is simply that one cannot be, do, and watch oneself being and doing all at the same time. Yes, if you go to watch yourself when they screen "rushes" (dailies).* But then you're the audience. You can watch yourself on the screen and think of yourself as another person. The event is occurring in the present. The scene you're looking at was shot the day before.

FB

I see. But as someone said, it worked, didn't it?

DC

It worked because you are a particular kind of person. You have no self-consciousness. You've probably never had any. You're very happy in your own skin. I don't know how you do it and my guess is that *you* don't know how you do it. This Jimmy Stewart thing you are is not something you consciously do. But how many others enjoy this kind of comfort with themselves? Not many. In this Class, no one else. In the late Bette Davis's immortal words: "Break all the mirrors in the palace." Worry less about the sight of your image and more about the tactics of the game. They won't let you down. Mirrors reflect the sight of you. Audiences reflect what they think of the sight of you. Neither one has anything to do with performing. The medium's the message and how well it's delivered. That's what defines great performing and it will always be so.

---

* From *The Random House Dictionary of the English Language*: "Dailies—a series of hastily printed shots from the previous day's shooting, selected by the director to be viewed for possible inclusion in the final version of the film; rushes."

Final Considerations

The work in my studio has evolved through many years of interchanges between myself and the actors, singers, and dancers who have worked with me. In the beginning a one-on-one relationship between teacher and student was the standard, even historical, method of study. The idea of working within a Class structure was daunting. Those of us in the first Classes were in agreement about good and great performances. They were there to be seen on Broadway stages and in films. But when we attempted to define them, agreement splintered into Babel. After all, what qualities define a great performance of a song? A good one? A fair one? A bad one? In the words of the late George Kaufman: "A forgettable one"?

Slowly, a workable definition was literalized out of questions asked, answers given, shaping and direction adopted, thrown out, reshaped and redirected until, without a conscious awareness that formulas and procedures were coming into focus, workable techniques were synthesized and codified. We, all of us, had invented methods that could be taught to newcomers. Once the technical skills were mastered, performances were put on the stage, sustained by those techniques—now invisible—but, nevertheless, supported by them.

Six work areas were defined, as follows:

1. No more did anyone ask, "Where do I put my eyes? Where do I look while I'm singing?" We had conceived the technique of a practical system we called, with an acknowledged lack of originality, "focus."* The experienced performer has no need for

---

* The word has been vulgarized by my students who came to refer to it as "spotting." I prefer "focus." Its true Latin meaning is "hearth" (a fireplace; an open fire; source of heat). Someone once said, "Without a hearth, where does one look for the center of a room?" It is reported that Kepler used the word in 1604 to describe, in the optical sense, the burning point of a lens or mirror. These allusions have a certain relevancy to the vocabulary of the theater: the heat implicit in connection; the concept of "to whom am I singing?"

this support system. He sings to the audience, and because they are alive to him and for him, he is in focus. The beginner, for any number of reasons (chiefly fear), has no sense of it. Self-consciousness preempts sane behavior; his eyes give him away.

2. No more did students ask, "What do I do with my hands while I'm singing?" They learned that body language responds to signals it receives from deep within the right brain (defined in *On Singing Onstage* as the "Two.").* Without an understanding of the *meaning* of what they were singing, they fell back on a limited vocabulary of stock gestures; without calling upon their imagination to furnish substance and distinction to the memorized lyric as it was recalled by the left brain, their bodies gave them away.

3. Music as scored decrees the melodies and the rhythms in which songs are sung. Lyrics as printed decree only the words. To make sense of language, it must be phrased. When the performer, slave to the printed music and lyric, sings without any understanding of how words group together to reveal clarity of thought, the awareness of only the words gives him away.

4. Further refinement of techniques brought with it the recognition that what they were going to say—rather than clinging to what they were saying until it was said and done—would ultimately affect the refinement of their physical life. Defined first as a concept and then translated into a technique (see *On Singing Onstage*—the "Three"**), it was a hard lesson to learn and harder still to execute. Before that day arrived, all thought and body language

    a) was nothing but a redundant charade of the lyric;

    b) arrived on the downbeat of each new line or, worse, on the active word within the body of the line; and

    c) moved in whatever time signature the song was scored. This became apparent when the "sound track" of the vocal and the accompaniment were *figuratively* turned off. There was no need to guess the time signature of the song being sung; the physical aspect of the performance resembled nothing more than a conducted version of the piece. Until he understood that

---

* The "Two" is a technical exercise and *should not be employed slavishly in the performance of a song.*

** Unlike the "Two," the technique of the "Three," once learned, is elemental to a graceful and stylish performance of all sung material.

the "Air" in the song could function as a time slot in which to set up the new line, late and indicative body language gave him away.

5. The dilemma of "what to sing" and "where and when to sing it" is with the performer throughout his career. It is obvious that all songs are not available to all performers. They may be denied us by virtue of our sex, our age, our appearance, our effect on the eye of the beholder—even our behavior justifies or impugns what we choose to sing. When we are ignorant of who we are, how we are seen, and how best to merchandise this information about ourselves, the choice of a "wrong song" gives away our innocence.

6. I have held to the belief that acting and singing, although related performing arts, are distinct and different ball games. Too many fine actors have learned, to their surprise, that although they know how to act, that knowledge offered next to nothing in the way of know-how when they sang what they had to say.* However, both forms of communication share one aspect of their disparate techniques: the cultivation of a rich imagination.** Imagination is the bank account from which all experiential and emotional withdrawals are put to the service of great performances.

I feel a sense of sadness come over me when a performance in my studio is "frozen."† The performer, having won approval, may discard the methods and means he used to achieve the good work and, in subsequent performances of the song will set about to clone the original. A more sensitive understanding of what the word "frozen" implies was expressed by a student after he completed a superior performance in Class. He said,

"My problem was once a question of 'freezing' the physical aspect of the performance and suffering the staged look that I knew was unsatisfactory. This performance today was the first time I surrendered to the trusting of the clarity of my 'thinking.' I knew who I was, I knew to whom I was singing, and I knew

* See *On Singing Onstage*, pages 55-62.
** The title of this volume pays respect to Stanislavski, the great Russian actor/teacher who first remarked that " . . . [an actor's imagination] is at the very heart of [his] work."
† The word applies to that moment, in late rehearsal, when the performance of a play or musical is ready for viewing by the public. It is then said to be "frozen." According to theater legend, when an eminent composer brought to the late Ethel Merman a new but tardy lyric during an out-of-town pre-Broadway engagement, she refused to learn it, announced that the show was frozen, and in her defense suggested he call her Miss Birds Eye.

why I needed to sing this particular song. And though I felt that, at times, my body was responding to whatever I was creating in my mind, I didn't plan any of it. I knew consciously the way to time the body language to gain its maximum effect. I suppose I've finally reached that place where I know I know what I know and, as I do in my acting, I have the technical knowledge to make it stageworthy."

I have always been uncomfortable when I tamper with a performance. It is my belief that what I like is not what the student-performer pays to hear. On the contrary, it is essential, at the start of his working life, that he begin to set down the definition of a value system he will use to gauge his own personal work. As his teacher, I can home in on what is incorrect, why it is incorrect, and how best to correct it, but I have learned to resist making any judgments based on what I may think is good or bad. The marketplace makes those judgments soon enough. When a sports announcer asked Ivan Lendl, the tennis champion, to describe his technique, he replied, "Instead of judging a situation, I observe it." I can think of no better advice to pass on to all players.

How to do anything is learnable. Once learned, the performer is best served by building the body of his work on the foundation of the recognition of his own uniqueness. In *Working in Hollywood* by Alexandra Brouwer and Thomas Lee Wright, the creature designer of E.T., Carlo Rambaldi, says, "I don't teach or give advice. . . . A chef could never create another chef like himself. In fact, if the truth is told, he doesn't *want* another chef to be like him." The quote is accurate but specious for, after all, chefs teach younger chefs in cooking schools and in restaurant kitchens. How to break an egg, how many eggs to break for recipes that require them, and how to make a soufflé rise are teachable data, able to be taught not because they constitute an art but because they are information.

I teach the above numbers 1 through 6 (information), and I am often called upon to give advice and edit performances (an art), which I attempt to do as honestly as I can, but beyond that I cannot create another teacher like me. It is not possible. In fact, if the truth were to be told, I am secretly pleased when I cannot see any of me in a performance of someone I have taught. I see the work and, in a sense, I know how it was achieved, but I recognize it for what it is—a personal statement of the performer that finds its language in the deepest roots of his history. This mass of private detail is denied me because I am not he and can never hope to be. I can imitate the externals of a successful or a failed performance but the root mystery of his cerebration will forever separate us. On the other hand, he knows what *I* am thinking because it is the task of a teacher to verbalize thought when it concerns the subject that has brought us together. The nature of this two-way street has always intrigued me for, although I have trained myself to speak out my mind, the student hears only what he is able to hear. A shifting functional deafness or an intentional misunderstanding protects his ego and protracts the study experience to the exact amount of time it will take for him to allow himself to hear what I say and to act on it. When a well-known actress I taught was taking her final leave of the Class, she thanked me for never telling her more than she was able to hear. I did not disabuse her of her re-write of our shared history. I had told her everything she had to hear, but she had sifted it and digested only what she allowed herself to hear. Thus do our minds conspire to protect us.

A Performer Prepares and the two books preceding it on performance techniques pertaining to the musical theater were published during the two decades of the eighties and the nineties. Their appearance was considered an irony, for during those years the musical theater, it was maintained, had begun to drift—had become too expensive to produce and to attend; that it was overblown and underendowed; that it lacked the unique casts, the wit, and the glamour of yesterday. To some extent the Lord Byron quote that "the good old times . . . [are gone]" was and still is true. However, we cannot change the times in which we are born. Apart from the elegiac inflection in some of the writing in my books,* it is my belief that the theater and, more particularly, the musical theater is far from comatose. Audiences flock to see the Phantom let loose his chandelier; gasp at a helicopter descending from the grid; applaud the "Cats" as they rise all over the world into the "flies" in spaceships; attend a refought French uprising; sigh over the Gershwin tunes reprised in *Crazy For You*; applaud, yet again, the *Guys and Dolls* of Frank Loesser; and continue to return to attend hit musicals over and over again. How else may we account

---

* See *On Performing*, pages 33-49.

for the astonishing runs of *A Chorus Line*, *Forty-Second Street*, *Evita*, *Les Miserables*, *Cats*, *The Phantom of the Opera*, and the revivals of old favorites that are dusted off the shelf and represented?* How else explain the recurring musical theater productions that can be seen, in repertory, on the stages of opera houses? And this activity takes place not only in our own country but around the world. Cameron Mackintosh began his ascent to his position as England's, if not the world's, preeminent musical theater producer with revivals of *Anything Goes* and *Oklahoma!* In Vienna, Austrians attend the latest Sondheim theater pieces and rehear Porter's *Kiss Me, Kate* almost as often as Puccini, and, in Japan, *Fiddler on the Roof* enjoyed phenomenal success. Australia, France, Scandinavia, Spain, and Mexico all thrilled to Lerner and Loewe's singing Higgins and Liza Doolittle. However, in two respects, Byron's "the good old times that are gone" rings true:

1. There are too few original musicals to feed the public what it demonstrably has indicated it wants. The "workshop" of the seventies was an idea whose time had come and now refers more to a preproduction of the musical rather than a trial balloon that can be retrieved if the theater gods are not beneficent. Established composers and lyricists have begun to experience the sneaking feeling they may be démodé. Whether their concern is justified can be debated, but there is no doubt that the language of the Gershwins, Kern, Berlin, Rodgers and Hart, Porter, Arlen and Harburg, among the many, no matter how much in evidence it may be, is not relevant or appropriate to today's young audiences. The composers and lyricists of the music and words they listen to have not made any significant moves toward the musical theater. At the moment, we are in stasis, playing the old and, too often, creating scores in the manner of. The handwriting on the wall that spells out the old established rules of the marketplace is known to us all: When supply is limited, competition for a place on stage stiffens. Of passing interest is the slow re-awakening of the film musical. As of this writing *Miss Saigon*, *The Phantom of the Opera*, *Les Miserables*, and *Evita* are in development phases; *Sweeney Todd* is to be directed

---

* *Guys and Dolls*, *Oklahoma!*, *Carousel*, *South Pacific*, *Kiss Me, Kate*, *Hello, Dolly*, *Gypsy*, *She Loves Me*, all the Sondheim musicals, and further back in time, *Babes in Arms*, *Pal Joey*, and *The Boys From Syracuse*, among others, are now recognized as part of our theater heritage. They are revived with the same respect and frequency as the plays of O'Neill, Williams, and Miller.

for the screen by Tim Burton; and *Into The Woods* will be filmed in collaboration with Jim Henson's puppet/creatures. Mr. Sondheim has written a new movie musical *Singing Out Loud* with William Goldman to be directed by Rob Reiner; Twyla Tharp, in collaboration with James L. Brooks, is at work on what is described as a "top secret" musical; and Bette Midler plans a three-hour television production of *Gypsy*.

2. I am often told that young would-be performers claim film as their preferred medium of expression, but I have not found this to be true. Wherever I teach I meet young actors, singers, and dancers as eager to work on the stage as those who have gone before them. In the words of a renowned actor, "A play [musical] needs and recognizes the presence of an audience but a movie doesn't give a damn if anyone's out front!" No, the problem does not lie in a lack of desire to perform but in finding adequate arenas in which to do it. With too few places for the beginner to learn his trade, he must turn to the ersatz environment of schools, conservatories, academies and institutes. Again, I have written about this at length.*

Admittedly, the marketplace is not bountiful. No longer is there the profligacy of employment that once afforded the fledgling performer an opportunity to build a career slowly. "Grab the money and run" is now the accepted shibboleth of show business. Henny Youngman in an editorial in *The New York Times* wrote, with no argument from this writer, about today's stand-up comedian: " . . . As Mr. Newspaper Headline came near, I figured he'd ask me a college boy question like, 'What makes a joke funny?' Instead, 'Mr. Youngman, what's the secret to *lasting*?' On that, I always give sound advice. 'Nem di gelt,' I said in Yiddish. 'Take the money.'" I agree with Mr. Youngman because I would give the same advice to the young beginner performer. Learn your trade as best you can with teachers you respect and admire, but when work is scarce, work when and wherever you can (there isn't that much of it around). " . . . Take the money," because along with the money you will be in front of audiences making mistakes you will never make again. Do not be afraid to leave the protection of the teacher. You can return. Take the money. Nothing is at stake when you wear water wings. Get out into the deep water where the

<hr>

* See *On Singing Onstage*, pages 207-209 and *On Performing*, pages 289-298.

risk is high but the rewards are based not on dog paddling but on swimming. The student has only the word of his teacher when he says, "Don't do that because . . . ." Audiences speak to actors, singers, dancers, and performers in a mysterious language. When, in *their* way, they say, "Don't do that . . . " one never forgets whatever it is he did—step on someone else's line, kill a joke or a laugh, up-stage a fellow member of the cast, miss a cue, dawdle on an entrance, exit too quickly or lose a "hand." The "Don't do that because . . . " may not be instruction in the classic meaning of the word, but it is an historic and powerful, never-to-be-forgotten lesson. Where but in performance can education like this be bought or found? Some cautionary words of advice: Stay away from auditions for the men and women who produce and/or cast major musical productions until you know your worth. Practice on stages that do not have the power to destroy. Learn to define your goals and the gauge of your personal aesthetic and do not sell them or yourself short.

On Singing Onstage, On Performing, and *A Performer Prepares*, the three volumes that describe my work, attempt to present to the young singer a broad coverage of a narrow field of interest—the performance of theater and contemporary music on and off a stage. During the years of writing them, the books have become texts in universities and conservatories. Like all textbooks that set down methodology, they should be handled with care. No matter how difficult it may be to learn a technique, it is only the beginning of a longer journey—one that the performer takes on his own. In the course of the pursuit of a career, it is essential that he must inevitably shed all dogma learned in schools and in studios in order to construct and put to use his own cognitive procedures and principles. Beyond and away from the allotted time for study that is an essential element in the life of every young performer lies the rocky road of a sustained career in show business.

The days are long gone when an actor, a singer, a dancer, or a performer could allow himself the luxury to declare that "I only want to work on the stage," " . . . on the screen," " . . . in nightclubs," " . . . on television" with any assurance that it might happen. As I have said, there is not that much of each part of the sum of show business to make those selective goals feasible. The most classical of artists can be seen selling soap even as he appears in the flesh selling Shakespeare. Soap operas and sitcoms are coveted by the working performer with the same zeal he once felt for seeing his name in lights on a Broadway marquee (a quaint reference to those gone good old times). Should this deter him? I do not believe so.

However, I do believe that, for the first time in the history of the performing arts, being unprepared is not a condition that counts one out. The sad truth is we are crowding the marketplace with mediocrity. Arrivals and departures occur with disturbing frequency; easy-to-come-by celebrity too often supplants excellence. These days, beginners eager to have excellence defined for them may have considerable difficulty finding it. The unprepared performer is too much with us. It is time that the young man in *A Chorus Line* who sang "I Can Do That" change his words, if not his tune. Third-rateism invites that nonsense. Had he seen Fred Astaire, he would have more correctly sung "I Can't Do That," or better, "I Want to Learn How to Do That" and "God! Someday I hope I'll be able to do that."

It is to him and to the performers yet to come that I address this volume.

ON SINGING ONSTAGE
New, Completely Revised Edition
by David Craig

"David Craig knows more about singing in the musical theatre than anyone in this country—which probably means the world. Time and time again his advice and training have resulted in actors moving from non-musical theatre into musicals with ease and expertise. Short of taking his classes, this book is a must."

—HAROLD PRINCE

In the New and Revised *On Singing Onstage* David Craig presents the same technique he has given to America's leading actors, actresses and dancers over the past thirty years. By listing the do's and don'ts of all aspects of singing onstage, you will be brought closer to the discovery of your own personal "style." That achievement plus information on how to get the most mileage out of an audition (what to sing and how to choose it) makes this book an indispensably practical self-teaching tool.

For anyone who has to (or wants to) sing anywhere, from amateur productions to the Broadway stage, *On Singing Onstage* is an essential guide for making the most of your talent.

AMONG DAVID CRAIG'S STUDENTS:

Carol Burnett, Cyd Charisse, James Coco, Sally Field, Lee Grant, Valerie Harper, Barbara Harris, Rock Hudson, Sally Kellerman, Jack Klugman, Cloris Leachman, Roddy McDowell, Marsha Mason, Anthony Perkins, Lee Remick, Eva Marie Saint, Marlo Thomas, Cicely Tyson, Nancy Walker . . . and many more

paper • ISBN: 1-55783-043-6

NOW AVAILABLE AS INDIVIDUAL TAPES

DAVID CRAIG

ON SINGING ONSTAGE

CLASS ONE: LECTURES

CLASS TWO: TECHNIQUE

CLASS THREE: SUBTEXT

CLASS FOUR: PROCESS/THE BALLAD

CLASS FIVE: PROCESS/THE UPTEMPO

CLASS SIX: PERFORMANCE/Q & A

EACH VHS TAPE IS 90 MINUTES
AND INCLUDES A 40-PAGE STUDY GUIDE, THE
LAST PUBLICATION WRITTEN BY DAVID CRAIG

$34.95 [$45.95 CAN] EACH

TAPE ONE
ISBN **1-55783-659-0**

TAPE TWO
ISBN **1-55783-660-4**

TAPE THREE
ISBN **1-55783-661-2**

TAPE FOUR
ISBN **1-55783-662-0**

TAPE FIVE
ISBN **1-55783-663-9**

TAPE SIX
ISBN **1-55783-664-7**

SPECIAL PRICE
COMPLETE SET
$184.95 [$240.95 CAN]
ISBN **1-55783-665-5**

"David Craig's class was one
of the most helpful and enjoyable
I have ever attended—and David
one of the most stimulating teachers
I have ever worked with."

—Lily Tomlin